Rethinking Private Higher Education

Studies in Critical Social Sciences Book Series

Haymarket Books is proud to be working with Brill Academic Publishers (www.brill.nl) to republish the *Studies in Critical Social Sciences* book series in paperback editions. This peer-reviewed book series offers insights into our current reality by exploring the content and consequences of power relationships under capitalism, and by considering the spaces of opposition and resistance to these changes that have been defining our new age. Our full catalog of *SCSS* volumes can be viewed at https://www.haymarketbooks .org/series_collections/4-studies-in-critical-social-sciences.

Rethinking Private Higher Education

Ethnographic Perspectives

EDITED BY
Daniele Cantini

Haymarket
Books
Chicago, IL

First published in 2016 by Brill Academic Publishers, The Netherlands.
© 2017 Koninklijke Brill NV, Leiden, The Netherlands

Published in paperback in 2018 by
Haymarket Books
P.O. Box 180165
Chicago, IL 60618
773-583-7884
www.haymarketbooks.org

ISBN: 978-1-60846-844-7

Trade distribution:
In the U.S. through Consortium Book Sales, www.cbsd.com
In the UK, Turnaround Publisher Services, www.turnaround-uk.com
In Canada, Publishers Group Canada, www.pgcbooks.ca
All other countries, Ingram Publisher Services International, ips_intlsales@
ingramcontent.com

Cover design by Jamie Kerry of Belle Étoile Studios and Ragina Johnson.

This book was published with the generous support of Lannan Foundation
and the Wallace Action Fund.

Printed in the United States.

10 9 8 7 6 5 4 3 2 1

Library of Congress Cataloging-in-Publication Data is available.

Contents

Acknowledgments

This volume grew out of a workshop I convened in Halle in November 2013, at the Research Cluster 'Society and Culture in Motion', and I am grateful for all the support, financial and moral, received there. I would like to thank in particular Matthias Kaufmann, Richard Rottenburg, Reinhold Sackmann and Werner Nell for their intellectual support, and Oliver-Pierre Rudolph for his practical support at different stages of this project. I would also like to acknowledge the role played by many graduate students, who enriched the conference by participating as discussants; in particular, Hami Imam Gümüs, Ronn Müller, Fazil Moradi, Daniel Pateisky, and Özgur Ücar. Finally, thanks are due to all the contributors to this volume, for their engagement and for the patience they bore at times in which the publication proceded slower than expected.

The volume benefited from the interest of researchers involved through other projects and venues. Among these, I wish to acknowledge the research project on Arab Universities, led by Seteney Shami of the Social Science Research Council in New York, in which I conducted the research on the October 6 Universities partly presented in this volume. The Transregionale Forum in Berlin, where part of this project was presented during its winter school on Education and Inequality organised in November 2014. The LOST (law, organisation, science and technology) research group in Halle, where a draft of the introduction was presented in July 2015; and the opportunity provided by a planned joint research project with the LAMES (Laboratorie Méditerranéen de Sociologie) at the University of Aix-en-Provence. I am grateful for the patience and the guidance provided by David Fasenfest, who also provided the index. Thanks are due to my competent editors at Brill, Rosanna Woensdregt and Kim Fiona Plas, as well as to Nick James, who proofread the entire manuscript. Lastly, I thank my wife for her patience and support through the vicissitudes of preparing the manuscript.

List of Figures

Notes on Contributors

Ayça Alemdaroğlu
(Ph. D. Cambridge 2011) is a sociologist and the Associate Director of the Keyman Modern Turkish Studies Program at Northwestern University. Her research has focused on Turkey and has engaged with a broad range of theoretical and ethnographic issues. These include youth culture and politics, gender and sexuality, constructions of space and place, experiences of modernity, nationalism, eugenics and higher education. The concern in much of her work is with the ways in which social inequality is produced and reproduced through bodies, places and institutions and informs the experiences of ordinary people. Before coming to Northwestern, Ayça was a post-doctoral fellow and a lecturer in the Anthropology Department at Stanford University. She was also a visiting scholar in the Department of Sociology at New York University between 2006 and 2008. Ayça was born and raised in Ankara and studied political science and sociology in the Middle East Technical University and Bilkent University.

Daniele Cantini
earned his PhD in Social and Cultural Anthropology at the University of Modena (Italy) in 2006, with a thesis on the Jordanian university system and its students. In 2007–10 was affiliated researcher at the CEDEJ (Egypt), where he worked on different projects dealing with university education and its privatisation, worries of citizenship, youth, religious minorities, and migration. In 2010, he was a researcher in the Social Science Research Council (USA) project on "Arab Universities: Autonomy and Governance". Since 2011 he is senior research fellow at the Research Cluster "Society and Culture in Motion" at the University of Halle (Germany). Between 2013 and 2016 he was the principal investigator in a BMBF sponsored project, managed through the Orient-Institut Beirut, on doctoral studies at Egyptian universities. He teaches at the University of Modena since 2008 and at the MLU Halle since 2012 different courses on the Anthropology of the Middle East, on Social and Political Anthropology, and on Ethnology of the Mediterranean. He is the author of Youth and Education in the Middle East: Shaping Identity and Politics in Jordan (London: I.B. Tauris, 2016). He co-edited a special issue on *Subjectivity and Islam: Anthropological Perspectives* (La Ricerca Folklorica, 2014). His articles appeared in *Anthropology of the Middle East, REMMM, CRES, Confluences Méditerranée*, in addition to different edited volumes.

Carmela Chávez Irigoyen

(Ph.D. candidate PUCP, 2015) is a teacher and researcher of the Social Sciences Department of Pontificia Universidad Catolica del Peru (PUPC). After some years developing studies related with civil society organizations and human rights agendas, her research has gone to sociology of higher education. In particular, studying the transformation of private universities. Her thesis project is focused in the study of low fee universities since liberalization process in Peru. She has participate in the Winter Academy "Inequality, Education and Social Power: transregional perspectives" invited by the Forum Transregionale Studien and the Max Weber Foundation at Von Humbolt University in 2014. Carmela has presented her research advances in international conferences as the 59th Annual Comparative and International Education Society in 2015 and the XXXIII International Congress of the Latin American Studies Association in the same year. Nowadays she works as a specialist in the Superintendencia Nacional de Educación Superior Universitaria (SUNEDU), a new public institutions product of the university reform in the country. She is part of a team that is developing a new evaluation model for academic careers. During 2016, she won a fellowship from the Chilean Government and is going to have a doctoral residence in Universidad Diego Portales in Santiago City.

Enrico Ille

Enrico Ille has a doctoral degree in Social and Cultural Anthropology from the University of Halle, Germany, and is a member of the Law, Organization, Science and Technology (LOST) Research Network. After holding positions as Assistant Professor at the Martin Luther University of Halle and at Ahfad University for Women, Sudan, he is currently Urgent Anthropology Fellow (The British Museum / Royal Anthropological Institute, London) with research on supply chains involving date production along the Nile in northern Sudan. He co-edited the volume *Emerging orders in the Sudans* (with Sandra Calkins and Richard Rottenburg, Langaa 2014) and published an annotated bibliography and a number of journal and book articles on the Nuba Mountains, discussing history, land issues and political economy, as well as development initiatives for agricultural production and water supply. His general research interest is the relation of state institutions, companies and communities in mineral resource extraction and food supply chains throughout Sudan.

Sylvie Mazzella

is a researcher at Aix Marseille Université of the LAMES, Mediterranean Laboratory of Sociology (CNRS, AMU). Sylvie Mazzella coordinated a research project based at the IRMC (Institut de recherche sur le Maghreb contemporain), focused on "Foreign students in the Maghreb and in the Euro-Mediterranean space. Towards which internationalization of higher education and towards which circulation of competences?" Sylvie Mazzella's book untitled *Globalization student. The Maghreb between North and South* (Karthala, 2009) includes contributions from researchers from Algeria, Morocco, Tunisia and France and describes the Transformation of student migration in the context of university competitions and selective immigration. Since 2005, she analyses the transformations of higher education in the Maghreb and the policies of hosting international students both in the Maghreb and in France. Sylvie Mazzella published two books on the transformation of higher education in the Maghreb, several articles on the privatisation of higher education in Tunisia and coordinated a recent issue of Cahiers québécois de démographie on the transformation of students' south-south mobilities and a special issue observing students' south–south mobilities is being published in the *Cahiers de la Recherche de l'Enseignement et du Savoir*.

Alexander Mitterle

is a research associate at the Institute for Sociology, the Centre for School and educational research at the Martin Luther University and member of the DFG-Research Group "mechanisms of elite formation in the German education system" (FOR 1612). From 2011 to 2014 he worked as a research associate at the Institute for Higher Education Research Halle-Wittenberg. His recent research focuses on the conditions and development of field stratification in the German higher education. He has also worked and published on the structure and time of teaching in German higher education and the governmentality of real-socialist higher education.

Annemarie Profanter

is an Associate Professor in Intercultural Pedagogy at the Faculty of Education of the Free University of Bolzano, Italy. She received her two doctorates in both Education and Psychology from the University of Innsbruck, Austria, and a master's degree in Psychology of Education from the University of London, UK. Since 2004 she resided periodically in the Islamic Republic of Pakistan and the Arabian Peninsula doing fieldwork and visiting fellowships for international institutions such as "The City University of Science and Information Technology" in Peshawar, Pakistan; the American University affiliated "Dhofar University" in Salalah, Sultanate of Oman; and "Prince Mohammed University" in the Kingdom of Saudi Arabia. She is working on projects addressing Arab women's educational opportunities in the Gulf and has recently published a documentary on polygyny in collaboration with the Ministry of Information in

Oman. Her current research includes Islamic integration and migration issues in Europe.

Susan Wright
(D. Phil. in Social Anthropology, Oxford) is Professor of Educational Anthropology at Aarhus University. She studies people's participation in large-scale processes of political transformation, working with concepts of audit culture, governance, contestation and policy. She coordinated the EU project 'University Reform, Globalisation and Europeanisation' and the EU ITN project 'Universities in the Knowledge Economy' in Europe and the Asia-Pacific Rim. She co-edits (with Penny Welch) the journal *LATISS* (Learning and Teaching: International Journal of Higher Education in the Social Sciences) and recently published *Policy Worlds: Anthropology and the Anatomy of Contemporary Power* (co-editors Shore and Peró, 2011, Berghahn).

Rethinking Private Higher Education: A Collection of Ethnographic Perspectives*

Daniele Cantini

The link between state formation, development, and education (including higher education) has become quite an established research topic in anthropology as well as in other social sciences in the past decades, and it has proved to be an interesting approach for deepening our understanding of societies all over the world. Universities[1] are a central feature of both the project of modernity, state-sponsored or global in scope, and of the construction of citizenship, as a gate institution granting access to professional life, regulating divisions among the population, and legitimising the state (Stevens, Armstrong and Arum 2008). A truly global form, the university is an institution found all over the world, partly due to the spread of globalisation and partly deriving from an older phase of global isomorphism, originating at the height of colonial power at the end of the nineteenth century. The growth of universities all over the world has been nothing short of a spectacular phenomenon, particularly so since the 1960s (Schofer and Meyer 2005). Moreover the university has been extensively and intensively institutionalised over the same period, making it an essential feature in most nation states (Meyer *et al* 2007).

Recently the link between university education and socio-economic development has become ubiquitous as many international agencies increasingly call for the need to 'build a knowledge society', which is now a key feature of development discourses. The usual argument is that a knowledge society contributes to social and economic development, and this finds its expression in publications, policies and programmes disseminated by the World Bank, the Organisation for Economic Cooperation and Development (OECD),

---

* Many people commented on earlier drafts of this introduction; I wish in particular to acknowledge the critical and insightful comments offered by Iman Farag, David Fasenfest, Patrick Lynn Rivers, Alexander Mitterle, and Neha Vora; I hope to have been able to address at least some of these in the text. All remaining faults are entirely mine.

1 A brief explication concerning the usage of 'higher education' and 'university' is necessary. The confusion derives from the empirical difficulty of determining what could keep together university, academy, institute, higher institute, as well as other denominations, and the actual meaning of the labelling is only properly understood in its context (Farag 2009). This volume deals with universities as case studies, and with higher education as the system within which universities find their place.

the United Nations and other international developmental agencies (Mazawi 2010). The current wave of reforms that are re-structuring universities anchors both the global north and south in the so-called global knowledge economy, where higher education is seen as increasingly crucial for economic development (Altbach and Levy 2005). Higher education occupies centre stage in the discourse on the global knowledge economy because "knowledge is treated as a raw material" (Slaughter and Rhoades 2004: 17). The argument that the future lies in a global knowledge economy was formulated by the OECD (Organisation for Economic Cooperation and Development) as a way for its members to maintain their competitive advantage over the rest of the world. The OECD developed indicators to measure its members' performance in positioning themselves for the inevitable emergence of a global knowledge economy, with quality as a crucial indicator (Wright and Rabo 2010). In short, universities become preferential sites for both the mining and the refining of the fundamental resource, knowledge, in a global knowledge economy that is both predicted and created by OECD policies (Mazawi 2010).

The global is configured as a knowledge economy where education, and higher education in particular, is perceived to be the central institution raising the standard of human capital, driving economic growth and playing a key role in securing a country's position in a global competition over knowledge (Nielsen 2012: 1). To meet the challenge, governments and universities worldwide are increasingly emphasising the need to internationalise their education systems and institutions, with new stratifications among countries and disciplines as well as new visions of competencies and capabilities the ideal student (and citizen) should possess emerging in the process. The second fundamental process occurring in this context is the increased privatisation of the higher education sector, both through partnerships between university, industry and governments (Etzkowitz and Leydesdorff 2000) and through the creation of private universities, the subject of this volume.

In the context of a steady growth of universities worldwide, private universities have been on the rise too, and are actually the fastest-growing segment of higher education, especially in countries where the state could hardly be described as encouraging liberalism (Altbach and Levy 2005). While the actual meaning of private varies internationally, as discussed extensively below, the upsurge is found in countries where enrolment rates are growing faster than the available seats at public universities, and the private sector fills in the gap, in a context of both massification of tertiary education and of a fundamental change in its funding. The rising social hunger for higher education and fiscal constraints, something detected by almost all studies mentioned so far, have meant that the state, in many national locations, can no longer meet demands; and the private sector is seen as a response to capacity challenges in both developed and developing countries (Morley 2014). While higher education landscapes are still largely national and regulated by states, private universities are seen as a challenge to the older, established notion of national universities catering to the broader public, despite the restrictions on access present in most countries; moreover, critics point to the risk of education becoming less of a right and more of a good to be sold and bought. This points to the first core element of this volume, namely to the necessity of understanding the entanglements of public and private, the new configurations of values and orders that are taking shape in the current historical phase.

"The market ideology of the private sector is often perceived as a contradiction to the core values of education for all, and critics fear that it will contribute to elite formation and social exclusion. Fears have tended to focus on the commodification of knowledge, instrumentalism in service of corporate needs and financial profits, the changing ethos, curriculum and values of higher education, a possible abdication of state responsibility, and the belief that new providers are compromising quality and standards by producing poorly regulated diploma mills" (Morley 2014: 14). The private sector is also conceptualised as a threat to social diversity and equality of opportunity, with the potential to exclude students from low socioeconomic backgrounds. On the other hand, students (and their families) in many low-income countries welcome the opportunity of having access to some forms of higher education (Ibid.).

While the general trajectory of this "reality that is here to stay" (Altbach and Levy 2005) has been already extensively discussed, there is an urgent need for deeper studies of particular contexts, in the attempt to make sense of the fears and hopes that private higher education raise, caught in a complex combination of opportunity and exploitation. This process is largely still to be studied, especially from an ethnographic perspective, as the intersections between states, international agencies and capital, changing conceptions of the state and of what is knowledge are all the more interesting. This is the second objective of this book, to offer ethnographies of private universities in different countries, with the aim of deepening our understanding of the actual processes of privatisation that are taking place, and of the different bordering processes between public and private. Such an objective is not only in line with the call to offer more qualitative research on "world model constructions and their enactments in local sites" (Meyer *et al* 2007: 213), but also following recent developments in social anthropology and related disciplines, namely the attention to contemporary configurations of values and orders.

Thinking through Private Higher Education

This volume offers fresh insights into the actual meaning of 'private' in different higher education contexts. While this might seem straightforward enough, matters become quickly complicated by the multiple meanings of private university, the different contexts and trajectories of higher education, as well as the many aspects that privatisation touches upon. It is precisely for these reasons that an ethnographic analysis is necessary, to shed light on these processes and contribute to a clearer understanding of the actual effects of global policies in local contexts.

As mentioned, universities are on the rise worldwide, and private universities have the lion's share of the growth; in East Asia (Japan, South Korea, the Philippines and Taiwan) 80% of students are enrolled in private universities, heavily regulated by the state (Altbach and Levy 2005). In the USA, 20% of universities are private, but are usually highly regarded and older than public ones.[2] While Western Europe is the least touched by the wave of privatisation, Central and post-socialist Eastern Europe are witnessing a steady rise in private universities. Overall, Latin America and Asia are growing fast, and Africa is following suit (Ibid.).[3] The Middle East and North Africa, not surprisingly due to the heavily centralised states that emerged after the colonial period, has been the last region to establish the private sector across the breadth of its countries. Supply and demand in private higher education has increased over the past 20 years in Southern Mediterranean countries, particularly in the Levant and, more recently, in North Africa. Although non-university private higher education already existed in many Middle Eastern countries, until the 1990s public education was the norm in all countries except Lebanon (Hanafi 2011). Since then, a massive academic boom in higher education has been taking place, with two-thirds (around 70) of the new universities founded in the Arab Middle East since 1993 being private, and more and more (at least 50) of them are branches of western, mostly American, universities (Romani 2009: 4, 2012; Miller-Idriss and Hanauer 2011).

---

2   The University of Phoenix is the obvious exception; I am grateful to Alexander Mitterle for this insight.

3   This growth is paralleled in the quantity of studies devoted to the topic; while in 1992 Daniel Levy could list only two significant monographs, a decade later a bibliography of private higher education comprised more than 250 pages; most of these, though, were national cases, rather descriptive in scope (Reisz and Stock 2008: 7).

These stunning figures notwithstanding, it is clear that the label 'private' has a variety of meanings. According to Reisz and Stock (2008),[4] Levy developed an analysis of the specific difference between private and public universities along three lines, the kind of financing, the control, and the orientation toward education, but these have been criticised for having only a limited relevance. Another 'extant definition' proposed by Levy (1986, quoted in Reisz and Stock 2008) is that universities are private when so defined by the public system. Altbach specifies that private universities are responsible for their own funding, but this too seems to be contradicted by some studies (also in this volume). According to Geiger, the third author examined by Reisz and Stock, private universities differ from the public ones in their functions; in order to differentiate from the public system, they have to offer "more, better or different" courses and disciplines (Geiger 1986, quoted in Reisz and Stock 2008; see Mitterle in this volume). Consequently the private differs at least partly from the public, with three typologies of combination, one with a "mass private and restricted public sector", such as in Japan, Philippines, Brazil and Colombia; a "parallel public and private sector", as in Belgium, Holland, Chile and Hong Kong; and finally a "comprehensive public and peripheral private sector", as in Germany, Sweden and France (Ibid.). Another distinction, proposed by Levy in his analysis of Latin American private universities, is in the origin of private universities; some originate from a Catholic background, others are elite institutions, while the third group is "demand compensating" (Levy 1986, quoted in Reisz and Stock 2008).

Matters are complicated by the fact that, while most private universities are national, being established and functioning in one country, there are also examples of cross-borders institutions, either through branch campuses, transplant campuses, or through various forms of linkage between two universities. There is a strong link between internationalisation and privatisation, exemplified by the private higher education global revolution described by Altbach and Knight (2007). Gulf countries offer the best example of the different ways in which universities are becoming international in the knowledge economy, where different kinds of private universities, both national and international, are mushrooming, funded by private capital with strong encouragement from governments (see Profanter in this volume). The recent expansion of satellite, branch and offshore educational institutions and programmes set up by foreign institutions in the region is unprecedented; of the estimated 100 branch campuses currently operating worldwide, over one-third are in the Arab region and the majority have opened within the last

---

4 Unless otherwise stated, translations are mine.

decade (Miller-Idriss and Hanauer 2011).[5] These institutions can be for or not-for-profit, can be small colleges offering courses in only a handful of disciplines, market-oriented, or full-fledged universities with stunning research records. Private corporate investments are also on the rise, and are mainly cross-national (see Alemdaroğlu in this volume). Financial arrangements of private universities often lack transparency, as many of these institutions operate as corporate identities (with consequences for the possibilities of doing research). The wide spectrum of institutions – from prestigious to garage-universities, of varying quality – makes it inappropriate to generalise.

What allows these institutions to be put under the same category is the series of normative prescriptions that circulate within the universities' institutional environments and that enunciate legitimate propositions, norms and standards that are to be adopted if the institutions want to appear rational and efficient (Musselin 2008, quoted in Farag 2009).[6] A famous analysis posited that universities are passing from a phase 1, knowledge for knowledge's sake, to a phase 2, knowledge for the market's sake. In 'mode 2', which is on a par with the Zeitgeist of a new global knowledge economy, knowledge is geared towards solutions to 'real-world' problems solved by transdisciplinary networks involving stakeholders outside academia (Gibbons *et al* 1994, quoted in Musselin 2008: 18–9). Despite the confusion over whether this is a description or a prescription (Mazawi 2007), it confirms the link between the global circulation of normative images of higher education and its privatisation.

Yet, even if older private universities are not taken into account, it is evident that it is not a single model spreading all over the globe. Private and public only make sense in relation to one another, and within the context of centralised

---

5   At most institutions, degree programmes are heavily focused on professional occupations, including business, engineering, technology and communications, although several universities also offer liberal arts programmes. In general, branch campuses tend to offer professional and occupational-type training, while the old- and new-style turnkey universities, and the single replica offshore campus, focus more on liberal arts training (Ibid.). Such transnational offshore educational institutions are often a cause of concern to local citizens in the Persian Gulf, worried about issues of cultural homogenisation and westernisation (see Profanter in this volume). The replacement of Arabic instruction with English-language instruction, the reduction or replacement of religious courses and the introduction of new fields of study which may threaten traditional local beliefs are but a few examples, with some ethnographies beginning to emerge dealing with the often unexpected cultural and social consequences of such universities (Vora 2015).

6   The prescriptions consist in "modifying the role of the State, transform universities into organisations, enhance the role of stakeholders, adopting logics of privatization and placing one's institution within a global perspective" (Ibid.).

political power, which has the necessary authority to credit and confer academic titles (Farag 2009); in this sense, it is necessary to have an historic depth in the analysis, in order to reveal the shifting meanings of public and private.

> Privatisation does not pass necessarily through a shift from the public to the private, but from an increase in the sphere of intervention of the former through the mobilization and the strengthening of the latter.[7]
> MUSSELIN 2008, in Farag 2009

For example, it has been widely noted that some modes of management derived from the private are applied to the public sector, leading to the university in question displaying an increasingly corporate character.[8]

This volume engages a discussion that rises above the normative cleavages usually associated with the issue of privatisation in higher education by examining the term's many meanings, as well as the heterogeneity of its practices (see Krücken and Serrano-Verde 2012). Each article in this volume exposes the limits of framing the issue of privatisation as a binary of 'private vs. public'. Not only are there many differences within the two terms – the state is far from being a monolithic actor, and private can mean many different things, for example it could refer to a for- or not-for-profit institution. These two are now so closely intertwined that privatisation can no longer be understood without taking state regulations and subsidies into account, or without considering the need for ideological support from the political realm (Ibid.). This seems to be a specific component of the current globalisation, in which particular components of institutions are reoriented toward global logics and away from historically shaped national logics (Sassen 2007). This process, by no means limited to the education sector, destabilises existing meanings and systems, in particular the social contract at the core of modern citizenship. The real object of analysis is thus less a coherent private logic, but rather the different layers of bordering between public and private.

---

7 Consider the standardising action operated by accreditation and evaluation agencies, which are presented as independent, technical and apolitical, and which typically work with both public and private establishments.

8 Shore and MacLauchlan (2012) identify several familiar features of the broader corporatisation of the university: the casualisation of junior academic staff; the adoption of auditing and New Public Management as disciplinary mechanisms that have pressed a more general 'proletarianisation of the professoriat'; as well as the increasingly powerful and central role of the administrator (see Cantini in this volume). The growth of the administration and relative decline of the professoriat provides a perfect illustration of how financial pressures are creating global isomorphisms.

Rather than concentrating on the typology, I follow Iman Farag in looking at the logics and practices of privatisation, which encourage the creation and development of private establishments catering to a paying public. The logic of the private is strictly complementary to that of the public (see Mitterle in this volume), with private establishments claiming to be offering education that is better, different or not available in the public sector. On the other hand, the logic of privatisations is market oriented – students, particularly those coming from abroad paying higher fees, are referred to as clients, if not directly as educational tourists (see Mazzella and Cantini in this volume),[9] while education is turned into a commodity that becomes a source of national revenue (Mamdani 2007).[10] These logics are often operating within the public system too – hence the need to conceptualise the private not in opposition to the public, but as different layers of borders in a relational perspective.

Almost all the studies presented in this volume deal with the newer form of private universities, something that originates in the past 20 years or so. These analyses reveal the ideological dimension of the privatisation of higher education. Since the 1990s, policy makers have viewed universities as catalysts for economic development and growth. In this light they become research-intensive organisations and training facilities for highly skilled labour, and, as such, are expected to generate added value for both individual investors such as businesses and students, and for society as a whole (Krücken and Serrano-Verde 2012). In many of the countries analysed in this volume, though, privatisation assumes a lower profile and seems to be geared toward different goals. There seems however to be a largely homogenous set of reforms in the education sector that are being implemented at a global level, usually adopting at least some themes originating in the neo-liberal ideology that has been largely dominant in the western world since the 1980s. From the other side, it seems

---

9   It is important to note that international student mobility is not always directed toward countries in the global north (Mazzella and Eyebiyi 2014). Student mobility can be encouraged by the state, with Gulf countries again being at the forefront in this market, Egypt being the most popular destination (Cantini 2014), followed by Jordan and the Maghreb countries (Mazzella, this volume).

10   Yet also speaking of commodification of higher education is far from being straightforward, since this word is used to "refer to different institutions, activities, processes and entities such as higher education services, educational products, intellectual property rights (e.g. patents and copyrights), and start-up firms" (Kauppinen 2013). For a thorough analysis of the marketisation of higher education and its implications for policies, see Teixeira and Dill (2011). This commercialisation needs to be situated in a wider historical context of political economy and global finance's relentless search for new sources of profit (see Alemdaroğlu in this volume).

that most of these states are rather lenient toward a governmental model that does not encourage, to say the least, political freedoms, and in which therefore the role of a 'private' education or of the 'knowledge society' has to be understood in its different contexts.[11]

The studies gathered in this collection deal first with states, and with national trajectories of higher education development. This national focus is necessary to explore the impact of global phenomena such as the current wave of privatisation, since it is at this national level that the most complex meanings of the global are being constituted; at the same time, the national is a key enabler and enactor of the emergent global scale (Sassen 2007). The different national settings are oriented toward global agendas and systems in complex and often contradictory ways, as the contributions to this volume make clear, and this adds to the necessity of understanding the historical circumstances that shape the current policies.

Reforming Universities – Neo-liberalism Going Global?

The reforms affecting higher education worldwide tend to present similar aspects, and this leads one to think that there is a global agenda operating behind these reforms, pushed forward by international agencies such as the World Bank, OECD and the European Union, despite the internal differences between them (Wright and Rabo 2010). Whether this is evidence of a "globally structured agenda of university reform" (Dale 2000, quoted in Wright and Rabo 2010) or more a case of convergence around a loosely shared set of international norms is heavily debated, as are the consequences of these processes, their homogenising effect on universities. My contention is that an answer to these questions is only possible if we look at the university as a global institution, the meanings and shapes of which originate in a process of increasing isomorphism (DiMaggio and Powell 1983). While I turn to a discussion of the university as an institution in the next section, here it is briefly necessary to discuss reforms within the framework of the nation state, since this is still the fundamental actor shaping them.

University reforms are a recurrent phenomenon. The mass university, particularly in developing countries where sustained population growth is resulting in larger cohorts entering university each year, could not keep up its promise of upward mobility, a factor which is also due to the changing economic policies

---

11   An extreme example is offered by the introduction of private universities in Pinochet's Chile (Bernasconi 1994, quoted in Reisz and Stock 2008).

that have reduced state intervention in the labour market. The newest 'international policy fad', the global knowledge economy, occurred at this particular point in history, leading the World Bank in particular to claim that developing countries should expand higher education as the 'latest way to leapfrog out of poverty', but that they should do so through privatisation (Wright and Rabo 2010). This new development created some resistance, since it conflicted with earlier models of the university and its relationship with the state.

> [The] circulation of educational ideas and ideologies is not merely a function of globalisation but involves actual historical processes, human agents, organisations, and governments within a framework of particular configurations of power and hegemonic relations.
>
> RIZVI 2006: 202, quoted in NIELSEN 2012: 8

According to Nielsen's analysis, Rizvi identifies four interconnected phenomena promoting what he labels a growing global convergence of educational policy ideas around neo-liberal precepts. First, a new kind of inter- and transnational policy space, shaped mainly by intergovernmental organisations.[12] Second, a neo-liberal imaginary supposedly becoming dominant through international conventions deriving from the likes of the IMF and World Bank, which put forward economic policy prescriptions for reforming developing countries. Third, consequent coercive measures, such as conditions attached to World Bank loans (see Cantini, this volume), which forced these countries to open up their markets to foreign private education providers (see Alemdaroğlu, this volume). Last, the establishment of new forms of cooperation between nations, as in the European Bologna Process, which aims to establish a European Higher Education Area and increase mobility and transparency within the region (Nielsen 2012).[13]

Despite the remarkable uniformity of reforms worldwide, rationales of internationalisation are negotiated and contested in the local contexts. What is yet largely to be accounted for are the changes that are taking place in the

---

12   Henry *et al*'s (2001) analysis of the OECD provides a good example of this: they argue that the OECD has played a major role in promoting the idea of internationalisation as a means for universities to "become more responsive to the OECD's interpretation of economic globalisation" (Henry *et al* 2001: 145, quoted in Nielsen 2012: 8).

13   While Rizvi argues that such cooperation promotes neo-liberal ideologies of marketisation, privatisation and competition even though introduced under a framework of collaboration, Nielsen notes that other authors have disputed a neo-liberal imaginary seen as too uniform and generalised (Nielsen 2012).

understanding of what is valuable knowledge nowadays, of the processes of internationalisation and of privatisation in the context of neo-liberal policies worldwide and within states that are normally not liberal, and of how international and local actors are trying to impose this new vision, to adapt to or resist it (Weiler 2011). This volume takes up precisely this challenge, by providing case studies highlighting various critical aspects of the privatisation and internationalisation of higher education worldwide. Before introducing the chapters that make up this volume, it is necessary to turn briefly to a discussion of what is meant by neo-liberalism, and how this volume contributes to the theoretical debate on actual existing forms of neo-liberalism.

Following up on a recent discussion, should neo-liberalism be analysed as a 'big Leviathan', a macro-structure or explanatory background against which other things are understood? Or should we rather analyse neo-liberalism as though it were the same size as other things, and trace its associations with them (Collier 2012)? In the second perspective, adopted by papers in this collection, the analysis could be linked to policy programmes, to trans-local channels of circulation carved by powerful institutions or peripatetic experts, to patterns of adoption and adaptation in various countries and sectors that produce new kinds of hybrid governmental formations (Ong and Hilgers 2005), as well as new borderisations between the public and the private (Sassen 2007).

The terms 'neo-liberal' and 'neo-liberalism' within contemporary anthropological scholarship have attracted a share of criticism (see JRAI 2015). Many critics of the use of these concepts concentrate on two points, its use as a 'term of choice' to describe the contemporary world, compared to 'late capitalism' for instance,[14] and, second, the concern that, if neo-liberalism explains and describes all contemporary socio-political-economic-cultural phenomena, then it loses any utility as an analytical category (Ganti 2014).[15] According to Ganti's analysis, the concept has four main referents; a set of economic reform policies (deregulation, liberalisation, privatisation); a prescriptive development model; an ideology that values market exchange as an ethic in itself; and a mode of

---

14   Whereas neo-liberalism is "truly an offspring of the Great Depression", late capitalism can be traced to processes of deindustrialisation and shifts from Fordist or Taylorist modes of production to more flexible forms of work organisation that began in Western industrialized democracies in the 1960s and 1970s (Ganti 2014).

15   In December 2012, the Group for Debates in Anthropological Theory (GDAT) at the University of Manchester debated the motion, "The concept of neoliberalism has become an obstacle to the anthropological understanding of the twenty-first century" (quoted in Ganti 2014).

governance (Ganti 2014). She notes as well that the term is ideologically and theoretically charged and most commonly employed in critique – of existing capitalist political-economic structures, modes of governance, an emphasis on bureaucracy, discourses valorising individual entrepreneurialism, or efforts to retrench the state's redistributive role (Ibid.).

The material effects of neo-liberal policies – the rise in global inequalities, the marginalisation of people out of the financial economy, the privatisation of public goods, the gentrification of cities and the reduction of social welfare programmes – are studied through the ways in which people cope with such transformations. However, studies on broader changes in the governance of the state and in conceptions of citizenship have shown that the impact of these reforms is not uniform, and that the state can stop expanding its authority in contexts of expanded cross-border and international traffic (Ibid.), with increased difficulty in distinguishing public and private elements in the bureaucracies that govern almost every aspect of social life (Graeber 2014).

Neo-liberalism may have become a hegemonic mode of discourse (Harvey 2005, quoted in Ganti 2014), but it appears to be functioning as a shorthand to signal a contemporary political-economic context; "Perhaps neoliberalism has been a little too convenient. It has become a handy way to bracket the global political economy without actively engaging it" (Schwegler 2009: 24, quoted in Ganti 2014). Moreover, it is becoming increasingly evident that neoliberal policies are far from being uncontested, sometimes effectively interrupted (Goodale and Postero 2013). Concepts such as 'market logics' or the 'free market' are treated as self-evident rather than interrogated, while anthropologists should "trouble [...] notions of any simplistic, economistic rationality", taking up the challenge of representing ethnographically the world system (Marcus 1995, in Ganti 2014). Moreover, neoliberalism is used as a prescriptive category that articulates a normative vision of the proper relationship between the state, capital and individuals, a structural or ideological force that has a tremendous impact on people's lives, life-chances, social relations and ways of inhabiting the world (Wacquant 2012).

Contributors to this volume have not been openly asked to address this question, and while some of them indirectly do (Alemdaroğlu, Cantini, Chavez) others do not. Nevertheless, all the studies presented here share a basic preoccupation of critical inquiry, namely the attention to changes in a variegated landscape of institutional, economic and political forms within the university. Each study presented here deals with national policy landscapes, and on how these local frames are intertwined with international ones; this analysis is a necessary step towards understanding the university as an institution, as a crucial site for developments that enable social progress (Meyer *et al* 2007).

The University as an Institution

This volume addresses changes in the governance, the structuring and the meaning of universities, in the context of the recognition that they are crucial institutions for modern nation states. In this context, understanding such changes becomes of paramount importance for comprehending contemporary developments, particularly given the current trend towards increased standardisation in governance and scope. I have tried elsewhere to present a comprehensive ethnography of a public university (in Jordan – see Cantini 2016), so here I will limit myself to a few cursory remarks. My aim was to establish the university as a crucial institution in the creation and maintenance of normative orders, at the same time being the very condition through which citizens are made, by being socialised into a network of rules necessary to live as subject, and through which critique emerges and new possibilities are created in a variety of ways that range from the actual structure of the university, the changes in policies, social and political lives of students, and the entrance into the labour market (Cantini 2016: 12–13). I am particularly interested in looking at the ways in which the university as a hub connects different institutional systems such as the labour market and the family, entrance into the professions and the sciences, the larger economy, the nation state and the global world. Higher education, despite its institutional strength, constitutes a paradox: "as a mechanism for the production of valuable credentials and official knowledge, it is simultaneously a powerful and a fragile social institution" (Stevens, Armstrong and Arum 2008: 137), an object of contestation with regard to its policies granting status and legitimising knowledge, to its workers as objects (and subjects) of political conflict and ideological controversy, and to its sources of revenue.

It has been noted that the new wave of universities is largely based on the model developed in the West in the last 100 years, without any political meaning but with a remarkable absence of local specificities, for example in the curricula (Elkana 2012). Each country has a peculiar history in terms of how universities became part of educational landscapes, and universities are also institutions deeply rooted in local logics and practices. Formal secular education is an essential component of nation building, through which the state produces competent citizens and workers; but 'social scientists have only begun to explore the empirical relations between the stratification, knowledge production and legitimation functions of higher education', and these are relegated to the same organisations, namely universities (Stevens, Armstrong and Arum 2008). Another line of inquiry has addressed the university not so much as an organisation but rather as an institution, the institutionalised locus of a

new knowledge system within the nation state, subject to transnational standardisation processes (Meyer *et al* 2007). Its success rests on the knowledge
it produces – not a specialised knowledge necessary to take up skilled posi-
tons in the labour market, a task at which universities have proved to be highly
inefficient, but rather as the core institutions sustaining "generalised notions
about universalistic values, human empowerment, scientific knowledge and
rationality" (Ibid.: 203). This line of inquiry emphasises the current transnational phase, in which organisational differences across universities are bound
to get narrower.

The university is part of globalisation, particularly if the latter is considered
as "partly enacted at various subnational scales and institutional domains" so
that "we can posit the possibility of a proliferation of borderings inside national territories" (Sassen 2005). Contrary to normal understanding of the border as "a geographic event and the immediate institutional apparatus through
which it is controlled, protected and generally governed" (Ibid.), Sassen argues
that the border is actually and heuristically disaggregating at multiple levels,
thereby allowing her to blur longstanding dualities in state scholarship, notably between the national and the global as well as between the private and the
public. She argues that

> the mix of processes we describe as globalisation is indeed produc-
> ing, deep inside the national state, a very partial but significant form of
> authority, a hybrid that is neither fully private nor fully public, neither
> fully national nor fully global (Ibid.).

As states participate in the implementation of cross-border regimes, whether
the global economic system or the international human rights regime, they
have at times undergone significant transformations, because this accommodation entails a negotiation. These negotiations and accommodations produce
new types of borders deep inside the territory of the nation state, changing
meanings and institutional apparatuses. In this sense, looking inside the
nation states does not entail a methodological nationalism, because of the
multiple and specific structurations of the global inside what has historically
been constructed as national. Particularly through the agency of specialised
types of private authorities, a distinct field is constituted, one that assembles
bits of territory, authority, and rights into new types of specialised structure.
Private universities fit particularly well within this theoretical framework,
which allows for an analysis that takes into account various ways in which the
state retains control over these institutions while relinquishing some aspects
that have been central to the understanding of what a university is. Studying

private universities is also, therefore, a way of studying contemporary sovereignties and contested spheres of legitimisation.

Beyond being a site of contestation, the university as an institution is inherently fragile, with its status continuously challenged by reforms, increased competition, uncertain economic perspectives, and in most countries examined here by the possibility of state violence. The notion of the fragility of institutions as necessary to provide both the possibility of order as well as of critique has been recently proposed by Luc Boltanski. In his words, such an approach involves

> abandoning the idea of an implicit agreement, which would somehow be immanent in the functioning of social life, to put *dispute* and, with it, the divergence of points of view, interpretations and usages at the heart of social bonds, so as to return from this position to the issue of agreement, to examine its problematic, fragile and possibly exceptional character.
> BOLTANSKI 2011: 61, emphasis in the original

A focus on their dominating effect downplays the fact that institutions, although bodiless, are far from being unequivocal, stable and neutral, but are actually rather fragile and ambiguous. While none of the contributions directly deals with this theoretical insight, the volume as a whole offers grounding for an analysis of private universities as being central in the discourses around citizenship and knowledge, as well as in the creation of values and orders.

Understanding Private Universities Ethnographically

The need for more qualitative research in this otherwise very well studied endeavour has been frequently raised, and this is precisely the second goal of this volume, namely to offer ethnographic analyses of how world model constructions play out in local sites. How concepts travel and what happens to them when they are translated into new cultural domains is a major topic of interest to anthropologists. The increasingly international character of the university has itself facilitated the spread of these new models and programmes, and universities are fertile grounds for disseminating new ideas, albeit not always good ones (Shore and MacLauchlan 2012).[16] The anthropology of the contemporary

---

16   The webs of international rankings and research assessments in which universities are entangled are a good example of this. These competitive rankings produce unreliable data that are only ever a proxy for quality, yet they continue to be used both as drivers

world increasingly faces the challenge of analysing global assemblages, to make sense of old and new differences in an increasingly interconnected and interdependent world. Recent studies focus on issues as diverse as state bureaucracies, conflict management practices, global health and indicators. My contention, shared by the other contributors to the volume, is that the university is an apt example of such global forms, clearly linked to the state and yet increasingly subject to the influence of global trends. It thus becomes particularly interesting to see what the effects of privatisations really are, particularly in countries that could hardly be characterised as promoting political liberalism.

Contributions to this volume follow in the footstep of an earlier collection of anthropological studies of university reforms (Wright and Rabo 2010). The chapters follow loosely what has been termed the "anthropology of policy" (Shore and Wright 1997), trying to understand education reforms as processes, dynamic assemblages that are translated into different contexts, being at the same time highly mobile and yet leaning toward a mimetic isomorphism. This volume takes the privatisation of universities as a way to dissect how they function, at a time in which their role is widely questioned, in the passage to the knowledge economy briefly outlined above.[17] In particular, each chapter, through the analysis of case studies, offers fresh material on different aspects of private universities. The topics presented range from the internationalisation and commercialisation of universities through transnational corporations (Alemdaroğlu); through the explosion of low-fee for-profit private universities (Chavéz); and through state intervention to attract foreign students (Mazzella). Different case studies are presented, in order to show what private actually means in different contexts, from the Sudan (Ille) to Egypt (Cantini) and Germany (Mitterle), concluding with the extreme case of Saudi Arabia (Profanter), where private meets the international, and universities are at the core of many social changes.

The volume offers new ethnographic explorations of campuses (in particular Ille, Cantini, Mitterle and Profanter), to understand how social and political dynamics interplay with education policies (following recent interest in the literature; see for example Cantini 2016, Dessouqi 2011; Kelly 2011, Tetrault 2011; Vora 2015, just to give a short selection based on Arab countries). This perspective sees campuses as unique social spaces, as life spaces where there is some social and gender diversity, as part of the city and as separate space, as a

---

of policy and as disciplinary tools for enforcing compliance (Shore and Wright 2000; Jöns and Hoyler 2013).

17   The shift from the idea of not-for-profit institutions producing 'public good' knowledge and education for critical citizenship to higher education increasingly being viewed as a private investment for the sake of employability, and as a way to promote economic growth.

space of reproduction and transformation (Farag 2009). A focus on universities allows an exploration of how citizenship, politics, identity and belonging are reconfigured within the classrooms and the diverse social spaces of these new universities, central institutions for the production of knowledge and subjects.

The papers adopt an ethnographic perspective in their analyses; despite the interdisciplinary character of this volume, social sciences increasingly rely on ethnographic and qualitative methods. This volume offers a deeper understanding of what private universities mean in different contexts, what are the layers of borderisation between the public and the private, and what are the points of contrast and debate, of confirmation and critique. The ethnographic perspective applied to such a topic enables the combining of the tools of research – participant observation, fieldwork, the adoption of the participants' point of view, observing their practices and interactions – to the discussion of problems usually addressed in the sociology of organisations or in political economy. Such a perspective enables the combination of matters pertaining to institutional theory – the structure of the university, its policies and reforms – with the analysis of the life-worlds of those working in it, those most influenced by the changes discussed in this volume. To understand fully the implications of global higher education reforms

> it is necessary to combine the already prominent macro-level, quantita- tive, or broad theoretical perspectives with an attention to those 'implicit, un-marked, signifying practices' ... [which] often slip below the threshold of discursivity but profoundly alter how bodies are oriented, how lives are lived, and how subjects are formed.
>
> GUPTA and FERGUSON 2002: 984, quoted in SHORE and DAVIDSON 2013: 6

The studies presented here discuss everyday practices as well as the wider political and economic contexts; such an approach has yet to become estab- lished, despite the fact that it opens up new lines of questioning and new forms of knowledge, even though there are studies going in this direction (see Bierschenk and Oliver de Sardan 2014).

Moreover, the studies presented here adopt a genealogical perspective in making sense of national trajectories of development in higher education; this involves analysis of the conditions of possibility that produce the present by delving into the past and the trajectory of particular rationalities and strate- gies that have culminated in the current order of things; thus each chapter of- fers a brief overview of national trajectories of higher education development. Such an approach maintains the "complex course of descent" in order to avoid romanticising the past, in order to see the inventedness of our worlds, and to highlight the political stakes in the process (Shore and Davidson 2013: 24–26).

Presentation of the Book

This book grew out of a conference organised in Halle in November 2013, and benefited from the interests of different researchers involved in other projects. The contributors, coming from different disciplines but sharing an interest in private higher education as well as a commitment to an ethnographic mode of research, present here different case studies, clustered around three main themes. Some of the chapters deal with the actual meaning of 'private' in different contexts, and highlight the many ways in which private and public overlap, thereby contributing to an understanding of the private as being structurally linked to the public, and to an in-depth analysis of the many levels of borderisation between the two. Others focus more on the notion of commercialisation and the commodification of higher education, with a chapter focused on the emergence of global companies with financial interests in the university market. Lastly, some chapters deal with the notion of internationalisation, notably from a 'global South' perspective, highlighting ways in which private universities are instrumental in attracting foreign students, and dealing with some of the problems, notably that of cultural authenticity, caused by the presence of transplant universities in contexts that appeared rather closed.

All of the contributions share the necessity of examining these issues through detailed ethnographic research, which allows movement beyond stereotypical assumptions and easy generalisations. Private universities are not easily understood by one simple definition, and are rather complex, dynamic and ambivalent institutions, functioning differently according to different internal structures – the low-fee for profit Peruvian universities discussed by Carmela Chavéz Irigoyen bear little resemblance to the transplant university in Saudi Arabia described by Annemarie Profanter, for instance – and according to different contexts. Practices at these institutions are diverse and heterogeneous, and so are their goals, both those officially stated and those which are understood by the people who inhabit them. These differences notwithstanding, in each context the emergence of private universities has not gone uncontested, and the shifting borders between the public and the private are bound to create new spaces of resistance and of critique.

Ayça Alemdaroğlu's contribution deals with one extreme example of the double effect of internationalisation and commercialisation of universities, namely the global expansion of higher education companies. She focuses on the largest such multinational, the US-based Laureate Education Inc., and its sudden entrance into the Turkish higher education landscape. In addition to highlighting how the global companies operate, she shows the concrete struggles in a country such as Turkey, where education is (still) profit-free. Understanding higher education as a new space for capital accumulation,

Alemdaroğlu looks ethnographically at how a transnational education company works, as well as at the overlaps between the trends of globalisation and the commercialisation of higher education. She calls for an agile approach from the sociology of education that not only recognises the urgency of analysing the processes of internationalisation and commercialisation in higher education in relation to the dynamics of global capitalism but also scrutinises the non-transparent dynamics of these entangled processes at the local level.

Carmela Chavéz Irigoyen introduces us to the mushrooming of low-fee for-profit private universities in Peru as part of two processes, the massification of higher education (reaching beyond the capital city, Lima) and the increasingly widely held view that links education with the necessity to make profit, particularly prominent since the mid-1990s when the law made this possible. This change, allowing the logic of commercialisation in the higher education sector, is happening in other countries too (see in this volume the case of Egypt), but in the Peruvian case is all the more interesting given the presence of private education before the 1990s, and the massive growth of universities (in Lima alone there are more than 50). Chavéz analyses the case of low-fee private universities that are at the forefront of the new rush to acquire a university education, partly linked to new market chances and to widespread expectations of mobility. She discusses the changes in the governance of universities and in the admission of students, as well as the difficulties of accommodating the new category in the existing systems of self-governance. She shows how these new social institutions accommodate new aspirations and desires.

Sylvie Mazzella discusses the role of the Tunisian state in sponsoring, regulating and orienting the private sector, in a context largely devoid of international institutional actors. Caught between the usual combination of a perceived crisis of the public sector and a growth in the cohort of potential university students, Tunisia is pursuing a middle path, allowing a national private sector to grow, unlike Algeria, but with heavy regulation from the state, unlike Morocco. Mazzella speaks of a hybridisation between the public and private sectors, demonstrating the various links between them through an analysis of career trajectories of presidents of private universities. Her contribution tackles another important issue, namely the role of Tunisian private institutions in attracting African students, thereby enhancing the internationalisation of higher education in the country, albeit in a south-south direction.

Enrico Ille discusses private universities in the Sudan, benefiting from his own experience as a lecturer in one such institution. He attempts to move beyond the public/private divide by reflecting on the economic, political and moral aspects of working at such institutions as experienced by his colleagues of the time. The 1989 revolution brought a renewed emphasis on political as well as cultural state control over education, universities being no exception, with an emphasis on authentic knowledge, e.g. respect for the beliefs of the Islamic revolution. Despite these specificities, Sudan experienced the same steady growth of higher education institutions observed worldwide – from five public universities in 1990 to 31 public and 51 private universities listed by the ministry in the year 2012/13 – with the usual combination of massive pressure to access higher education with a discourse on its decreased quality. Government spending on higher education has decreased in the past 20 years, but its control over the sector has continued to grow, including cases of violent harassment of students and lecturers – in this sense Sudan is an apt example of how privatisation does not proceed hand in hand with liberalisation. In this difficult context, a moral distinction is operated between private for-profit and private but communal oriented universities, with the latter enjoying a higher status.

My contribution discusses the role of private universities in Egypt, with the aim of presenting a critical approach to the understanding of the mutual relation between institutions of learning and social and political change, in a context in which public education has usually been seen as a security issue by the political regimes. My analysis shows that the commodification of education is well underway, and privatisation is simply one aspect of this; it is the commercialisation of knowledge, the idea that the priorities should be set by the market, which is more troubling. The privatisation and commercialisation of the university does not inhibit the role of the state, nor its capacity to control the sector, which is crucial to its own legitimacy; the paper shows clearly how much control this kind of private universities allows for. The case study of the October 6 University, a recently established, private, low-fee for-profit institution, shows how such universities are part of state developmental goals toward new satellite cities in the desert, as well as new instruments in the effort to create a different student population, less politically conscious and active.

Until 1996 the Kingdom of Saudi Arabia was remarkably absent from the higher education landscape of the Arab region; this changed when the new king set entrance into the knowledge economy as one of the major goals of his reign. Profanter analyses the role of the newly established private universities, which include transplant universities as well as public-private cooperation, in the internationalisation and liberalisation processes that are at the core of the knowledge economy. While the private sector is growing steadily, the for-profit in particular, it remains firmly in the control of the state despite its frequent links with institutions abroad, mainly in the USA. Defining what counts as a private university in the kingdom is challenging, and causes ambiguity in official statistics, so she first discusses issues of funding, ownership, orientation, functions and governance. Her case study, the Prince Mohammad Bin Fahd University, located in the eastern part of the country and which allows females as well as males to enrol, enables Profanter to deepen her analysis of the contradictions inherent in the willingness to open the higher education sector up to private and international actors within a socially and politically highly conservative context. This chapter provides a clear example of the practical difficulties of higher education transplant, even in a context where budgetary worries are not an issue and where there is a clear political will to create the necessary conditions for private enterprises to flourish.[18]

Alexander Mitterle examines the expansion of private higher education in Germany, a phenomenon still marginal but indisputably growing in the last decade, and yet understudied, particularly when it comes to making sense of this growth, and to comparing private universities with the overwhelming public sector. While private universities have been present in Germany since the nineteenth century, particularly as linked to the various churches, both the legal status and the meaning of 'private' have varied considerably, and acquired a new understanding in the past 20 years, at the same time as most of the case studies presented in this volume. Another similarity with other cases is that such private universities do not arise in a political vacuum but in a context of highly regulatory state power – they are not private *per se* but private by public will. In a context in which public universities have a strong presence, are almost free of charge, and offer good quality, private universities struggle to thrive, opting for innovative subjects of study (half of them in the business administration sector, however) and trying to offer better conditions. Alexander offers a new way of understanding the private, through an analysis of bordering practices, which he explains by reference to admission policies, location and student ambassadors. This shows how continuities between the public and the private sector may become more diffuse in the coming years, thus eliciting further analyses on the actual meaning of private universities.

Conclusion – What Ethnographies of Private Higher Education Reveal

In the current global knowledge economy, universities are supposed to be, or to become, the factories in which the new basic resource is refined. To this end, everything within them, from modes of governance to their relation with the state, is increasingly made to resemble corporate structures, focusing on efficiency and quality. In this context, internationalisation is a necessity to

---

18   It is interesting to compare this study with the overall ethnography on how branch campuses in the United Arab Emirates have an important relationship with emerging forms of racial consciousness, identity and politicisation among students, both citizens and foreign residents (Vora 2015).

augment international student enrolment as a source of income and of respectability; at the other end of the academic production line, the employability of students has become a socially decontextualised signifier, a fundamental performance indicator in higher education, something on which the quality of the education received is evaluated (Krause-Jansen and Garsten 2014). Private universities are part of this context, and are subject to the same constrains as everyone else; a need to be productive and efficient, with heavy repercussions for the teaching staff, for instance, coupled with an increase in managerial personnel and an ubiquitous obsession with measurement and rankings to secure quality (Shore and Wright 2000).

This volume takes the university as a core institution in the project of modern nation states, which is currently undergoing a serious revision through a different understanding of its functions and of its desired outcomes. Higher education has to be understood through the political, economic and social forces that both support it and attempt to shape its sense of mission and purpose, and politics is central to comprehending the institutional, economic, ideological and social forces that give it meaning and direction (Giroux 2016). Particularly in not-so-liberal settings, such as many of the cases explored by contributors to this volume, it is interesting to examine the actual implications of privatisation and internationalisation policies. While some of the reforms taking place could be described as a mere political spectacle, "largely intended to satisfy demands by competing stakeholders with which the state is embattled to ensure its survival" (Mazawi 2007: 262), the effects of privatisation and internationalisation policies are acutely felt in many different contexts, and are more likely than not "here to stay" (Altbach and Levy 2005; Morley 2014).

This volume makes at least two important contributions to the growing field of studies that seek to understand this phenomenon, happening worldwide almost simultaneously, albeit under very different political and social circumstances. First, it shows clearly how the 'private' cannot be understood without a 'public', and that rather than positing the private as something completely different it is more interesting to look at the different layers of borders within the two.[19] Secondly, it shows the benefits of an ethnographic methodology in allowing for a deeper understanding of what is actually happening in the field. In this way, the volume contributes to several current debates in the social sciences. The rise of private universities is a recent phenomenon, still

---

19   It is interesting to see how privatisation and internationalisation are happening within
      the public universities too; in this volume this is hinted at by Mazzella and Mitterle, but
      there are studies that start to address the issue (see for example Cantini 2016, in particular
      Chapter II).

understudied, especially in comparative perspective, and particularly when it comes to ethnographic case studies. This volume is a first attempt at providing case studies, understood within their own national settings, but keeping the focus on dynamics that can be detected all over the world. Despite the national specificities, the contributions collected here examine in detail a number of issues usually associated with privatisation. In this sense, the volume offers a comparative overview that retains the polyphony (and polysemy) of the different contexts, enhanced by the fact that the contributors come from a variety of social science backgrounds.

Works Cited

Altbach, P. and J. Knight. 2007. "The internationalisation of higher education: motivations and realities". *Journal of Studies in International Education* 11 (3/4): 290–305.

Altbach, P. and D. Levy. 2005. *Private Higher Education: A Global Revolution*, Rotterdam: Sense Publishers.

Behrends, A., S.-J. Park and R. Rottenburg. 2014. *Travelling Models in African Conflict Management*. Leiden: Brill.

Bernasconi, A. 1994. "La privatización de la educación superior chilena y la regulación a través del Mercado". *Estudios Sociales*, 82 (4): 9–24.

Bierschenk, T. and J.-P. Oliver de Sardan (eds). 2014. *States at Work: Dynamics of African Bureaucracies*. Leiden: Brill.

Boltanski, L. 2011 [2009]. *On Critique: A Sociology of Emancipation*. Trans. by Gregory Elliott. London: Polity.

Cantini, D. 2014. "Une université privée égyptienne dans le nouveau marché international de l'enseignement supérieur". *Cahiers de la Recherce sur l'Education et les Savoirs*, 13: 167–179

Cantini, D. 2016. *Youth and Education in the Middle East. Shaping Identity and Politics in Jordan*. London: I.B. Tauris.

Collier, Stephen. 2012. "Neoliberalism as big Leviathan, or ...?" *Social Anthropology* 20 (2): 186–195.

Dale, R. 2000. "Globalisation and education: demonstrating a 'common world education culture' or locating a 'globally structured agenda for education'?" *Education Theory* 50 (4): 427–448.

Dessouqi, N. 2011. "Cairo University" (in Arabic). Report prepared for the project *Governance and autonomy in the changing landscape of higher education in the Arab world*, New York: Social Science Research Council.

Di Maggio, Paul and Walter Powell. 1983. "The iron cage revisited: institutional isomorphism and collective rationality in organizational fields". *American Sociological Review* 48 (2): 147–160.

Elkana, Y. 2012. "The university of the 21st century: an aspect of globalisation". In J. Renn (ed.). *The Globalisation of Knowledge in History*. Berlin: Max Planck Research Library for the History and Development of Knowledge.

Etzkowitz, H. and L. Leydesdorff. 2000. "The dynamics of innovation: from National Systems and 'Mode 2' to a Triple Helix of university–industry–government relations". *Research Policy* 29 (2): 109–123.

Farag, I. 2009. "La privatisation de l'enseignement supérieur dans le monde arabe. Etat des lieux et questions de recherché". Higher Education in the Arab region, http:// arabhighered.org/wp-content/uploads/2015/11/Farag-French-Privatizaton.pdf.

Ferguson J. and A. Gupta. 2002. "Spatializing states: toward an ethnography of neoliberal governmentality". *American Ethnologist* 29: 981–1002

Ganti, T. 2014. "Neoliberalism". *Annual Review of Anthropology* 43: 89–104.

Geiger, R.L. 1986. "Finance and function: voluntary support and diversity in American private higher education". In: Daniel Levy (ed.) *Private Education: Studies in Choice and Public Policy*. Oxford: Oxford University Press.

Giroux, Henry. 2016 [2012]. *Twilight of the Social: Resurgent Publics in the Age of Disposability*. New York: Routledge.

Gibbons, M., H. Nowotny and C. Limoges. 1994. *The New Production of Knowledge: The Dynamics of Science and Research in Contemporary Societies*. London: Sage.

Goodale, Mark and Nancy Postero (eds.) 2013. *Neoliberalism, Interrupted: social change and contested governance in contemporary Latin America*. Stanford: Stanford University Press.

Graeber, D. 2014. "Anthropology and the rise of the professional-managerial class". *HAU: Journal of Ethnographic Theory* 4 (3): 73–88.

Hanafi, S. 2011. "University systems in the Arab east: publish globally and perish locally vs. publish locally and perish globally". *Current Sociology* 59 (3): 291–309.

Harvey D. 2005. *A Brief History of Neoliberalism*. Oxford: Oxford University Press.

Henry, M. *et al.* 2001. *The OECD, Globalisation and Education Policy*. Oxford: IAU Press, Pergamon.

Jöns, H. and M. Hoyler. 2013. "Global geographies of higher education: the perspective of world university rankings". *Geoforum* 46: 45–59.

Kauppinen, I. 2013. "Different meanings of 'knowledge as commodity' in the context of higher education". *Critical Sociology* 40 (3): 393–409.

Kelly, M. 2011. "Balancing cultures at the American University of Kuwait". *Journal of Arabian Studies: Arabia, the Gulf, and the Red Sea* 1–2: 201–229.

Krause-Jensen, J. and C. Garsten. 2014. "Introduction: neoliberal turns in higher education". *Learning & Teaching* 7 (3): 1–13.

Krücken, Georg and Kathia Serrano-Verde. 2012. "Editorial". *European Journal of Education*, 47 (2).

Levy, Daniel. 1986. *Higher Education and the State in Latin America: Private Challenges to Public Dominance*. Chicago, IL: University of Chicago Press.

Mamdani, Mahmood. 2007. *Scholars in the Marketplace: the Dilemmas of Neo-liberal Reforms at Makerere University 1989–2005*. Cape Town: HSRC Press.

Marcus GE. 1995. "Ethnography in/of the world system: the emergence of multi-sited ethnography". *Annual Review of Anthropology* 24: 95–117.

Mazawi, A. 2007. "'Knowledge society' or work as 'spectacle'? Education for work and the prospects of social transformation in Arab societies". In L. Farrell and T. Fenwick (eds). *Educating the Global Workforce*. London: Routledge, 251–267.

Mazawi, A. 2010. "Naming the imaginary: 'building an Arab Knowledge Society' and the contested terrain of educational reforms for development". In O. Abi-Mershed (ed.). *Trajectories of Education in the Arab World*. London: Routledge, 201–225.

Mazzella, S. and E. Eyebiyi (eds). 2014. "Observer les mobilités étudiantes Sud-Sud". *Cahiers de la Recherche sur l'Education et les Savoirs* 13 (special issue).

Meyer, John *et al.* 2007. "Higher education as an institution". In Patricia Gumport (ed.). *Sociology of Higher Education*. Baltimore, MD: Johns Hopkins University Press, 187–221.

Miller-Idriss, C. and E. Hanauer. 2011. "Transnational higher education: offshore campuses in the Middle East". *Comparative Education* 47 (2).

Morley, L. 2014. "Inside African private higher education: contradictions and challenges". *International Higher Education* 76: 14–15.

Musselin, Christine. 2008. "Vers un marché international de l'enseignement supérieur?" *Critique internationale* 39 (2): 13–24.

Nielsen, G. 2012. "Higher education gone global". *Learning & Teaching* 5 (3): 1–21.

Ong, A. and S. Collier. 2005. "Global assemblages, anthropological problems". In S. Collier and A. Ong (eds). *Global Assemblages: Technology, Politics, Ethics*. Malden, MA: Blackwell.

Reisz, Robert and Manfred Stock. 2008. "Private hochschulen – perspektive der forschung". *Die Hochschule. Journal für Wissenschaft und Bildung* 2: 6–18.

Rizvi, F. 2006. "Imagination and the globalisation of educational policy research". *Globalisation, Societies and Education* 4 (2): 193–205.

Romani, V. 2009. "The Geopolitics of Higher Education in the Middle East: Frame and Prospects". Crown Center for Middle East Studies, http://www.brandeis.edu/crown/publications/meb/MEB36.pdf

Romani, V. (ed.). 2012. "Enseignement supérieur, pouvoirs et mondialisation dans le monde arabe". *Revue des mondes musulmans et la Méditerranée* 131 (special issue).

Sassen, S. 2005. "When national territory is home to the global: old borders to novel borderings". *New Political Economy* 10 (4): 523–541.

Sassen, S. 2007. *Territory, Authority, Rights: From Medieval to Global Assemblages*. Princeton, NJ: Princeton University Press.

Schofer, Evan and John Meyer. 2005. "The worldwide expansion of higher education in the twentieth century". *American Sociological Review* 70: 898–920.

Schwegler T.A. 2009. "The bankrupt framework of neoliberalism: a bailout of anthropological theory". *Anthropology News* 50: 24.

Shore, Cris and Miri Davidson. 2013. *Methodologies For Studying University Reform and Globalisation: Combining Ethnography and Political Economy*. Aarhus: EPOKE, Aarhus University.

Shore, Cris and Laura McLauchlan. 2012. "'Third mission' activities, commercialisation and academic entrepreneurs". *Social Anthropology* 20 (3): 267–286.

Shore, Cris and Susan Wright. 2000. "Coercive accountability: the rise of audit culture in higher education". In M. Strathern (ed.) *Audit Cultures: Anthropological Studies in Accountability, Ethics and the Academy*. London: Routledge, 57–89.

Slaughter S. and G. Rhoades. 2004. *Academic Capitalism and the New Economy: Markets, State and Higher Education*. Baltimore, MD and London: Johns Hopkins University Press.

Stevens, M., E. Armstrong and R. Arum. 2008. "Sieve, incubator, temple, hub: empirical and theoretical advances in the sociology of higher education". *Annual Review of Sociology* 34: 127–151.

Teixeira, Pedro and David Dill (eds). 2011. *Public Vices, Private Virtues? Assessing the Effects of Marketization in Higher Education*. Rotterdam: Sense Publishers.

Tetrault, M.A. 2011. "Identity and transplant-university education in the Gulf: The American University of Kuwait". *Journal of Arabian Studies* 1(1): 81–98.

Vora, N. 2015. "Is the university universal? Mobile (re)constitutions of American academia in the Gulf Arab states". *Anthropology & Education Quarterly* 46 (1): 19–36.

Wacquant, L. 2012. "Three steps to a historical anthropology of actually existing neoliberalism", *Social Anthropology*, 20 (1): 66–79.

Weiler, H. 2011. "Knowledge and power: the new politics of higher education". *Journal of Educational Planning and Administration* 25 (3): 205–221.

World Bank. 2002. *Constructing Knowledge Societies: New Challenges for Tertiary Education*. Washington, DC: World Bank.

Wright, Susan and Annika Rabo. 2010. "Introduction: anthropology of university reform". *Social Anthropology* 18 (1).

Wright, Susan and Chris Shore. 1997. *Anthropology of Policy: Critical Perspectives on Governance and Power*. London: Routledge.

CHAPTER 1

The Global Trade in Higher Education: A Tale of an American Company in the Middle East

Ayça Alemdaroğlu

On 20 November 2006, employees and students of Istanbul Bilgi University, a medium-size, non-profit, private university in Istanbul, woke up to the news that 50% of their university had been sold to an American company, Laureate Education Incorporated. The members of the Bilgi faculty and students had not been aware that their university was for sale, nor did they know universities could be bought and sold. Despite the rumours that had been circulating in the corridors about the financial bottleneck, nobody anticipated that the way out of the distress would be the sale of the university. The next day, the university administration denied the news of the sale and declared that the new relationship with Laureate would merely be "a strategic cooperation" with the goal of transforming the university into a global institution. The strategic cooperation that started on that day in 2006 ended with the company's takeover of the university in 2009.

Today, along with Istanbul Bilgi University, Laureate owns over 85 campuses and online universities around the world. These institutions vary in size and scope, ranging from a community college in San Jose, California, to a design school in Italy, from a health sciences school in Brazil to a comprehensive university in Malaysia. Headquartered in Baltimore, Maryland, Laureate is the largest higher education company in the world, with a commercial presence in 28 countries and educating more than a million students in Europe, Africa, Asia, and the Americas. Despite its size, Laureate has managed to keep a low profile in the US and remained immune from the public scrutiny and governmental pressure that have impacted on other higher education companies such as the Apollo Group, DeVry, and Corinthian over the last five years. According to 2015 numbers, for-profit colleges educate 11% of all higher education students, but get 26% of all student loans and produce 43% of all loan defaulters in the US. There are plenty of lawsuits against these colleges for high tuition fees, poor educational outcomes, aggressive marketing strategies, exploitation of federal student loans by the enrolment of students with inadequate qualifications to degree programmes that they cannot complete, leaving many with life-long debts. The US Government has introduced new regulations that hold colleges accountable for preparing students for gainful employment, mandate graduation and job placement disclosures, impose new rules to protect students from misleading or overly aggressive recruiting practices, and ensure that only eligible students receive federal funds. After the enactment of these regulations, many of the private suppliers encountered difficulties. For example, one of the nation's largest for-profit college chains, Corinthian, announced the closure of its 28 campuses in April 2015 upon a $30 million fine levied by the Department of Education against the company for publicising falsified data that were misleading to students. Laureate's relatively smaller commercial presence in the US, and its heavy reliance on student tuition fees rather than federal loans, protects it from the troubles of its counterparts.

However, the company's acquisitions in countries such as Turkey, Mexico, and Chile are puzzling, simply because the laws in these countries ban for-profit institutions in higher education. This paper unpacks the Laureate phenomenon as a new creature of commercialisation and globalisation in higher education. By focusing on Laureate's acquisition of Istanbul Bilgi University, I examine below the macro and micro processes by which higher education emerges as a global space of capital accumulation and transnational governance. How did Laureate acquire a non-profit school in a country that bans for-profit institutions? What happens to an institution when its leadership is transferred from domestic entrepreneurs and academics to a foreign management company? What are the overlaps between the two trends of globalisation and commercialisation of higher education?

To explore these questions within the framework of the Bilgi case, I draw on my recurrent fieldwork in Istanbul and Ankara between 2011 and 2013. During this period, I conducted in-depth interviews with the head of Laureate's operations in Turkey and a number of past and present members of the Board of Trustees, administrators, and faculty of the university. I also interviewed bureaucrats at the Council of Higher Education (Yükseköğretim Kurulu or YÖK), a regulatory state institution that oversees Turkish universities. Finally, I examined the company's operations by studying its website, public communications and financial reports. In the following, I will examine the macro and micro context of the acquisition of the university, the business strategy, and the political work of the company in achieving legitimacy and successfully transforming the university.

Higher Education as a New Space of Capital Accumulation

The end of the twentieth century coincided with a fundamental transformation in the functions and organisation of higher education. In the most general sense, as Patricia Gumport (2000: 67) points out, this was the transformation of "the dominant legitimating idea of public higher education from higher education as a social institution to higher education as an industry". Higher education has become increasingly seen as an economic enterprise, being governed and organised in accordance with the economic principles of profitability, accountability, and efficiency. Scholars have named this new phenomenon 'academic capitalism', and have argued that in this new order, knowledge has been transformed from being treated as a public good, produced and used for social benefit, into a commodity bought and sold for profit (Slaughter and Rhoades 2009; Slaughter and Leslie 1999). Slaughter and Rhoades (2009) argue that market-like behaviours, marketing and selling a wide range of products, have become a prominent characteristic of higher education institutions in the US. In addition to earlier practices of selling non-academic consumption items (such as logos, T-shirts, mugs, etc.), colleges are now also looking for ways to generate revenue from their core research and teaching functions. Academic capitalism entails practices such as opting for types of knowledge-production that produce patents and copyrights; forming partnerships with private companies for research and development; and bringing in professional administrators who can boost the institution's competiveness, brand name, and revenue. There is a sizeable literature on the adverse effects of this commodification process, led by the US colleges, on institutional autonomy, objectivity of research, and the social ideals of the university (Bok 2004; Kirp 2003; Readings 1996; Slaughter and Leslie 1997; Slaughter and Rhodes 2004). While this literature mainly focuses on public and non-profit private institutions, there is very little on the most extreme form of commodification in higher education, namely, for-profit private institutions (Kinser and Levy 2007).

Laureate Education Inc. is a distinctive player in the global for-profit higher education sector. Formerly called Sylvan International Universities, it was established in 1998 by the publicly traded Sylvan Learning Systems. Laureate began acquiring universities globally in 1999, first with the Universidad Europea de Madrid, a comprehensive private university in Spain. In the early 2000s, the company reported record growth rates, increasing its revenues over 30% each year and growing its stock price at significant rates on the NASDAQ. In 2004, the company adopted its current name 'Laureate' after separating higher education from its core K-12 tutoring, educational testing, and corporate education operations. The *Chronicle of Higher Education* reported on the arduous marketing research that the company undertook to find its new name, sifting through French, Spanish, Italian and Portuguese dictionaries for a word that might suggest "achievement," "a sense of internationality" across national borders, and in particular a sense of 'Europeanness' – deemed an asset in the countries in which the company operates.[1]

Laureate ventured into the Turkish market in 2006. Turkey was attractive for Laureate as its economy was undergoing extensive privatisation of the public sector. After coming to power in 2002, the Justice and Development Party (AKP) governments launched a "massive privatisation" campaign similar to Mexico and Argentina in the 1990s, selling leading public enterprises in block sales to major private sector consortia (Öniş 2011). As a result, the country became more open to international trade and investment, and the per capita GDP rose significantly, from around $3,000 in the early 2000s to about $10,000 by the end of the decade. However, while the economic restructuring promised a myriad of opportunities in many sectors of the economy, such as banking, finance, energy, and communication, higher education was not necessarily one of them: First of all, the Turkish Constitution (1982) bans for-profit institutions in higher education. The Law of Higher Education (no. 2547, 1981) allowed private foundations to establish and operate higher education institutions, provided that they were not-for-profit. Secondly, about 90% of higher education in the mid-2000s was taking place in public universities. Turkey witnessed a rapid expansion of public universities in the 2000s, making the country seem less than an ideal place for investment. Thirdly, higher education is a financially, administratively, and ideologically heavily regulated field in Turkey. The military rulers following the 1980 coup created the Council of Higher Education as a regulatory state institution in order to plan, administer, and audit higher education institutions. Financially, the Bylaw for the Foundation(al) Higher Education Institutions (article 26) specifies that 'foundation universities' should not directly or indirectly transfer revenues obtained from educational, consultancy and commercial operations to the foundation or to third parties. If it is proven that this has occurred, the bylaw mandates the closure of the university. Administratively, university admission in Turkey is done through a centralised system based on a nation-wide competitive exam executed by YÖK. The YÖK maintains tight control over most aspects of student recruitment, determines the quotas of academic programmes, and sets the base-line scores for student acceptance. Finally, the military regime also deemed the Council to be an ideological panacea against political mobilisation in universities, which became the hot bed of political conflict between leftists and ultra-nationalist groups throughout the 1970s. Legally the YÖK can close universities based on ambiguous provisions such as non-compliance

---

1   Goldie Blumenstyk. 2004. "Sylvan Learning Systems caps its metamorphosis into a higher-education company with a new name". *Chronicle of Higher Education* (17 May).

with the principles of Ataturk such as secularism or undermining the unity of the nation. With its laws against for-profits and its centralised system, Turkey would seem to be an inhospitable place for Laureate.

However, despite its seemingly inhospitable legal framework, Turkey's international commitments made it an attractive place for Laureate. Among all the service sectors that the General Agreement on Trade in Services (GATS) addresses, the World Trade Organisation (WTO) members are the most reluctant to make commitments in education (Bashir, 2007). Less than one-third of the 149 member countries made commitments in education, in contrast to banking, financial services, business, and telecommunications, in which 70% to 95% of all members commit (Kemp, 2000). Turkey is among only 32 countries that signed up to the four provisions, including (a) cross-border supply – from the territory of one member into the territory of any other member, and includes any type of course and testing service that can cross borders through distance education or commercial franchising; (b) consumption abroad – involves the education of students in foreign countries; (c) commercial presence – the actual presence of foreign investors in a host country, including foreign universities setting up campuses and institutions; (d) presence of natural persons – the ability of people to move between countries to provide education services. Hence, Turkey was fully committed to the liberalisation of trade in higher education mandated by GATS.

The global and national policy contexts in the late 2000s were also favourable for further privatisation of Turkish higher education. The major proponent of Turkey's privatisation of higher education has been the World Bank (WB). In its country study reports, the bank has advised the government to take measures to increase private investment in education. The bank promoted this policy based on the growing demand for higher education in the developing world and the failure of states to cater to such demand. Worldwide, the number of students in higher education institutions nearly doubled from 99.7 million in 2000 to 198.6 million in 2013, with about 90% of those students in countries outside the US, according to the United Nations Educational, Scientific and Cultural Organisation. According to the World Bank's "The Strategic Direction for Higher Education in Turkey" (Report No. 39674, 2007):

> Turkey devotes 1.1 percent of GDP to public spending on tertiary education, comparable with many countries and above many others, but below the Scandinavian countries. Turkey is unlikely to increase this percentage substantially, especially as the government faces competing educational priorities at the basic and secondary education levels. At the same time private spending on tertiary education is .1 percent of GDP,

on par with the Scandinavian countries but well below any of the other countries [such as Australia, Korea, USA]. Without increases in the overall share of GDP devoted to tertiary education, it will be very difficult for Turkey ... to expand its system. Such an expansion is likely to entail a significant increase in private spending. (p.9)

In the context of the government's feverish privatisation campaign, the Ninth Development Plan (2007–2013), compiled by the AKP government, states that "the establishment of private higher education institutions will be permitted provided that an efficient quality assessment and supervision system is set up".

While these planned changes are promising for foreign education companies, and to some extent explain Laureate's interest in Turkey, the question remains how the company acquired and operates a college in Turkey. In order to answer that question, one needs a micro approach, focusing on a local context where the aforementioned global blueprints play out. For this purpose, we shall now turn to the actual conditions of the Laureate's acquisition of Bilgi University and the political work the company engaged in to achieve legitimacy in Turkey.

Buying a University Overseas

Istanbul Bilgi University was established in 1994 as the Istanbul School of International Studies, a branch of Portsmouth University in England. For two years, the university operated as a 'pirate university', without the necessary permissions from the YÖK (Arslan ve Odman, 2011). In 1996 it acquired the status of a 'foundation university', and launched its first campus in Kuştepe, a lower-class neighbourhood in central Istanbul, with a focus on arts and social sciences. The founder of the university, Oğuz Özerden, was a young entrepreneur who made his fortune from the Alo Bilgi, a variety of premium call-in phone lines, mostly offering phone conversations with celebrities. Academics who took part in the founding of the university were former faculty at the prominent public universities of Turkey, and many of them had been dismissed or had resigned from their positions because of their left-leaning opposition to the military regime following the 1980 coup. In the 2000s, the university recruited faculty members with PhDs from prominent American and European research universities. This composition rendered the university a politically and intellectually lively and progressive place to work, especially for social scientists.

During the 2000s, the university and its faculty harboured politically progressive yet controversial ideas and events in Turkey. In 2005, the university hosted what came to be known as 'the Armenian conference', when the original organisation at the Bosphorus University – a prominent public university in Istanbul – was cancelled by a last minute court order. The Minister of Justice publicly denounced the conference organisers for "stabbing the Turkish nation in the back" for not subscribing to the official denialist position on the Armenian genocide.[2] However, President Abdullah Gül, and Prime Minister Recep Tayyip Erdoğan, along with the European Commission, decried the court decision as an anti-EU provocation referring to the ongoing legislative efforts to punish the denial of the genocide in European countries. This helped the organisers to circumvent the court ruling by moving the conference to Bilgi University. Liberal intellectuals and academics welcomed the event as a taboo-breaking milestone on the road to the democratisation of the country.[3] The following year, the university hosted what came to be known as 'The Kurdish Conference', the first conference to explicitly name the Kurdish problem in its title at a time when the majority of Turks denied its existence. Bilgi University also adopted a liberal approach to the issue of 'veiling', despite the regulations prohibiting its use in public institutions and the constant anti-veil pressure from YÖK.[4]

In addition to increasingly becoming a venue for democratic conversation in Turkey, the university also pursued community-friendly policies. Unlike many public and foundation universities, which began to subcontract their service jobs in the 1990s, Bilgi staffed its own security, cleaning, and transportation personnel, even employing a couple of carpenters, favouring workers from the unprivileged neighbourhoods that surround its campuses.

Bilgi was also a financial outlier in Turkey's higher education field. If we categorise Turkey's foundation universities in terms of their institutional and financial composition, were three main categories at the time of Laureate's arrival on the market. First, universities owned by large multi-national family holdings, such as Bilkent, Koç, and Sabancı, which rank among the top universities in Turkey in terms of research and students' success. Second, universities founded by faith-based or business organisations, such as TOBB, Fatih, Izmir Ekonomi; and finally, universities that emerged from the private secondary

---

2   http://www.hurriyetdailynews.com/armenian-conference-finally-gets-under-way-at-bilgi
    -university.aspx?pageID=438&n=armenian-conference-finally-gets-under-way-at-bilgi
    -university-2005-09-25.

3   http://armenianweekly.com/2014/05/07/heterogeneous-memory-vs-homogeneous-nation
    -memory-revisited-turkey/.

4   Over the last two decades, the issue of the veil was at the centre of political contestation between Islamists, liberals and democratic leftists on the one side and secularist and nationalist groups on the other.

institutions, such as Atılım, Yüce, TED.[5] In comparison to these three groups, Bilgi lacked the strong financial and/or institutional backing available to others. Rifat Sarıcaoğlu, the current chairman, who first contacted Özerden on behalf of the company in 2004, explained Laureate's interest in Bilgi based on a similar mapping of Turkish foundation universities.[6]

In 2004, the university launched SantralIstanbul, a new campus project to include a contemporary art museum and an energy museum in a defunct power station. The project became possible through Özerden's personal efforts to persuade then -Prime Minister Tayyip Erdoğan to obtain the rights on the site from the Ministry of Energy and Natural Resources for 20 years. The new campus project was also seen by the founder as a project to transform education in the social sciences there by injecting it with the dynamism and creativity of art. Influenced by the Gulbenkian Commission's report, "Open the Social Sciences" (Wallerstein 1996), with its critique of nineteenth-century departmentalisation in particular and the university as an institution in general, Özerden explained the goal of the project:

> The university is a very conservative institution like the church. It does not like change. There has been a crisis in the social sciences in the last ten years; it is for that reason that we do something at the intersection of the social sciences and the arts. This is in a way to challenge and open up the university. This is a project to break up the formal structure in the university.[7]

The progressive approach and the liberal environment that Bilgi cultivated over the years placed the university in a special position relative to other foundation universities in Turkey.

Laureate first contacted Bilgi in 2004, around the time the SantralIstanbul project was launched. However, Özerden declined this first offer, which he later described as "indecent".

---

5 This categorisation summarises the state of the foundation sector in 2004. Since then Turkey has witnessed a boom in foundation universities, many of which were founded by companies and businesspeople and located in places that are obscure to the general public.

6 Interview with Rıfat Sarıcaoğlu, 18 October 2010, İstanbul.

7 Interview with Oğuz Özerden, "Zaman zaman pişman oldum". *Radikal*, 21 September 2007. http://www.radikal.com.tr/haber.php?haberno=227582&tarih=21/07/2007.

Laureate was after buying an entity that legally cannot be bought or sold. They are like American cowboys, the law does not matter as long as they want something and there is an opportunity.[8]

Over the next two years, however, the opportunity for Laureate ripened as campus construction unexpectedly cost over 50% more than the budgeted US $30 million. This financial burden was aggravated by the low student intake in 2006 when the YÖK raised the acceptance score for four-year colleges, leading to a significant fall in the earnings from tuition fees at private universities.[9] The increasing sense of financial risk turned Laureate's 'indecent proposal' into an opportunity for Özerden and his team as an alternative source of funding.

Bilgi University was also under pressure from the YÖK in connection with the bylaw (Article 26), which mandates that courts can close down any university if it is proven to have contradicted the Principles of Ataturk, such as secularism and loyalty to the unity of the nation. The vagueness of the language in the bylaw gives great discretionary power to the YÖK. The university had already received a warning from the institution in the late 1990s, at the peak of the pressure exerted on universities to ban veiled students from attending classes. The coupling of the political situation with the financial bottleneck intensified Özerden's sense of risk of losing the university.

In addition to the pressure from the YÖK during the expansion of the university, Özerden and his entourage faced increasing pressure to set up more formal institutional norms and procedures. The team's extemporaneous involvement at every level of decision making made it difficult to respond adequately to the needs of the faculty, students, and personnel. For instance, if a faculty member needed funding, she had to talk personally to Özerden or one of his close associates. Thus, the faculty members closer to Özerden had access to more resources, causing resentment among the rest over time. However, even though Özerden and his team were aware of the necessity to establish more formal procedures, they were unwilling or unequipped to change the established relations and power structure within the university. In this context, they revisited Laureate's offer, now seeing it as a chance to monetise the value of the institution.

After negotiations, the legal consultants were eventually able to formulate the 'indecent proposal' into a legal deal. In 2006, Bilgi and Laureate declared a partnership. The deal was announced to the Turkish public as a "strategic cooperation" and "the integration of 'Bilgi' into a global network". Özerden stated

---

8   Interview with Oğuz Özerden, 19 October 2010, İstanbul. .
9   *Radikal* 21 November 2006.

that, with this cooperation, Laureate would help Bilgi open vocational schools, embark in online and adult education, and sell services in these two areas.[10]

In the press release about the partnership, Douglas Becker, chairman and CEO of Laureate, stated:

> We are excited that Istanbul Bilgi University has joined the Laureate net-work to serve increasing numbers of aspiring students in Turkey and the region. Bilgi's academic and social mission will significantly add to the cultural and academic richness of Laureate's international network.[11]

In the same press release, Laureate announced to its stockholders that Bilgi University is a non-profit foundation university, and therefore, the transaction would not materially impact on the company's 2006 and 2007 earnings out-look. The terms of the deal remained undisclosed. However, we know that the company acquired seats on the board of Bilgi and signed a management deal to sell services to the university. In my interviews with Bilgi administrators in Istanbul, I could not identify which services these were. 'Buying services' from another Laureate company was likely to have been a cover for transferring funds out of Bilgi until Turkey legalises commercial universities. Laureate's annual filings to the US Securities and Exchange Commission (SEC) confirm my initial understanding.

In the 2005 filing, the company stated the following risk factor in countries such as Mexico and Chile, where for-profit universities are banned by appli-cable law:

> In order to efficiently transfer funds out of the universities in these coun-tries, the Company has entered into management agreements with the university. Under these agreements, the management company would be paid for providing services to the university. There is no assurance that the governments would continue to permit this type of arrangement at all or would not require the Company to revise the amounts charged for the services provided.

In June 2007, six months after the announcement of its partnership with Bilgi, an investment group led by private equity firm Kohlberg Kravis Roberts (KKR) and Laureate's CEO Douglas Becker bought out the company by collecting

---

10   *Radikal* 21 November 2006.
11   http://www.laureate.net/NewsRoom/PressReleases/2006/11/IstanbulBilgiUniversity
        Partnership.aspx_.

all its shares on NASDAQ. The buyout was significant for two reasons. First, it epitomised the growing interest of big financial institutions in higher education. In 2010, the KKR announced in a memo to its investors that the 2007 investment in Laureate had increased in value by 45%.[12] The increasing interest of big financial institutions in higher education, and in particular in Laureate, became more striking when the International Finance Corporation (IFC), the investment arm of the World Bank, made a $150 million investment in the company in 2013—announced as the largest investment in education by the IFC. Second, the buyout marked a turning point in Laureate's global expansion. In 2006, just before the transaction, the company held 31 universities in 16 countries. In the following eight years, the company tripled the number of institutions it managed. Once owned by a lightly regulated private equity firm, Laureate was relieved of the need to disclose its accounts and operations to the SEC. Hence, the buyout allowed the company to gain flexibility in the pursuit of fast-tracked global expansion.

Since the buyout, no public information has been made available about how the partnership with Bilgi impacts Laureate's earnings. In my interview with the chairman, Sarıcaoğlu, in 2010, he mentioned that the returns from Bilgi were well below some of the other Laureate universities, adding that the company expects a different value-added, especially in the early years of the transaction. He claimed that Bilgi University adds prestige to the network and facilitates the company's access to new markets by attracting students from Eastern Europe, Central Asia, and the Middle East, expanding Laureate campuses and programmes both in Anatolia and in the wider region.

From Strategic Cooperation to the Takeover: The Legitimacy of Laureate in Turkey

The strategic cooperation announced in 2006 ended in the company's takeover of the university, by replacing 80% of the board seats at the university's parent foundation, the Bilgi Education and Culture Foundation, and the majority of the university's board of trustees and top administration in 2009. Despite the deal, the actual transfer of the university turned into a strenuous legal struggle when Özerden went to court demanding its cancellation on the grounds that it was contrary to the provision of Foundations Law that restricts the replacement of the Foundation Board. The court case lasted a couple of years. Despite

---

12   http://www.bloomberg.com/news/print/2014-01-06/clinton-pitches-kkr-backed-college
      -chain-amid-controversy.html.

the lower court's favorable decision and the Courts of Appeal's earlier favorable ruling in a similar case, Özerden lost in the appeal process.[13]

However, how Laureate has achieved legitimacy in Turkey is still a pertinent question. Let me turn to my ethnography at the YÖK to shed some light on this. In my conversations with YÖK board members and bureaucrats overseeing the Foundation Universities in September 2011, I realised that they, purposefully or not, refrain from acknowledging that Laureate is a for-profit management company and that it had purchased Istanbul Bilgi University. Instead, YÖK bureaucrats repeatedly utilised the word 'network' that Doug Becker used twice in his announcement of the Bilgi deal quoted above. (quoted on p. 36), to explain the relationship between the university and the company. For them, the relationship was one of academic collaboration, which aligns with the Council's recent policy that aims to make Turkish universities 'global' by promoting international research collaboration and student exchange. Nonetheless, the question here hardly is whether or not Bilgi has become a part of a global network. Rather, it is the nature of this collaboration and the ways in which term such as 'network' or 'academic collaboration' are employed so as to misrecognise the fact that an American education company bought a university in Turkey, where universities are still non-tradable entities by law.

Echoing the neoliberal discourse circulated by the WB, IFC, and WTO, my interlocutors at YÖK claimed that private investment in higher education is necessary in order to share the state's burden of innovation and response to the increasing demand for higher education. In that framework, while they were evasive about the nature of the relationship between the company and the university, they were enthusiastic about the legalisation of for-profits in the new draft Higher Education Law. During my conversations at the Council, I became aware that a free zone for higher education was also on the agenda. Two members of the board who were responsible for overseeing foundation universities explained to me that the possibility of establishing a higher education zone similar to Dubai's International Academic City[14] was on the Board's table. The zone, at the time planned on the Konya Plateau, would attract foreign investment to Turkey by tax exemptions and easy transfer of earnings abroad.

While YÖK members were evasive about the case of Laureate itself, and denied its for-profit nature, they explained to me that the legalisation of

---

13   Interview with a founding member of the Bilgi Foundation, September 2013.
14   http://www.diacedu.com.

for-profits would help YÖK "separate the wheat from the chaff" ("*sapla samanı birbirinden ayırmak*") by allowing universities to "show their true faces" ("*gerçek yüzleriyle ortaya çıkması*"). Even though I was told YÖK audits the accounts of foundation universities every year, there is very little transparency. A recent qualitative study conducted in foundation universities reveals the ways in which university funds are unlawfully used to profit private individuals and businesses and the extent to which these universities fail to fulfil their teaching and research functions (Vatansever and Gezici-Yalçın 2015). The YÖK board members I talked to argued that legalising for-profit operations and private gains in higher education will allow the state to tax these institutions and individuals, hence ensuring that they pay their dues. However, despite a certain degree of agreement about legalisation, I also observed some confusion and lack of comprehension about the potential implications of such commercialisation. When I mentioned some of the mal-practices and the national debate, which later led to a Senate Committee Investigation of for-profits in the United States, one member stated: "Honestly, we're trying to wrap our minds around this business, thinking where the devil is".

The decision process at YÖK, however, is not independent from Laureate's political work in Turkey. The next section will explore the company's efforts to shape its public image and relations with politicians and state institutions.

Laureate's Political Work

In my role as Honorary Chancellor of *Laureate International Universities,* I have had the privilege of meeting students, faculty and alumni at Laureate Institutions in Brazil, Germany, Malaysia, Mexico, Peru, Spain, Turkey, and the United States … One of the most inspiring characteristics of the Laureate community is its commitment to social change. The impact Laureate students have on their communities is profound. In my own work with the Clinton Global Initiative, we seek to foster collaboration among governments, and non-governmental organisations, sharing *best practices* and knowledge and securing specific commitments to address the world's most pressing problems. Students and communities throughout the Laureate International Universities network are engaged in similar work, and I am proud to be a part of their efforts.

President WILLIAM JEFFERSON CLINTON, Honorary Chancellor of Laureate Universities[15]

---

15   http://www.slideshare.net/ruthec/laureate-international-universities.

As the honorary chancellor of Laureate International Universities, President Bill Clinton visited Istanbul Bilgi University with Laureate's CEO Douglas Becker on 2 October 2010. During this visit, he spoke with Turkey's leaders in government, education, and business and addressed Bilgi students, alumni, and faculty. In his address, Clinton praised the government's ability to sustain growth in the face of global economic crises. He stated that he has been a keen proponent of Turkey's EU bid, and that the EU would make a big mistake if it turns down Turkey, which it needs for manpower, dynamism and culture to build a better future.[16] Clinton's visit to Bilgi was only one of his many tours accompanying the CEO Becker to Laureate campuses in countries where the company needs a little backing in PR in order to solve problems and establish 'good' relations with governments and regulatory bodies.[17]

Laureate hired Clinton in 2010. By this time there were several other people from his administration working in key positions in the company, such as Richard Riley, the former secretary of education, and Joseph Duffey, the former head of the information agency. While Clinton's compensation is undisclosed, Becker explains the former president's work for Laureate as being based on his belief in the company's "strong social mission".[18] This 'social mission' unites Becker and Clinton in other ways. Laureate sponsors the Clinton Global Initiative (CGI), an initiative of the Clinton Foundation, which states its mission as to bringing together global leaders, including heads of states, Nobel Prize winners, leading CEOs, heads of major NGOs and philanthropists, and pursuing them to make commitments to the implementation of "innovative solutions to the world's most pressing challenges". Laureate sponsored the first CGI meeting held outside the US and has made a number of commitments to the Foundation since 2007. Laureate's charitable work with CGI allows the company to capitalise on Clinton's political influence while conducting business around the globe.

Laureate's political work involves other channels of influence. In May 2010, Universidad Europea de Madrid, Laureate's first university, awarded Recep Tayyip Erdoğan then Turkey's prime minister, now the president, an honorary

---

16   For a video-recording of Clinton's speech at Bilgi: http://www.youtube.com/watch?v=Ot DoajWIVPA.

17   For President Clinton's other trips, see: http://www.laureate.net/AboutLaureate/President Clinton#t2.

18   http://www.bloomberg.com/news/print/2014-01-06/clinton-pitches-kkr-backed-college -chain-amid-controversy.html.

doctorate for his support of projects that promote understanding and reconciliation between peoples, religions and cultures.

In the ceremony, Halil Güven, then the rector of Bilgi University, gave the
commendation. In his speech, he praised the prime minister for "making important advances" in democratisation, economic growth, and the prevention of
corruption, and for his ability to position the country and himself as "a partner
of trust in international relations". For those who follow Turkish politics, these
praises for Erdoğan are dubious at best.[19] An honorary degree from a European
university affirms Erdoğan both at home and abroad, advancing Turkey's bid
for membership in Europe while bridging the West to 'the Muslim World'. In
return, Erdogan's government has turned a blind eye on the company's operations in Turkey. The silence at YÖK about Laureate suggests that the company's
political efforts do aid its *de facto* legitimacy.

In my visit to YÖK, I also spoke with Professor Yekta Saraç, then the vice-
president and now the president of the institution. Saraç's narrative about
Laureate was no different from those of the other YÖK officials I interviewed.
However, during my visit I observed a report on his desk prepared by the
Association of Foundation Universities (Vakıf Üniversiteleri Birliği-VUB), an organisation that was unknown to me at the time. The VUB was founded in 2008
to represent the common interests of foundation universities and to strengthen
their solidarity. Since 2009, the Chairman of Bilgi University's Board of Trustees,
Rifat Sarıcaoğlu, also chairs the association homed in Bilgi's Santral Campus.
In 2013, only 26 out of 69 foundation universities were members of the VUB,
and the most prominent ones in terms of educational standards and research
funding, such as Bilkent and Koç ve Sabancı, were not among them. The VUB's
website showcases Sarıcaoğlu's activities as the leader/chair of the association,
which centre around participating in and influencing the decision-making
processes regarding the planned reform to the higher education system.[20] In
its report on the proposed changes to the Higher Education Law by YÖK, the
association criticised the draft law for failing to respond to the problems and
demands of the foundation universities, and asked for revisions that incorporate their interests.[21] Among the legal changes that Sarıcaoğlu's VUB called for

---

19   For an account of Turkey under Erdoğan: https://www.theguardian.com/world/2016/aug/
      30/welcome-to-demokrasi-how-erdogan-got-more-popular-than-ever?CMP=share_
      btn_fb
20   http://www.vub.org.tr.
21   For the report, see: http://www.vub.org.tr/?cat=4.

were permitting universities to operate as branch campuses of international universities, allowing the current foundation universities an option to convert their status to private universities (read as 'for-profit'), authorising them to set up or invest in companies, removing the restrictions on online and distance education, extending and institutionalising adult education, licensing higher education institutions to diversify and organise as teaching or research institutions and reducing the 30% full scholarship requirement in the draft law to 10%.[22] Finally, the VUB also called for the installation of a ranking system in Turkey akin to that in the US, in which universities are evaluated on the basis of academic performance, scientific production and student/parent satisfaction. The draft law proposed by YÖK in 2012 was revised in 2013. The new version has incorporated many of the VUB suggestions, including the legalisation of for-profit and foreign institutions, the reduced full scholarship requirement, and allowing universities to specialise as research or teaching institutions.

'Best Practices', Transnational Governance and the Transformation of Bilgi

In various public communications, Laureate defines its role as being to leverage, enhance, and incorporate "best practices" in management and academics across its global network.

> The implementation of Laureate's unique global strategy gained significant momentum in 2005. We extended our leadership by launching innovative academic programs, leveraging *best management practices* (my emphasis) across our network, expanding capacity and entering new markets. (Laureate Press Release, Quarter Ending 31 December 2005)
>
> Every institution within Laureate's network defines its identity, programs and approach based on the needs of its students, and community ... Relationships among our universities are enhanced through shared curricula and degree programs, student and faculty exchanges, academic *best practices* (my emphasis), scholarships and an active online network.

---

22   The proposed changes regarding foundation universities can be viewed in two texts: 'Vakıf Üniversiteleri Birliği'nin Yükseköğretim Kanun Taslağı Üzerine Görüşleri' and Rifat Sarıcoğlu'nun. 'YÖK'ün Yükseköğretimin yeniden yapılanmasına dair açıklaması üzerine görüşler'. http://www.vub.org.tr/?p=476.

We are focused on preparing our students to meet the real-world needs of employers in our increasingly interconnected global society.[23]

The term "best practices" is used throughout Laureate's public communication material. Nowhere, however, does one find a definition or description of what these practices actually are. The question is not only what these practices really are, but also how they are transferred from one country to another. Moreover, it is also a question how "best practices" are compatible with the company's claim that "every institution within Laureate's network defines its identity, programs and approach based on the needs of its students, and community". A glance at the changes at Bilgi since 2009 will help us figure out how best practices take shape on the ground.

Since its acquisition by Laureate, Istanbul Bilgi University has been transformed from a social science university to a comprehensive, multi-faculty one, with a growing emphasis on vocational education. It has opened over 40 new vocational programmes, has a new school of engineering and architecture, and has embarked on opening new branch campuses in Bursa, Antalya, Adana and İzmir.[24] The growth of Bilgi, in a sense, can be seen as an epitome of Laureate's unfettered global growth in vertical and horizontal educational markets across geographies. Together with the growth, the company also introduced new management practices to reduce operational "inefficiencies" and costs by expanding the "flexible, teaching-focused faculty led by an experienced local management team".[25] After the Bilgi takeover, the new board of trustees appointed a new rector, Halil Güven, an engineering professor known for his accountability measures in the previous higher education institutions that he led in Istanbul and Northern Cyprus in 2009. Professional human resources and marketing managers were transferred from the corporate world to lead the university's marketing strategy and to reduce inefficiency in HR management. These new appointments completed the transfer of the faculty management from the founder and his circle to the Laureate representative and a small to a small group of professional managers. The new administration laid off faculty who were known to have close relationships with the previous administration, and tens of academic support and service personnel; they adopted new

---

23 http://www.laureate.net/AboutLaureate/~/media/Files/LGG/Documents/Media%20 Kit/2%20Pager/Laureate%202%20Pager.ashx.

24 "Bilgi dünyadan sonra Anadolu'ya açılıyor", *Hürriyet*, 23 July 2010, http://hurarsiv.hurriyet .com.tr/goster/haber.aspx?id=15395115&tarih=2010-07-23.

25 http://sec.edgar-online.com/laureate-education-inc/10-k-annual-report/2006/03/16/ section2.aspx.

faculty performance and reward-management regulations; and introduced measures to increase faculty workload and reduce salaries. These new appointments were not welcomed by the faculty, and during my interviews with them I repeatedly heard stories about how the new corporate managers were not intellectually up to the task of bringing change to the faculty's practices.

Indeed, the transformation of the university led to the mobilisation of the academic and support staff, and ultimately to the formation of a labour union, — the first of its kind in a foundation university in Turkey. Although the union has not gained collective bargaining power, it became a concern as well as an impetus for the company in restructuring the university. Aslı Odman, one of the union organisers, describes the momentum of mobilisation:

> After a long and ambiguous process of developments (following Laureate's takeover), the most concrete incident that brought us together was the rumours about the transfer of 340 jobs in cleaning, security and technical support services (of the university) to subcontractor companies. On the one side these colleagues were actively working and on the other side the subcontractors were going around the campus and bidding.[26]

This created widespread indignation among the left-leaning faculty, who took pride in the distinction of Bilgi as a university that provided stable service jobs with social security to hundreds of people recruited mostly from the low-income neighbourhoods that host the university campuses. Three-hundred-sixty of the 500 faculty members signed a petition against subcontracting these services. The petition was successful: It not only stopped the process of subcontracting but it also constituted a formative moment with regard to the unionisation that followed. The main idea driving the process was that the university should not be organised in accordance with market principles and the measure of profitability. As Odman further explains:

> We were encountering the language of the market and accountancy. To replace 'the student' with 'the consumer' is not something that we can accept. The question of 'how much education, knowledge and science did you produce?' cannot be the same as in the retail sector.[27]

Sarıcaoğlu did not take the news of unionisation well at first, but after consultation with the company's European director, he agreed that he could work

---

26   "Dili Bozuk Ekipten İlk Sendikal Hareket", *Birgün*, 30 May 2010.
27   Ibid.

around the union to achieve the management goals. In fact, the chairman became more tactful in dealing with resistance. A major asset to the company in
the process of restructuring the university and dealing with opposition was
the 'native' group of faculty who had a distant relationship with the previous
administration and had often been irritated by its arbitrary ways and favouritism. One of the newly appointed top-rank administrators, Professor Mehmet,
said he was offered the position after attracting the chairman's attention in
a faculty meeting with his knowledge of finance and understanding of management issues. Mehmet was positive about many of the changes carried
out by the new administration, such as the accountability and transparency
measures, and decentralisation, which gave deans and departments autonomy
over their budgets. He believed that these new measures were necessary in
order to rationalise the university's operations. Laureate, he observed, is a
company that is mainly interested in the financial and marketing aspect of
the university. He likened the company's relationship to the faculty to the relationship of a hospital management to the doctors. He said: "Laureate sees the
deans as the managers of the departments, gives them autonomy in spending
and does not intervene with the scholarship". Professor Mehmet responded
to my questions about the disapproval and suspicion circulating on the campus about the changes introduced by Laureate by drawing a slightly different picture of the change than my other interviewees. While, for instance, I
heard frequent complaints about Laureate's attempt to introduce spreadsheets
as detailed as including the cups of coffee and tea consumed by the faculty,
Professor Mehmet had a different take on the new budgeting system. He said:
"In fact, budgeting is not something restrictive. It can be liberating. It gives you
freedom from fawning over the boss".

However, there were issues that seemed problematic even to him and other
faculty members supportive of the changes. Anecdotes were rife, such as how
Laureate recruited a new HR person from the retail industry, who claimed to
be introducing performance measurement to the faculty but who had to resign
after accidentally emailing a list of 'to-be-fired' to the wrong people; or the new
marketing specialist who did not know what graduate study was, or how she
"foolishly" cited Mustafa Kemal Ataturk, hoping to impress the faculty without
being aware of the political critique that many of the Bilgi faculty spearhead
about the democratic deficiencies of the regime he established in the 1920s
and 1930s. Laureate's new recruits in human resources, marketing and finance
came under particular fire as a "spectacular failure", in Mehmet's words. He
explained that the company prefers people who can manage "corporate talk"
and "who are able to solve problems in Ankara" —in the government and the
YÖK—but who do not know how to work in a university.

In 2011, the rector had to step down after firing three faculty members in the visual communication and design faculty, following controversy that erupted over a student's final thesis project.[28] A 'insider' professor of economics was appointed as the new rector, which to an extent eased the discontent about Laureate at the university. The company also adopted a more aggressive approach to suppressing unionisation, threatening and firing some of the academic and support personnel who joined the union. Among them were 15 research assistants, whose contracts were cancelled despite the opposition of their departments. By getting rid of them, the administration not only disposed of some of the most active union members but also acquired leverage in redefining the terms of contract with non-tenure track academic positions, making them more precarious and short-term. The Laureate administrators' deliberate attempt to hinder unionisation can be seen as an another example of the company's violation of Turkey's constitution, which guarantees the right to join trade unions under article 51 and the Turkish Criminal Law (article 118), which stipulates that threatening workers into not joining a union is punishable with up to two years imprisonment.

The union, as a first of its kind in a foundation university, received a lot of media attention and support from the faculty in other universities. Union activists organised many mass events, such as the petition campaign against subcontractors, the Labour Day rally, and the 80-day sit-in on campus to protest against the layoffs, all of which contributed formatively to the unionisation process. However, the union gradually lost its appeal due to a number of challenges, including the difficulty in representing the diverse interests of the faculty and service workers in the university, the loss of trust between the leaders of the union (Sosyal-İş) and union members, and the more tactful methods that the Laureate administration developed over time in dealing with resistance.

Turkey's legal context, Bilgi University's peculiar history, and the composition of its faculty have imposed certain limits on and challenges to the Laureate management. Despite these challenges, the company has gradually been making changes in the university in order to increase enrolment and decrease cost. These goals define the management of Laureate Institutions across the board. Angélica Buendía Espinosa (2012) observed similar changes after Laureate's

---

28   http://www.hurriyetdailynews.com/default.aspx?pageid=438&n=response-to-porn
      -scandal-by-istanbuls-bilgi-university-violated-academic-freedom-protesters-say
      -2011-01-10.

takeover of the University del Valle de México (UVM), the company's largest single university in Latin America, where the company gets approximately 60% of its revenue.[29] The number of campuses has grown more than threefold, from 12 to 37, since Laureate acquired the institution in 2000. She writes that, under Laureate's control, the university became more market-oriented in its focus:

> The primary growth strategies centered around the fulfillment of 'enroll-ment goals' using aggressive publicity strategies to 'win' more market share: these strategies were based on the benefits of 'UVM's international-isation ... The academic plans that were created on the campuses always depended on the 'achievement' of enrollment goals, which in some cases were excessive.
>
> ESPINOSA 2012: 88, 89

Laureate claims to be hands-off on academic issues, preferring to leave those decisions to local needs and experts. However, the cases of both UVM and Bilgi show that the pressure for enrolment growth and the profit motive inevita-bly have an impact on academic decision-making, the faculty, and students. The university administration, for instance, decided to increase the tuition fee more than 50% over three years in 2009, leading to 1,600 letters from students asking for a reduction. Students set up a Twitter hashtag, #28bintlyebilgidei-simne ('what business do I have at Bilgi for 28 thousand'), receiving hundreds of tweets. One student tweeted "Dear Bilgi students, you can add to your CV 'opened a university', cause we are funding the Bursa campus with the tuitions we pay". Another one chimed in with "We want a school not a company".[30] Many others expressed their discontent with the university operations, the high prices, and lack of adequate facilities for teaching. After the 1,600 students undersigned a letter to the rector protesting the tuition increases, the admin-istration backed down and announced that the increase in tuition would be adjusted to the inflation rate.[31]

Despite such local problems – the rising concerns of students about the quality of education, the increasing concerns of the faculty about the effects of commercialisation on academic ideals, and the company practices that violate

---

29   https://www.insidehighered.com/news/2013/10/10/laureates-growing-global-network -institutions.

30   https://twitter.com/hashtag/28bintlyebilgideisimne?src=hash.

31   http://www.habervesaire.com/news/gercek-enflasyona-gore-zam-2305.html.

Turkish law – at a global level, as Kevin Kinser observes, "there's an aura of quality that surrounds the Laureate name". Kinser argues that this is because the company has been "successful on a global scale for awhile without having regulatory controversies follow them around".

> They've been able to navigate the regulatory minefields in the 30-something countries that they're now in without there being a major scandal and perhaps without there being a minor scandal. I'm sure there are some things here and there.[32]

Laureate operations in Turkey are among the "things here and there". But Turkey is certainly not the only country to which this applies. A 2012 report by a committee of the Chilean Chamber of Deputies names Laureate universities among others as defying the law that requires universities to be non-profit. However, according to *Inside Higher Education*, the Chamber of Deputies, the lower house of the Chilean Congress, subsequently rejected the report. Similar to Turkey, this indicates a tendency on the part of the Chilean political authorities, purposefully or not, to misrecognise Laureate.

The company achieves this aura of legality and "aura of quality", as Kinser puts it, not only by way of political influence but also by deploying the discourse of 'best practices' to explain its goals and operations. Originated from the investment and portfolio management, 'best practices' became a management buzzword in the 1990s and has been picked up as an operational rationale expanding to a wide variety of commercial and social organisations ranging from government agencies to hospitals, from the military and police forces to universities. This transferability across sectors is based on another assumption: that production and management processes are uniform enough that 'best practices' seen to yield good results in one industry or company, are adoptable by others. As many of its critics have pointed out, however, 'best practices' are often based on "selective observations" (Overman and Boyd 1994: 69) or "anecdotes" (Greene 2012) that are applied "randomly, subjectively and without any justification" (Arnost Vesely 2011). Its practitioners present 'best practices' as scientific and value-free technical knowledge that will help institutions to achieve presumably common objectives such as cost effectiveness and consumer satisfaction. The problem, however, is that the assumption of transferability undermines specific goals, accumulated know-how,

---

32   https://www.insidehighered.com/news/2013/10/10/laureates-growing-global-network
      -institutions.

and established practices of individual organisations. The assumption is that the ultimate goal of every organisation is to attain competitive advantage in its field of operation. However, as Wendy Brown (2014) argues, 'best practices' involve more than infusing metrics into public institutions. Indeed, "bundling up, and ... formally attending to a number of different concerns such as of transparency, legality, accountability, efficiency and competitive advantage" enable

> the absorption of public and political concerns into markets, and consequently the elimination of the need of legal political or ethical interferences from the state or any other political source.[33]

Ultimately, as Brown sums up, 'best practices', presented as a value-neutral working formula of governance, contributes practically to spreading neoliberalism across different economic sectors and countries.

Conclusion

Today, the conversation about higher education involves two main topics: commercialisation and internationalisation. Laureate Education Inc. is perhaps the most extreme form in which these two processes are entangled. In this paper I have examined the Laureate phenomenon at the intersection of micro and macro processes by focusing on its operations in Turkey. In conclusion, I would like to briefly discuss the significance of the Laureate case for the sociology of education.

Laureate Education Inc. provides a case study which helps us to think about the relationship between education and economy at a new intersection at which education becomes a commodity that can be bought, sold, and traded across borders. This calls also for a modification of two prominent ways in which social scientists have traditionally studied the relationship between education and the economy: first, in terms of the educational outcomes of the economy – the impact of economic growth on educational opportunities; and second, in terms of the socio-economic outcomes of education, such as individual salaries, class structures, social mobility, and economic growth

---

33   Brown's lecture, entitled "Governmentality in the Age of Neoliberalism" at the Pacific Center for Technology and Culture on 18 March 2014, http://pactac.net/2014/03/wendy-brown—governmentality-in-the-age-of-neoliberalism/. See also Brown (2015).

(Brinton 2005). In this new era, however, education, independent from its outcomes, becomes a source of economic activity and growth.

Laureate's business model is dependent on the constant expansion of its market. Transnational treaties such as GATS and global institutions such as the World Bank are prominent agents in laying the groundwork for the transformation of higher education field into a sphere of international trade. Prominent in the efforts to achieve global expansion is the desire to tap into the growing demand for higher education in developing countries, which local institutions fail to meet, and where millions of young people's aspirations are tied to getting a college degree. In this context, due to the global prominence of American universities, US brands deliver higher hopes for better jobs, upward social mobility, and a brighter future. Whether or not Laureate institutions actually deliver the promised knowledge, experience and labour market outcome, in a context where educational opportunities expand faster than jobs, they are highly unlikely to fulfil the hopes of many.

Finally, as Arthur Stinchcombe (1990) has argued, universities, just like banks, are "fiduciary institutions", which help us trade and mediate between the present and the future. He explains:

> In both banks and universities, we have to trust the institutions to run for us the risks we are not competent to run (or do not want to run) ourselves, so that we can buy a reliably liquid degree in engineering that can be cashed in for a job ... or so that we can reliably collect our savings account with interest when we want to make a down payment on a house ... And it is because we have to trust them to act for us in markets that we can't ourselves manage that I call them both 'fiduciary' institutions.

In the aftermath of the 2008 economic crisis, the comparison of universities to banks is certainly unsettling. As we continue to face the dire socio-economic consequences caused by the failure of banks in fulfilling their fiduciary roles, one wonders whether the expansion of higher education companies worldwide is also prone to crisis, with bankrupt universities on the one side and letdown humans on the other. In that sense, the Laureate case calls for an agile approach from the sociology of education that not only recognises the urgency of analysing the processes of internationalisation and commercialisation in higher education in relation to the dynamics of global capitalism, but also scrutinises the non-transparent dynamics of these entangled processes at the local level.

Works Cited

Arslan, Hakan and Asli Odman. 2011. "İstanbul Bilgi Üniversitesi'ndeki Şirketleşme ve Sendikalaşma Süreci". In Fuat Ercan and Serap Korkusuz Kurt (eds). *Metalaşma ve İktidar Baskısındaki Üniversite*. Istanbul: SAV, 593–653.

Arslan, Hakan and Asli Odman. 2012. "Metafordan Gerçeğe Üniversite A.Ş". In Çetin Bolcal *et al* (eds). *Üniversite, Üniversitelerimiz Nereye Sempozyumu*. Istanbul: İstanbul Kültür Üniversitesi, 269–297.

Bok, Derek. 2004. *Universities in the Marketplace: The Commercialization of Higher Education*. Princeton, NJ: Princeton University Press.

Brinton, Mary C. 2005. "Education and the economy". In Neil J. Smelser and Richard Swedberg (eds). *The Handbook of Economic Sociology*. Princeton, NJ: Princeton University Press, 575–602.

Brown, Wendy. 2015 *Undoing the Demos: Neoliberalism's Stealth Revolution*. Cambridge, MA: MIT Press.

Eğitim Sen (2012) *Yükseköğretimin Yeniden Yapılandırılmasına Karşı Görüş Metni*, http://www.egitimsen.boun.edu.tr/site/wp-content/uploads/2012/10/Eğitim-Senin -Yükseköğretimin-Yeniden-Yapılandırılmasına-Karşı-Taslak-Görüşü.pdf

Espinosa, Angélica Buendía. 2012. "Change or continuity in the Mexican private sector? The case of laureate – the University of the Valley of Mexico". In Hans G. Schuetze and Germán Álvarez Mendiola (eds). *State and Market in Higher Education Reforms*. Rotterdam: Sense Publishers.

Gumport, Patricia. 2000. "Academic restructuring: organizational change and institutional imperatives". *Higher Education* 39: 67–91.

Harkin Report (2012), http://www.harkin.senate.gov/help/forprofitcolleges.cfm

Kinser, Kevin and Levy Daniel. 2007. "For-profit higher education: U.S. tendencies, international echoes". In James J.F. Forest and Philip G. Altbach (eds). *International Handbook of Higher Education*. Berlin: Springer, 107–119.

Kirp, David L. 2003. *Shakespeare, Einstein, and the Bottom Line: The Marketing of Higher Education*. Cambridge, MA: Harvard University Press.

Öniş, Ziya. 2011. "Power, interests and coalitions: the political economy of mass privatization in Turkey". *Third World Quarterly* 32 (24): 707–724.

Readings, Bill. 1996. *The University in Ruins*. Cambridge, MA: Harvard University Press.

Slaughter, Sheila and Gary Rhoades. 2004. *Academic Capitalism and the New Economy: Markets, State, and Higher Education*. Baltimore, MD: Johns Hopkins University Press.

Stinchcombe, Arthur L. 1990. *Information and Organizations*. Berkeley, CA: University of California Press.

Vatansever Asli and Meral Gezici-Yalçın. 2015. *"Ne Ders Olsa Veririz:" Akdemisyenin Vasifsiz İşçiye Dönüşümü*. Istanbul: İletişim.

Vesely, Arnost. 2011. "Theory and methodology of best practice research: a critical review of the current state". *Central European Journal of Public Policy* 5 (2): 98–117.

Wallerstein, Immanuel. 1996. *Open the Social Sciences: Report of the Gulbenkian Commission on the Restructuring of the Social Sciences*. Stanford, CA: Stanford University Press.

CHAPTER 2

Free Market and Higher Education: The Case of Low-Fee Universities in Peru*

Carmela Chávez Irigoyen

The purpose of this chapter is to clarify the implications of practices and discourses surrounding the creation of a new institutional offer of higher education in low-fee private universities (LFU) in the city of Lima. This phenomenon is part of the process of the massification of higher education in the country and the expansion of the private market. The study focuses on how these institutional and non/institutional discourses and practices around the LFU are transforming universities themselves but also the social valuation of higher education. The chapter contains two levels of analysis: the institutional, related to public images and narratives that are part of the formal discourses of the university authorities and managers; and the students' views, in particular their expectations of higher education, and the role of such expectations in social mobilisation. The hypothesis is that the new discourses and practices of the LFU have transformed education into a private good that includes a new perspective on the education system, seen as a market, and also on university students, treated as clients.

> (Querer) que las universidades sean privadas, pero sin fines de lucro, (...) demuestra una ignorancia, un desconocimiento total de cómo funciona el capitalismo, que si inviertes dinero, tienes que ganar dinero. De eso se trata una inversión. Es como si a los que venden autos o refrigeradoras les dijeran que no pueden ganar dinero porque hay una demanda social de por medio. O que tendrán utilidades hasta un límite establecido por el Estado. Es un absurdo. Entonces el mercado se viene abajo, fracasa. ¿Quiénes son los más perjudicados? El pueblo.
>
> ALBERTO BEINGOLEA, Peruvian Congress Representative[1]

* This research would not have been possible without the sponsorship of the Research Management Direction of Pontificia Universidad Católica del Perú (PUCP) during 2014 and without the enthusiastic support of my advisor Martin Benavides. Thank you both.

1 English translation: "To wish for a university to be private without profit interests denotes ignorance of how capitalism works. It means that when you invest money, you have to win

This phrase, spoken by a Congressman from the Popular Christian Party during the debate on the new university law in 2014, articulates well a common view that is prevalent in an important sector of Peruvian society, concerned with the naturalisation of profit in educational organisations. It represents the emergence of a new discourse: that education is a commodity. This chapter explores the transformation of private universities since the start of the economic liberalisation process in the mid-1990s. In particular, it considers a relatively new organisational phenomenon in the Peruvian higher education system, the Low Fee Universities (LFU). LFU are private universities which were created during the 1990s, with monthly fees which are much cheaper than the average among private institutions (at least 50% less). These may or may not be for-profit institutions, but they all have some variables in common, including high flexibility of access, a limited teaching career structure and a strong professional profile informing the design of careers.

The main argument is that LFU have transformed universities as educative social institutions, particularly because of their discourses about higher education in an environment of economic liberalisation. Also the organisational transformation that has occurred has led to students that value education as a way to improve their life conditions, to raise social mobility and to obtain educational credentials. Fieldwork has therefore been undertaken in two LFU during 2014–2015, applying semi-structured interviews and institutional ethnographies. All the evidence was analysed using qualitative techniques in an attempt to build an institutional analysis from an interpretative perspective. This means revealing the meaning assigned to actions by the actors themselves (Gonzáles 2001: 245).

The study concentrates on universities created after law 882 was introduced in 1996. Also those chosen are all part of the low-fee group (LFU) that settled in Lima, because of its numerical dominance in the country.[2] The research has been designed as a comparative case study in which we want to find similarities and differences that can be trusted, and with valid data (Ying 2015: 47) that

---

money. This is what investment means. If not, it will be as if you tell cars or refrigerated salesman you can sell, but you can't win, because there is a social interest in between. Or as you say 'you can have gains, but with a profit limit'. It is absurd if you do this, the market will fall, will fail. And who is going to be the most damaged? The people will be". Available in: "Beingolea: Ley Mora liquida inversión privada", *Expreso* 8 May 2014, http://www.expreso .com.pe/noticia/2014/05/04/beingolea-ley-de-mora-liquida-la-inversion-privada.

2 Lima has 44 of the 90 private universities in the country, and more than half have developed as a consequence of law 882.

allow us to develop an explicative model (Sartori 1999: 243) of the institutional transformation of Peruvian universities.

Also this reflection fits into a bigger global debate about how universities have changed within a global tendency towards massification of higher university education (on the demand side) and of institutional diversification (on the offer side). Processes at the local level have been developed in the context of economic liberalisation policies. I suspect that LFU is the institutional product of a bigger tendency: the mercantilisation of higher education as a private good that serves either for social mobility or as credential for social prestige.

The Expansion of Higher Education in Peru

The university as educational institution has accompanied the formation of the nation since colonisation. The Universidad Mayor de San Marcos was the first university in America, established in 1551, and during the colonial period universities were founded in principal cities in the Andes, the Universidad Nacional San Cristóbal de Huamanga en Ayacucho in 1677 and the Universidad Nacional San Antonio Abad del Cusco in 1692. But the arrival of independence marked the point at which the university really became established as an institution for the academic attainments of elites, and during the nineteenth century, six universities were founded.[3] In this context, the first private non-profit university was founded in 1917, the Pontificia Universidad Católica del Perú.

But it was at the dawn of the twentieth century that the university as an institution for higher education grew all over Peru. That phenomenon was part of the modernisation cycle that occured throughout Latin America in which the development discourse and the entrance of important international and national organisations led to the establishment of the model of 'import substitution', inspired by the dependency paradigm, in which the principal point was the economic development of the region's countries in order to enter into the dynamic of the new productive modernisation process in the Cold War period. That was the time of the emergence of important international economic organisations such as the World Bank, the Inter-American

---

3 The Universidad Nacional de Educación Enrique Guzmán y Lavalle (1822) in Lima; Universidad Nacional de Trujillo (1824); Universidad Nacional de San Agustín (1828) in Arequipa; Universidad Nacional del Altiplano (1858) in Puno, and the Universidad Nacional de Ingeniería (1876) and Universidad Nacional Agraria de La Molina (1902), both in Lima.

Development Bank (IDB) and, with a more important role in the region, the United Nations Economic Commission for Latin America and the Caribbean (ECLAC), in which the principal goal of the international advocacy agenda was the modernisation of the productive structures of the Latin American countries. In Peru, however, its influence came 20 years later, with the liberalisation process at the beginning of the 1990s.

As a consequence of this, the role of higher education was seen as a priority, and the universities were supposed to be the crucial first stage in the production of the new intellectuals, businessmen and public managers who would lead the process of taking the country into this international framework that national governments embraced with enthusiasm. Thereby, in the 1960s and 1970s, university was the place for regional elites who could afford the expenses and economically support their youngsters in the capital or other cities of the country (also in private elite universities) looking for social mobility and social recognition as professionals but also, as a new social class in terms of changing education level, career paths, access to urban services and economic capacity relative to their parents.

In the last two decades there are two factors that have increased both the 'offer' and the 'demand' of university higher education. In the first place, the transformation of Peruvian society because of internal immigration processes and a demographic boom (these phenomena have come together since 1950) that have increased the overall population by 300%. In 1960 there were about 10 million people in Peru, in 1980 the figure was about 18 million, and in 2014, about 30 million. Furthermore, the population growth has been urban. In 1960 the urban population constituted about 47% of the total, in 2000 it was about 72% (INEI 2001). These two mutually dependent situations, a demographic bonus plus an urbanisation process, have transformed the whole education system, expanding demand for all levels of formal education not just in the capital but also in cities inside the Andean and Amazon regions.

After the transition from military rule in 1980 and in the frame of the new constitution of 1977, law 23733 was passed in 1983 establishing a new institutional frame for universities, both public and private. It established that all of them had to have instruments of governance such as a University Council and University Assembly, with student representation and a teacher career structure with merit accreditations. Also, the law established a non-tax policy for non-profit private universities, and a regulatory body over all universities that was called the National Rectors Association. Institution formed by all the rectors of all universities that worked as a "self-regulation" space with out any interference from the state. But with public competences as the emission of official academic grades, a national university information system and with competences for institutional accountability.

This institutional and juridical frame worked until Fujimori's government self-putsch in 1992, when he decided to close down the congress (both chambers) and to establish a new Constitution, which was introduced in 1993. Between 1992 and 1996 six for-profit universities were founded, two of them being the most expensive in the city of Lima.

I have to take into account that during the 1980s, public universities experienced deep institutional problems. As the final report of the Truth and Reconciliation Commission pointed out, the state neglected education for decades, being without any real modernisation programme and full of traditional authoritarian pedagogies. In this panorama, new radical anti-system paradigms raised, paradigms that were sustained in dogmatic Marxism manuals that provided a basis on which the extreme left ideologies that were exploited by Shining Path (SP) could be developed. This was the most radical left army and political party in South America, responsible for almost 54% of the deaths and disappearances of people during 20 years of armed conflict in Peru. It used the education system as a major space in which to proselytise, especially in secondary schools and higher education institutions. SP filled up the university public system during the 1970s and 1980s, taking over student councils, university federations and also some university welfare directorates in order to develop clientelist networks, especially among students with less opportunities and rural family roots who were systematically discriminated against in urban societies. The way in which the state responded to this situation was very unfortunate: military interventions, political confrontation with teachers' unions (which engaged in lengthy national strikes), stigmatisation of left-wing student movements within the universities and, even worse, serious violations of human rights. Two emblematic cases were the disappearance and assassination of almost 100 teachers, workers and students of the Universidad Nacional del Centro (UNCP) in Junin, a region in the middle of the Peruvian Andes, and the massacre of eight students and one teacher in the Universidad Nacional de Educación "La Cantuta" in Lima. Both were the direct responsibility of the state. Also, at least seven public universities experienced military interventions on their campuses during the 1990s (Truth and Reconciliation Commission 2003). As a consequence of these developments, it has become a commonly held view since the 1990s that public universities are not safe places to study.

However, this is not the only factor behind the increased popularity of private universities: entrance into a public university is very competitive.[4] The

---

4 In Peru each university has its own entry system, incorporating special treatment with direct access for students obtaining the best grades at first level private schools, and special

proportion of applicants for places in a public university who are successful is one fifth, while for private universities the proportion is four fifths.[5]

But maybe the most important factor that has increased the size of the private higher education sector has been Legislative Decree 882, whose aim is to promote investment in education, and which allows for-profit associations to operate within the education sector. This came about at a time of economic liberalisation, and the subsequent transformation of the state from being the primary economic advocate (1979 Constitution) to playing a subsidiary role. This uncontrolled spurt of private universities led to the passing of law 29971, which established a moratorium on the creation of new universities.

Evolution of the University System

The for-profit university has generated a new organisational model that leaves out standard elements of university governance, teaching career structures, academic bodies, and student participation inside the university. The traditional model has been replaced by a management structure without academic departments, and teachers who are hired by the hour, and who do not really form an academic establishment. Also, because they are private enterprises or private associations, there have been many difficulties with regard to supervision and control of expenses, despite the fact that they have benefitted from a special non-taxes policy. As they don't pay taxes, they are not required to present a report (the one all Peruvians are obligated to present to the Tax Office) on their income and expenditure. This has been accompanied by difficulties in self-regulation for the National Rectors Association that has been faced with both governance problems in public universities (involving battles with groups frozen in positions of power)[6] and less transparency and accountability in private institutions.[7] In this respect it is interesting that the only institution that

---

exams in their own pre-university academies. But they also run institutional entrance exams in which any student can participate.

5   More information at: http://rankings.americaeconomia.com/mejores-universidades-peru -2013/ranking/.

6   Interview with Zenón de Paz *Programa Otra Mirada* 13 June 2013 Major references at: http:// www.otramirada.pe/content/entrevista-zen%C3%B3n-depaz-nueva-ley-de-universidades -s%C3%A1bado-15-de-junio.

7   Morereferencesat:http://rankings.americaeconomia.com/mejores-universidades-peru-2013/ escala-de-grises/.

has sanctioned private universities is the National Institute for Competence Defence and Property Rights, over issues related to consumer rights. Between January and September 2014, 22 private universities were sanctioned for 18 infringements because of bad quality of service, non-attendance to complaints, and also bullying behaviour related to students' demands.[8]

Since 2009, however, some important steps have been taken to reverse some of these problems. These include the creation of the National System for the Evaluation, Accreditation and Certification of Educational Quality (SINEACE) which has instituted a policy of developing national education standards by accreditation processes. Also in this context, discussions took place regarding the need for a new law to place limits on universities and to ensure minimum standards of quality in university education.

The debate about the need for a new university law was finally settled in 2013 when the Congressional Education Commission led by president Daniel Mora presented a new University Law to the Congress, number 30220. This was approved in 2014, and resulted in some changes in the university system. The most important was the formation of a central office called 'Superintendencia Nacional Universitaria -SUNEDU' as a rectoral administration office that is also under the auspices of the Education Minister.

This means that the frame of the higher education system is changing, going from the self-regulation paradigm to a structure which incorporates more state control. The new law also established guidelines for the creation of new universities which must build a quality guarantee system for careers and lay down minimum requirements for university teaching (i.e. dedication, academic grades, years of experience). The implementation of the new university law will impose a fundamental transformation in the contract modalities of these institutions.

Finally, the new law proposes a new way of electing authorities for public universities, trying to counter the old, established groups that have been involved in the bad practices of non-transparency and corruption. The law was publicly supported by the president,[9] and was finally approved on 9 July 2014.

However this process was not accepted without much resistance from universities (especially from the National Rectors Association and the Federation

---

8   More information at: https://corresponsalespe.lamula.pe/2014/08/05/estas-son-las-universi dades-sancionadas-por-indecopi-en-lo-que-va-del-ano/corresponsales.pe/.

9   Available at: http://www.rpp.com.pe/2013-12-16-humala--muchas-universidades-estan-enga nando-y-estafando-a-los-jovenes-noticia_655467.html.

of Private Institutions of Higher Education, that groups universities), and politicians, including congressman who were owners of private universities themselves. The opposition's principal argument was that this 'intervention' will remove autonomy from public universities, and block economic freedom in the case of private institutions. At the end of 2014, a new rector's association was created, the Association of Universities of Peru – ASUP-[10] containing most of the old rectors.[11] In January 2015, 13 amparo actions were presented to repeal the new law,[12] and every one of those was approved.[13] However in November 2015, the Constitutional Audience have resolved these amparo actions, establishing the constitutionality of the university law and its total validity.

How to Study Peruvian Universities?

One of the first things we have had to do in studying Peruvian universities is to recognise that we are faced with an immense diversity of private higher education institutions that are differentiated by quality, selectivity, prices, process of institutionalisation or institutional projects (see figures 2.1, 2.2. and 2.3). In this context, the main objective of this research is to establish the relationship between the low-fee universities and new university students, particularly in terms of how these two discourses, the institutional and the aspirational, converge into a new institutional model. How has the social construction of the new low-cost private universities come about, taking into consideration the dynamics and tensions surrounding them and that they respond to, and what are the consequences of all of this in terms of the creation of a new type of Peruvian university student?

---

10   Avaliable at: http://www.asup.edu.pe/.

11   Also the representative of the public universities elected to ASUP has faced important claims of corruption in his own university, and has also been elected as part of the National Council of Judges. More information at: http://www.rpp.com.pe/2014-11-06 -trujillo-congreso-denunciara-a-rector-de-la-unt-orlando-velasquez-noticia_739826. html.

12   More information at: http://www.iloaldia.com/index.php/actualidad/noticias/politica/ 40433-ley-universitaria-existen-trece-acciones-de-amparo-contra-la-norma.

13   This case was a judicial scandal because the judge that accepted the amparo (meaning that the NRA has to be restored and the new law repealed) is the son of one of the deans of the university that presented the legal action. He also has a brother and a sister working in the same institution. More information at: https://redaccion.lamula.pe/2015/01/23/ guerra-contra-la-calidad-universitaria/mnavarro/.

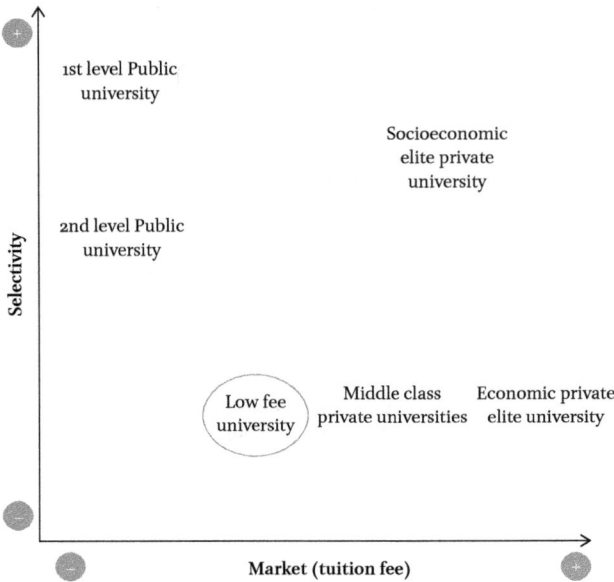

FIGURE 2.1 *Diversity of Peruvian universities by selectivity for entrance*
SOURCE: CARMELA CHAVEZ IRIGOYEN

This picture changes if we see how private universities which cater for the socio-economic elite perform around academic quality rankings.

However it is not possible to understand the phenomenon just by looking at the 'offer' side of the equation. If we also look at the 'demand' side we also find that the number of higher education institutions has grown all over the country. In 1993 the number of students engaged in higher education in Peru was 1.5 million, in 2005 it was about 2.3 million (Diaz 2008: 103). Also the number being enrolled each year has increased: in 2005 there were 559,000 (Diaz 2008: 101), in 2010 there were almost 800,000 (INEI – ANR 2011). Of these, more than 60% enrolled in private universities in 2010.[14] Beyond this, there are also more people trying to enter universities: in 1970 4.4% of the population between 17 and 20 years took university entry exams (almost 64,000), 30 years later more than 12% of the population did so, almost 411,000 people (Diaz 2008: 86).

---

14   The same phenomenon is found in technical education, in which the registration index has grown in the private sector.

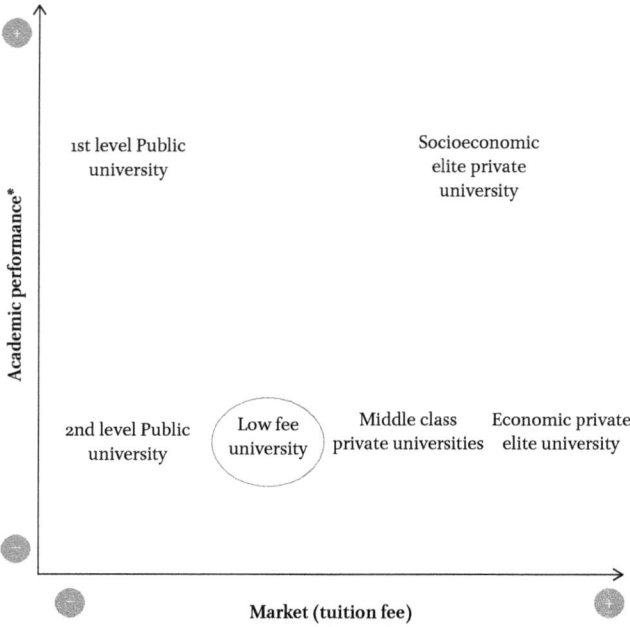

* Quality indicators: QS Ranking 2016/Scimago

FIGURE 2.2 *Diversity of Peruvian universities by quality performance*
SOURCE: CARMELA CHAVEZ IRIGOYEN

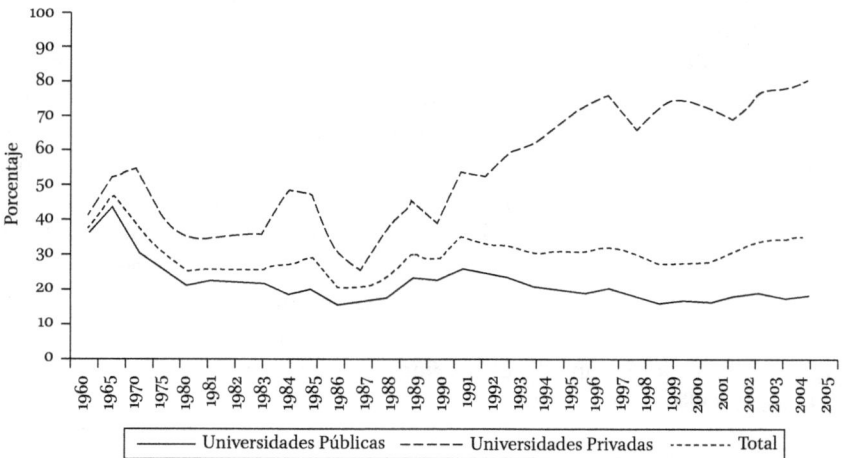

```
—————— Universidades Públicas  ————— Universidades Privadas  -------- Total
```

FIGURE 2.3 *Evolution of the admission level to universities by type of university (public/private)*
1960–2005.
SOURCE: DIAZ, JUAN JOSÉ (2008) EDUCACIÓN SUPERIOR EN EL PERÚ:
TENDENCIAS DE LA DEMANDA Y LA OFERTA EN: BENAVIDES, MARTÍN (ED).
ANÁLISIS DE PROGRAMAS, PROCESOS Y RESULTADOS EDUCATIVOS EN EL
PERÚ: CONTRIBUCIONES EMPÍRICAS PARA EL DEBATE. LIMA. GRADE.

So in 2014 there are not just more people at university but also more people trying to enter. However this demand has not been accompanied by the expansion of places in the public system, as Juan Jose Diaz remarked. The admission index in public universities averages less than 42% (Diaz 2008: 92), while in the private the figure is more than 60%.

This means that at a time when many people want to enter university, public institutions are maintaining the same level of entrance requirements, while the private sector has made entrance more widely attainable.

The New Private University: The Low-Fee Universities

The process of transformation and expansion of higher education occurred in Peru during the 1990s under Fujimori's government. It took place in the context of economic reform related to the Washington Consensus, which was based on an economic adjustment programme with the principal goal of reducing public expenditure. This included, on the one hand, the closure of public enterprises and the reduction of the state's role in the economy and social investment in public services (such as education and health). On the other hand, it involved the liberalisation of the economy, promoting the private investment in fields which were hitherto the province of the state, together with the creation of new rules. In other words, flexibilisation of the conditions for private capital in almost all economic sectors.

In 1996, Law 992 was introduced. It was part of the economic liberalisation process whose principal consequence was to allow profit from investment projects in education. Not only was the market opened up, it was also unregulated. The only mechanism for controlling the formation of new universities was the National Rectors Association, a self-regulated civil association with public functions. In ten years it authorised the establishment of almost 80 universities – 50 private and 30 public, many of them without any kind of quality certification, including almost 50 with only provisional operation licenses. While in the 1990s public universities represented 50% of the total, in 2014 they represent just 35%, and are facing serious financial problems (Arregui 1994: 20).

This escenario of deregulated liberalisation provided an important space for a new actor in the education market, one that wanted to provide for the high demand for higher education: LFU. Besides the cost, around 700 nuevos soles (200 euros) per month, LFU all have some characteristics in common. First of all, they are institutions with no access filter, having access levels of 100% (all the students who take the access exam get in). Secondly, most of the teachers are hired just for the hours they teach. On average fewer than

5% are full time teachers. Thirdly, they don't usually have any institutional bodies related to research or innovation, having a very low level of academic performance, fewer qualified teachers, less internationalised, and with fewer resources invested in research initiatives (Benavides 2015: 41).

It is difficult to say exactly how many LFU there are in Peru. Unfortunately the institutional cost of the universities is not made public, and there is no public information system dealing with the issue.[15] But looking at the national list we can affirm that LFU are the principal actor in the massification of higher education. This process has a special impact in the city of Lima, which has congregated almost the same number of private universities as the whole of the rest of the country, with 44 of the 90 private universities. Of these 44, 44.57% are for-profit universities, most of them LFU.

Not just universities have changed, university students have also changed. The profile of university students has changed accordingly, with more and more students coming from new social strata, a product of the economic growth process in Peru during the last decade, and also students with non-academic backgrounds looking for professional and technical training at university level. It is estimated that three out of every four university students are first generation students.[16]

This process has been followed by a rise in the number of job offers from the formal businesses in the country,[17] and an improvement in salaries for professionals who have a university degree. On the social side, after a sustained economic growth cycle in the country, a new urban socio-economic sector has emerged, whose members have significantly increased their monetary income. Moreover, this new sector reproduces important expectations regarding the social mobility that can be achieved through education (Cuenca 2012: 6), which is their best route for achieving the new social and cultural capital that they desire.

All these expectations are based around private universities: both 65% of the higher education 'offer' and 60% of the 'demand' (measured by university enrolment). Despite this situation, and unlike other countries such as Brazil (Benedito 2013; Bittaer 2006; Mc Cowan 2004), Chile (Rodriguez 2012; Brunner

---

15   However, this is going to be built by the Education Ministry in the frame of the new university law.

16   For more information see: https://ricardocuenca.lamula.pe/2015/03/22/universitarios-de -primera-generacion/palimpsesto/.

17   Almost 80% of employment nationwide is informal. These jobs are not covered by employment law and do not generate tax payments. More information at: http://peru21.pe/ economia/inei-79-empleo-peru-informal-2173107.

2007) or Argentina (Iriarte 2008), so far there are few studies focused on private universities. The debate is more concentrated on the urgent need to build a university system that can ensure quality and even equal opportunities.

As we have seen, over the last 30 years the major change that has affected the Peruvian university panorama has been the rise and dominance of the private university. The majority of these institutions are run as businesses and cost less to attend than their traditional counterparts. They are for-profit universities that are being set up and promoted by new educational businesses (who often own other pre-school centres, schools, technical colleges, etc.), important national and international corporations and even political leaders from national political parties. These new universities have been developed in a completely different way to traditional ones and have created new institutional models in terms of administration and new organisational frames for the academic community. They have also removed any kind of student participation mechanism within the universities.

Within this context, it is important to study the transformation of the private university into a key institution in preparing new generations to be young professionals, and to its development as a new type of educational institution more broadly. Applying a sociological framework of new institutional theory, we consider private universities as social institutions that even though they are part of the social education system develop institutional discourses which treat education as a private good. This tendency is more present in for-profit educational organisations, mostly focused on the 'promise' of either economic or social success.

For this analysis I start from the point of view that education is a social institution and because of that constitutes a channel of actions either for the social reproduction of groups or for individuals. In many ways social institutions in education are also networks of information and a space of exchange of identities. In this sense, institutions have to been understood as entities that help individuals take decisions and classify elements of social life such as values, taste and beliefs (Douglas 1996: 39).

As Douglas says, it is important to understand institutions as structures which don't have minds of their own (Douglas 1996: 19). This means that they are highly adaptive to the environment in which other institutions are also settled. This adaptation process needs formal and informal norms that have to be more or less accepted by the community and the individuals in order to become real in the field and that are reinforced by a system of incentives and sanctions depending on the compliance or opposition of individuals or groups.

In the middle, between social norms and individuals, are the organisations (Brinton and Nee 1998: 31) – schools, universities – which normalise behaviours and social practices, building cultural narratives about the social world around and allowing social relations between individuals (Dahrendorf 1994) There are three aspects to this.

Namely, social institutions are always in a position of tension between tradition and innovation, production and reproduction. This dynamic has consequences in the transformation of the social relations that are going on inside them (Ramirez 2012). This means that studying institutions forces us to seek the social origin of individual preferences and what standards apply to personal choices in a restrictive scenario (Gómez and others 2010: 2) In this sense, social institutions are rules (North 1990: 3) that structure the exchanges related to social change, power, cultural legitimacy and social reproduction (Powell and DiMaggio 1991: 23).

For institutional sociologists, organisational environments have a high dependence on cultural processes that are the bases of local practices and the realities of daily life (Meyer y otros 2005: 7–9). This approach will be useful in understanding the isomorphic process of adaptation between institutions and social structures that reproduces and legitimates beliefs, discourses, values and actions (DiMaggio and Powell 1983: 150). University has changed as an institution and moved away from its traditional role of forming academic social elites and citizens to producing professionals who are looking for technical training in the search for jobs (Tilak 2009: 450). Also the education process has changed because the internationalisation process of higher education models that are being driven by huge transnational tendencies, and in particular the CMA, which have been appropriated very fast for educational institutions included universities (Thorn and Soo 2006: 7). Because of this, competencies based education is now the imperative model which all the new universities, but also the old ones, are taking as a pedagogical model to implement in their curricula. (Rodriguez 2007: 147). This pedagogical model, which comes from public management education (Rivenbark and Jacobson 2014: 182), has impregnated most of the higher education system. Because of this, most debates about educational quality refer to the educational model, institutional mission and aims, and the fulfilment of certain standards regarding institutional functions and activities in terms of teaching and academic programmes.

Some Evidence from the Field

The research was begun by contacting two universities in the city of Lima. Both universities were part of the economic group devoted to technical educational which had settled in downtown Lima (in the historical centre) and that were able to be funded from the late 1990s, in the context of Law 882. Both are settled in a low/middle class neighbourhood near historical downtown Lima. One of them, the Engineering Private University (EPU), has around 13,000 students and offers 31 careers (20 in engineering), while the Health Technical University (HTU), has around 5,000 students and offers 11 careers (seven in health sciences) (INEI 2010).[18]

With the objective of having a common element for comparison in both universities I decided to look into one career option that is common to both, and that is the Law School,[19] trying to analyse the formal and informal practices of all the educational actors in the institutions (primarily authorities, deans, managers, teachers and students).

I have also decided to combine qualitative techniques with institutional analysis. In terms of qualitative techniques, I have used personal interviews, participant observation, and it is in the plan to include focus groups. In the first fieldwork, during July 2014 and January 2015, I undertook nine interviews, including five with university authorities and teachers and four with students in both centres, and two campus visits. The interviews differ depending on the person concerned, dealing with topics related to the institutional and organisational frame, academic and administrative bodies, career syllabus modelling, pedagogical practices, the profile of teachers and students, expectations about higher education, etc. In terms of the institutional approach, I have studied all the public information regarding the institutions that is contained in the II University Census of 2010, all the institutional information contained in the websites, and the public registration records.

In addition, developing the fieldwork wasn't an easy job from an ethnographic point of view, especially because of the internal processes of the universities arising from the adaptation process with regard to the new university law. One of the limitations I faced arose from the institutional fear of private universities about revealing themselves to external eyes because of the internal changes they had developed in the framework of the new university law.

One of the variables that are part of the relationship between the researcher and the subject of the research is that I was from a peer organisation, another university. Not just that, I was from one of the most prestigious private

---

18   To protect institutional information, we are not using the universities' real names.

19   In Peru, Law Schools have the highest rate of inscription in all the country, with almost 150,000 students. Source; Diaz, Juan José. 2008. Educación superior en el Perú: tendencias de la demanda y la oferta. In Benavides, Martín (ed). Análisis de programas, procesos y resultados educativos en el Perú: contribuciones empíricas para el debate. Lima: Grade (p. 105).

university in the country, and that variable was a sensitive thing in some of the interviews, leading to distrust and discomfort in some of the universities I contacted. Although I sent several official communications trying to get interviews with authorities and principal managers in at least seven institutions, it was quite hard to finally get appointments. However, for one of the institutions that form part of the study, this credential plus the fact that I were using ethical tools (for example, oral personal consent) was an important aid in developing a trusting relationship, and this institution authorised me to talk with some of the teachers, directors and managers working there.

Some of the universities that were part of a first sampling exercise don't provide public information concerning the names and emails of university authorities, give incomplete addresses and telephone numbers on their web pages, and also operate poor corporate services, for example with regard to re-direction of calls between the central phone and the annexes, keeping records of formal letters, and so on. Such things may be just anecdotes from the first steps of the fieldwork, but they don't give a positive impression of institutions that are training young people who are going to work in organisations, and who will be expected to be professional, and respectful of the people they are going to be dealing with. In this sense, these experiences are little windows that allow us to see daily behaviours that constitute some of the informal norms of many LFU.[20]

With regard to the interviews with students, I faced some challenges to get the universities' official registration lists, and indeed I still haven't received any of them. Therefore it was problematic to have a rigorous sample of the student profile. Many of the students work during the day, and therefore classes are at night, a factor that limits the potential free time available for them to be interviewed. However, I was able to talk with some of them, three male students who were in the middle of their careers. They were contacted in public spaces such as by the entrance door, or places near the university, and this was one the reasons why it was difficult to catch women students to speak with us. Hopefully, with more contact and having official permission to talk to staff and students, I will overcome these difficulties and be able to strengthen the research.

---

20   One extra variable that wasn't among the experiences I expected during fieldwork was to face informal practices related to gender and generational discrimination. In my case, and because I am a 'young' woman researcher (in my late 30s) and many of the authorities are older men (in their 50s) it consisted of inappropriate behaviour during the first contact, such as making jokes and personal comments outside the scope of the research. These were the most uncomfortable experiences I had during the fieldwork.

The Low-Fee Private Universities Discourse

Both universities are for-profit enterprises and they have developed an organ-isational structure that includes a board and a principal manager that are more senior than the rector. In this new chart, a student participation mechanism has disappeared completely, and there is no institutional space for student representation like in the traditional universities, which have local centres of student university federations. Also they have built an institutional order with a prevalence of management business administration processes based, at least in the formal sense, on the search for efficiency, and that use strategic planning to design not just the administrative bodies but also the academic ones.

However, LFU, even for-profit LFU, are not homogenous. There are some dif-ferences related to internal organisation, but also in formal discourses. These variations are related to the type of management and institutional culture that managers employ in their labour relations with the academic authorities and workers. In this respect, important data has emerged from the fieldwork in the sense that alongside their formal institutionalisation – as low-fee for-profit private universities – universities can be very different *inside*. Heterogeneity is bigger than we thought.

One of the first differences is related to the type of board in the university. For now they have built two institutional models: the family enterprise model and the corporate business. In the first case I find that the HTU is a family business with just the owner – the father – and his sons and daughter as board members. One of his daughters is also the general manager. The Careers Director observed that the fact that the university is a family enterprise permeates the whole or-ganisation, in which family values such as loyalty, esteem, generosity and ser-vice vocation are part of the informal organisational structure. One example of this is how the principal places in the academic or administrative board are selected by personal invitation, with people that are part of a circle from whom trustworthiness is expected. So the managers and the authorities selected by the managers spread the idea that the organisation has to operate and to work as a family. Also the Careers Director talked about how important it was that on Christmas Eve and on institutional feast days the workers were given domestic electrical goods. I wonder how this familial approach actually operates in the context of institutional design in the sense that family relations are based on emotions and principles of authority, and do not follow the bureaucratic *Webe-rian* way (which involves designing a road to get to a determinate goal) which is generally considered to be appropriate in modern organisations.

In the second case, the EPU has been undergoing institutional change since the beginning of 2014, when one of the most important national economic groups bought the university as part of its corporate expansion. They are in the middle of a re-engineering process in which not just administrative procedures are changing but also new departments and posts are being established, such as Quality Directorates, Vice-rectorships, Academics Coordinators' offices, etc. The action board has as a principal manager a person who comes from the corporate business world, who is in charge of the university, developing a parallel corporate education training system for the workers of the economic group, and trying to implement institutional values such as efficiency, impacts, results, management processes and quality of service at each level of institutional governance.

A third point is the type of corporate image the board and principal managers want to build. Both universities have a new institutional discourse associated with the value of entrepreneurship, and a social narrative about personal overcoming through education. In this sense, the education promise is not related to the process of education itself or to the development of personal or academic skills, but more to the permanent need to develop professional market-oriented skills.

Management Practices and Corporate Identity

LFU has developed internal procedures which are managed by organisational schemes (based on flowcharts, regulations, duties, procedures, etc.) outside of the functional structures. For example, curriculas that are designed by Quality Education Offices instead of Academic Departments. One of the consequences of this institutional model has been the implementation of monitoring at all levels, including a system of teacher evaluation. This means that education management is also going on inside the academic departments. In the same way each organisation is trying to develop a corporate image based on the promise of social mobility by enabling students to get a good job after completing their studies. An important clue in this respect is the existence of agreements with institutional networks that can hire students as 'practicantes' (i.e. instructors) in their organisations.

In the case of HTU, most of these arrangements are made with public institutions such as ministries, local government offices, decentralised offices and, in particular, with the justice sector. Eagerness to pursue this course has also led to bilateral certification initiatives between the university and some public institutions, whereby certain credentials of excellence can be granted by the university. For example HTU is preparing to work with the Justice Ministry to provide certification enabling a career in law, certification that is going to be based on the value of public management competences even though the public office concerned isn't an academic institution able to provide educational accreditation in its own right. Also the UHT has established a quality management system (ISO 9001 certified) that is included in the public information on the university website. Apparently they want to introduce an accreditation process by 2015.

However the EPU is not looking for such arrangements because they are trying to consolidate the internal process. Because of the changes, with a new board and new managers, they are concentrating on enforcing the new administration procedures and on adjusting the relationship between these and the academic system. In this sense, they are focused on developing intermediate levels of coordination between teachers and academic authorities, standardising pedagogical content and didactic materials, and providing special course coordinators.

Also I find that the pedagogical models chosen by universities are relevant in establishing similarities and disparities. Both universities have taken an ultra-professionalised pedagogical model, the Competencies Modeling Approach (CMA), which is a way of designing careers but also a technique of teaching that can ensure that students are developing skills to address 'real' problems and to propose solutions to them.[21] CMA is the new official discourse through which LFU (but not only LFU) are entering into the realm of learning indicators. CMA includes detailed professional profiles in the design of careers and course curricula that have to be aligned to the professional profile in content, teaching methodology, and the evaluation process itself. One of the institutional explanations for the use of CMA is related to the profile of the students: they don't have any academic background and the university doesn't have any access restrictions, therefore the university and its academic departments need to be able to guarantee professional and personal skills at the completion of the academic process.

Education management at both institutions is also related to normalisation processes such as maintaining records of activities, number of class hours, number of students, the obligation to use educational devices such as PowerPoint or *prezi* presentations, videos, intranets, *moodles, blackboard* devices, etc. which are more and more required of the teachers and which are covered in their performance evaluations. They have also implemented systems of 'integral evaluations' based on surveys, not just of students but also of the area coordinator (another teacher, who conveys information about their

---

21   Frida Diaz. 2014. "Strategies for the CBA development", presentation at the International
       University Conference. 23 October. PUCP.

performance to the next level in the hierarchy), peers, administrative secretaries, etc. So it is not only organisational life that has been 'bureaucratised', but also the educational aspects, meaning that organisational government weighs upon academic governance. All of this is part of the plan of develop corporate management in the university, through formal and established procedures, and through monitoring bodies which supervise the adaptation process.

Finally, the kind of progress that the graduates of their schools are able to make after graduation is of great importance for the universities. Because both institutions are relatively new in the university 'market', they are trying to develop their own professional profiles that can be attractive for future generations of students. Of particular importance to the new role that universities have taken on in terms of institutional performance is their ability to successfully insert their new graduate students into the labour market.

Students' Expectations of Higher Education

Talking with the students you find diverse backgrounds, including those who are second generation university students in the family and those who are the first. In some cases their mothers are housewives, while others are professional women. Some come from public schools and some from private ones, and they live either in the peripheral areas of the city, in low class neighbourhoods, but also in some middle class ones. Some of them are already working full time, and don't want to leave their job because they are scared of being out of work, but others are still thinking about what they want to do when they become professionals. Some of them entered university at the average age for university students (18), and some had already had another educational experience, such as having studied for a technical career and entering university for this purpose. Also they chose university for different reasons. In some cases they chose that particular university because it was affordable, or because it was near home, or because it was easier to get into relative to the university they really wanted. So we are talking about students with different academic and social trajectories. Social heterogeneity seems to be the norm in LFU.

All these students have two things in common. First of all, they are investing in a private university. Bearing in mind that the average salary in Lima is about 1,400 nuevos soles (about 400 euros),[22] the investment in a LFU, at about 200 euros, is not negligible.

---

22   For more references see: http://elcomercio.pe/economia/peru/sueldo-promedio-limenos
        -subio13945-entre-junio-agosto-noticia-1632070.

Second, they all recognise that university education – despite technical formation for example – is worthwhile in enabling them to have better professional opportunities, better jobs and a better chance of economic mobility.[23] In addition, one of the students said that "university education is good for having discipline, making people think, and having more prestige in society".

Third, although many of them say they have another vocational interest such as literature or art, they have chosen Law for a practical reason: to have better choices when they enter the labour market. They see clearly how they want to design their careers with professionalisation as their objective. With this intention, they affirm that law school is important both to learn law and to have good connections. These good connections come via teachers, who are the link between the university and the labour market. One of the students observed that:

> teachers are the most important thing. You can learn from books, they will always be there (...) but (the tricks) that teachers can teach you from their own experience and the contacts they have (in the institutions that can hire me) are fundamental.

Fourth, in terms of future expectations I found that LFU students want to obtain 'good jobs', working in prestigious institutions, earning large amounts of money and, if possible, becoming managers. They are looking for professional success, which means having a socioeconomic status through which "you can gain respect through your professional title".

In summary, I found that students' discourse relates higher education to their professional futures, and that they are aspirational in the sense that they are investing time, energy and money looking for a 'better' future that is full of commonly held images of success, social recognition and improved cultural level.

Conclusions: LFU and New Discourses in Higher Education in Peru

With regard to the initial question about how private universities have changed since the liberalisation process in the 1990s, I can say that, at least in the case of

---

23   In Lima a person with a university degree earns on average about $1,000 (US) per month, a person with technical level qualifications, $480, and with just secondary level, $360. For more information see: http://www.mintra.gob.pe/mostrarContenido.php?id=152&tip=548.

LFU, they have not just become commercial enterprises, but they work along similar lines to any other private business.

This means that LFU are adapting their internal organisation and academic design to the demands of their new 'clients': the young aspirational students looking for social mobility and social recognition through job security. They immerse them in a social and cultural environment that values pragmatic and quick responses to personal demands and social needs, preparing them for the uncertain scenarios of their professional futures. In the interviews I frequently heard terms such as 'socioeconomic sector', 'culture of service', 'segmentation of the market', 'management orientation', 'indicators and measurement' to refer to the changes that have taken place inside the universities. They are becoming pragmatic in the sense of themselves taking on a discourse of business management that can lead to the provision of good services. So the universities transform into a place for good practices, with administrative and pedagogical systems that can be measured against national and international goals (rankings, accreditations processes, ISO, indexes, etc.) and that develop institutional mechanisms to ensure results in the short term.

But also universities as social institutions have transformed the common outlook of their students, who are full of expectations about how to fit in with the needs of the labour market, the necessity of having higher education credentials and social networks to enable entry into the social dream of a secure job. However, this is more than just pragmatism or utilitarianism, these students seem to be under a lot of pressure from family concerns about social mobility and the goal of better life conditions. We have to take in account that most of these students are the first ones in their families that have gone to university. Many of them, inter-generationally speaking, no longer live in an economically precarious situation. While they have high expectations of achieving social ascendency via higher education, they also have limited capacity for competing at an academic level (for example, for competing to enter a national (public) university, where the chance of securing admission could be as low as seven to one against). They also aspire to a university degree as the entrance point into the job market. This all leads to investment in the private sector and, for many families, a significant dent in the family income. What the students I interviewed are looking for in a LFU career is not just economic security and socioeconomic mobility, but also prestige, something that they can't get if, for example, they enter a technical profession.

On the 'offer' side, the LFU is an institutional product that has been created to cater for and reproduce a new demand for social and economic emergence by the canal of education, supposedly giving credentials to successfully access the labour market, with better chances for economic security and social recognition. Its institutional model depends on its institutional projection at a market level, taking advantage of existing legislation as much at the organisational-administrative level as in terms of the organisation of the academic community and student participation.

In terms of 'demand', there has been a change in the social valuation of higher education by all the actors in the education process, but in particular from the students and their families. Although this research is still in progress, I have established that LFU are part of a global tendency, incorporated in the paradigm of 'knowledge societies' where education is transformed into an object that is dressed in credentials of social recognition but which hides the fact that education is actually a good for exchange in a capitalist economy.

I understand that this new type of university responds to the conjunction of at least four variables. The first is the rise of a new, socially and economically emerging social group, with high expectations of receiving professional training and entering higher education, but with a limited capacity to finance this, and with limited abilities to gain admission to or remain within the public university sector. Secondly, the more widely available offer of university education provided by the profit-making universities/businesses (or the equivalent in non-business universities belonging to one person or family) which are developing organisational models that do not comply with traditional university standards. A third factor is the extremely flexible legislation regarding the Peruvian higher education system, that is incapable of regulating the proliferation of university-businesses, and has no academic quality control or accountability mechanisms. And finally, the existence of a group of businesses and investors interested in investing in the formation and expansion of low cost, private universities, and who also have roles of authority within the universities themselves.

In many ways the research is facing a phenomenon related to the 'democratisation' of university education that has emerged as part of the logic operating under liberal economic principles that hide enormous inequalities in societies that have become more and more globalised within the knowledge, innovation and scientific development framework. Since the start of this period, the university as a traditional institution concerned with the higher education of social and cultural elites has changed, developing new organisational models, pedagogical paradigms and institutional discourses. As I have seen, in LFU this configuration has removed the possibility of a debate about education as a public right and universities as institutions for critical thinking (Labaree 2007: 104). This process is occurring in the middle of an international wave of 'think-tanks' that are spreading a discourse of efficiency in educational management. In a national scene of profound crisis in the public universities it has led to the emergence of the private organisations as synonymous with quality and efficiency (Tilak 2008: 450).

We find ourselves in the debate over whether or not higher education is a public good or a private exchangeable good. Over the last few years, this debate has gained force in the American region due to the severe restrictions on, and even prohibition of, the university-business concept. Today, in 2014 in Peru, we have on offer institutions that can satisfy the demand for university education. This is possible because of flexible legislation that allows for a type of institutionalism that is willing to sacrifice certain elements of academic life in order for graduates to be able to experience a more rapid insertion into the labour market; the preference for private education (motivated by how difficult it is to get into a public university, their supposed loss of prestige, or the belief that private universities are better) and a market with more and more university graduates willing to work as university professors. However, there are serious doubts about the quality of this type of higher education and the medium-term consequences of it in terms of how these new professionals will then access a labour market that is constantly more and more competitive and demanding.

Finally, one of the topics that arises from this discussion concerns the impact of this precarious diversification on educational inequalities. Contrary to what one may assume to be the case about LFU students, that they are students coming exclusively from poorer sectors of society, they are in fact more heterogeneous and less segregated than those at public and elite private universities. Recent research (Benavides 2015) confirms that although Peru is in the process of reducing its high levels of inequality in terms of access to higher education, the dynamics of segregation has in fact been transferred between types of universities.

Although our research hasn't addressed this problem, it seems that Peruvian higher university expansion is facing a democratisation with low and fewer standards. What this means is that the major diversification of the institutional 'offer' doesn't actually mean more equitable access.

Works Cited

Arregui, Patricia. 1994. "La situación de las universidades peruanas". *Notas para el Debate* 12.

Asociación Nacional de Rectores. 2014. *Directorio de Universidades*. Lima: ANR.

Balarín, María. 2014. "The changing governance of education: a comparative political economy perspective on hybridity". *American Behavorial Scientist*. 21 May.

Benavides, Martín. 2004. "Educación y estructura social en el Perú. Un estudio acerca del acceso a la educación superior y la movilidad intergeneracional en una muestra de trabajadores urbanos". In GRADE *¿Es posible mejorar la educación peruana? Evidencias y posibilidades*. Lima: GRADE.

Benavides, Martín and Manuel Etesse. 2012. "Movilidad educativa intergeneracional, educación superior y movilidad social en el Perú: evidencias recientes a partir de encuestas a hogares". In Ricardo Cuenca (ed.). *Educación superior: movilidad social e identidad*. Lima: IEP, 51–92.

Benavides, Martín *et al.* 2014 *Desigualdades educativas y segregación en el sistema educativo peruano. Una mirada comparativa de las pruebas PISA 2000 y 2009*. Lima: GRADE, 10.

Benavides, Martín *et al.* 2015. *Expansión y diversificación de la educación superior universitaria, y su relación con la desigualdad y la segregación*. Lima: GRADE.

Benedito, C. 2013. "Reconfiguring higher education in Brazil: the participation of private institutions". *Analyse Social* 208: XLVIII.

Bittar, E.C.B. 2006. *Estudos sobre ensino jurídico: pesquisa, metodología, diálogo e ciudadania.* (2nd ed.) Sao Paulo: Atlas.

Boons, F. and L. Stranegard. 2000. "Organizations coping with their natural environment: a laboratory for institutionalization?" *International Studies of Management and Organizations* 30 (3): 7–17.

Brinton, Mary and Victor Nee (eds). 2001. *The New Institutionalism in Sociology.* Palo Alto, CA: Stanford University Press.

Brunner, J.J. and D. Uribe. 2007. *Mercados universitarios: El nuevo escenario de la educación superior*. Santiago de Chile: Ediciones Universidad Diego Portales.

Castro, Jorge, Gustavo Yamada and O. Arias. 2011. *Higher Education Decisions in Peru: On the Role of Financial Constraints, Skills, and Family Background*. Lima: Centro de Investigación de la Universidad Pacífico.

Coomans, Foons and Antenor Hallo de Wolf. 2005. "Privatisation of education and the right to education". In Koen De Feyter and Felipe Gómez Isa (eds). *Privatisation and Human Rights in the Age of Globalisation*. Antwerp: Intersentia.

Cuenca, Ricardo. 2012. *Educación superior, movilidad social e identidad*. Lima: IEP.

Dahrendorf, Ralph. 1994. *Ley y orden*. Madrid: Civitas.

De Sousa Santos, Boaventura. 2006. *La universidad poopular del siglo XXI*. Lima: Fondo Editorial de la Facultad de Ciencias Sociales UNMSM.

Diaz, Juan José. 2008. "Educación superior en el Perú: tendencias de la demanda y la oferta". In Martín Benavides (ed.). *Análisis de programas, procesos y resultados educativos en el Perú: contribuciones empíricas para el debate*. Lima: GRADE.

DiMaggio, P. and W. Powell. 1983. "The iron cage revisited: institutional isomorphism and collective rationality in organizational fields in organizational fields". *American Sociological Review* 48: 147–160.

DiMaggio, P. and W. Powell. 1991. *The new institutionalism in organization analysis*. Chicago, IL: University of Chicago Press.

Douglas, Mary. 1996. *Cómo piensan las instituciones*. (2nd ed.). Madrid: Alianza editorial.

Edu-Factory and Universidad Nómada (comps) 2010. *La Universidad en conflicto. Capturas y fugas en el mercado global del saber*. Navarra: Traficantes de sueños.

Flores Barboza, Jose. 2001. "El Decreto Legislativo 882 y la desnaturalización de la Universidad". *Investigación Educativa* 5 (8): 8–15.

Galcerán Huguet, Montserrat. 2010. "La mercantilización de la Universidad". *REIFOP* 13 (2): 89–106, http://www.aufop.com/

García Guadilla, C. 2003. *El difícil equilibrio: La educación superior como bien público y comercio de servicios*. Lima: Universidad de Lima – Columbus.

Gonzáles, José. 2001. "El paradigma interpretativo en la investigación social y educativa: nuevas respuestas para viejos interrogantes". *Cuestiones pedagógicas: Revista de ciencias de la educación* 15: 227–246.

Guerrero Serón, Antonio. 2003. *Enseñanza y sociedad. El conocimiento sociológico de la educación*. Madrid: Siglo XXI.

Gutmann, Amy. 1987. *Democratic Education*. Princeton, NJ: Princeton University Press.

IELSAC. 2007. *Educación Superior y Sociedad*. 1 (12).

INEI. 2014. *Estadísticas oficiales*. Main references at: http://www.inei.gob.pe/estadisticas/indice-tematico/expenditure-of-education-sector/

INEI – ANR. 2011. II Censo Nacional Universitario Lima, http://www.inei.gob.pe/estadisticas/censos/

Iriarte, A. 2008. *Cambios epocales y transformaciones en el sistema de educación superior. La universidad Argentina y los nuevos desafíos*. Buenos Aires: Teseo.

Labaree, F. 2007. *Education, Markets, and the Public Good*. Abingdon: Routledge.

Lemaitre, María José and María Elisa Zenteno. 2012. *Aseguramiento de la calidad en Iberoamérica. Educación Superior. Informe 2012*. Santiago de Chile: CINDA.

Mattei, Ugo. 2013. *Bienes comunes. Un manifiesto*. Trotta: Madrid.

McCowan, T. 2004. "The growth of private higher education in Brazil: implications for equity and quality". In *Journal of Education Policy* 19 (4): 453–472.

Meyer, John *et al.* 2007. "Higher education as an institution". In *Sociology of Higher Education*. Baltimore, MD: Johns Hopkins University Press, 187–221.

North, Douglas. 1990. *Institutions, Institutional Change and Economic Perfomance*. Cambridge: Cambridge University Press.

Ramírez, F. and Christensen, Tom. 2012. "The formalization of the university: rules, roots, and routes". *Higher Education* 65 (6): 695–708.

Rivenbark, William C. and Willow S. Jacobson. 2014. "Three principles of competency-based learning: mission, mission, mission". *Journal of Public Affairs Education* 20 (2): 182–192.

Rodriguez, E. 2012. "La educación superior en Chile y el rol del mercado: culpable o inocente?" *Ingeniare* 20 (1).

Sartori, Giovanni .1991. "Comparing and miscomparing". *Journal of Theoretical Politics* 3 (3): 243–257.

Sota Nadal, Javier. 2004. *El sentido de la II reforma universitaria en el Perú*. Lima: ANR.

Thorn, Kristian and Maarja Soo. 2006. "Latin American universities and the Third Mission: trends, challenges and policy". *World Bank Policy Research Working Papers* 4002, http://siteresources.worldbank.org/EDUCATION/Resources/278200 -1099079877269/547664-1099079956815/LAC_universities_wps4002.pdf

Tilak, J. 2009. "Higher education: a public good or a commodity for trade?" *Prospects, UNESCO's Journal of Comparative Education*: 449–466, http://www.kritischestu denten.nl/wp-content/uploads/2011/09/higher-education-a-public-good-or-a -commodity1.pdf

Tomasevski, Katarina. 2005. "Globalizing what? Education as a human right or as a traded service?" *Indiana Journal of Global Legal Studies* 12 (1).

Truth and Reconciliation Commission. 2003. "Conclusions and recommendations". In *Final Report*. Lima: The Commission, http://www.cverdad.org.pe/ifinal/

Ying, Robert K. 2013. *Case Study Research: Design and Methods*. (5th ed.). Los Angeles, CA: SAGE.

CHAPTER 3

Challenges and Stakes in the Construction of a Private Market in Higher Education in Tunisia

Sylvie Mazzella

International trade in higher education services has increased significantly over the past 20 years following the inclusion of education services in the negotiations of the General Agreement on Trade in Services (GATS), which came into force in January 1995 under the auspices of the World Trade Organisation (WTO). This is occurring not only through the traditional means of international mobility of students and teachers, but increasingly through foreign investment by educational institutions. The international education market has become increasingly diversified and is progressing at a greater rate in developing countries than in industrialised nations.[1]

Comparative and empirical studies (Leclerc-Olive, Scarfò Ghellab, Wagner 2001; Mazzella 2009) challenge the prevailing doxa according to which destinations in the Maghreb are considered a default option. The increase in supply and demand in private higher education, and the opening of markets to foreign investors (who welcome the creation of international campuses) are global phenomena that have also been experienced by countries in the Maghreb region, in particular Tunisia and Morocco.

This study examines the evolution of the private university sector in the Maghreb: a sector that is currently gaining in strength and recognition. The past decade has seen the expansion of private international courses established by institutions operating within the Maghreb region. How can these new types

---

1   Supply and demand in private higher education has increased over the past 20 years in Southern Mediterranean countries, particularly in the Near East and, more recently, in North Africa. In the Near East, Lebanon is without doubt the country where the practice of establishing foreign private universities is the longest-running (e.g. foundation of the American University of Beirut in the nineteenth century prior to the opening of a foreign university in Cairo in 1908) and has the highest enrolment rate among such universities, accounting for more than half of the total number of enrolments. Other countries, such as Jordan and Egypt, have achieved nearly 15% enrolment by increasing the number of places they offer at private universities. The Maghreb region (in particular Tunisia and Morocco) has a comparatively lower enrolment rate in private higher education institutions (around 10%) despite the student population having doubled in three years (Ministry of Higher Education, Tunisia and Morocco, 2013).

of courses be defined? Are they a real substitute for studying abroad or simply chosen in the absence of a better alternative? What new type of South-to-South student mobility will they lead to? Finally, what partnerships are forged with foreign universities (until today exclusively French universities) and more broadly with foreign investors? Is it merely a question of market-driven logic?

The hypothesis put forward is actually one involving the hybridisation of public and private approaches to the operation of these institutions. Commercial logic and national and international entrepreneurial management principles overlap with the approach of public institutions and public services, or the sense of citizenship and civic participation in a post-revolutionary context in the Tunisian case. This chapter aims to explore the complex issue of the interdependence of public and private approaches in light of the 'hybrid' path adopted by project leaders, in this case the founding presidents of such private institutions. The study brings together the information necessary to analyse the way in which these parties engage in trans-Mediterranean knowledge based entrepreneurial activity, and the resources and networks that they mobilise.

This article focuses more closely on the situation in Tunisia,[2] at a time when the issues facing the country – as in Morocco and in Algeria – centre on the new balances in terms of the economy (between interventionism and liberalism), politics (between authoritarianism and the democratic process)[3] and education (between 'Arabisation' and internationalisation). The reform of higher education in Tunisia, and of private higher education in particular, is in my opinion the main challenge that the first elected government of the second Tunisian republic (after 4 February 2015) has to deal with.

Tunisia represents a particularly interesting case due to the political stance adopted toward private higher education during fifteen years, having found a sort of middle ground compared to other Maghreb countries – between the great openness to it of Morocco since the 1980s and the reluctance of Algeria.[4] Through the state endorsed process of privatisation in Tunisia (and more

---

2 This research project is based on case studies conducted regularly since 2005 in the Maghreb (including a two-year stay in Tunisia) consisting of in-depth interviews with the heads of private higher education institutions and those in charge of public higher education, and from statistics sourced from government documents, and also student enrolment forms from private institutions. The results of these studies have been published several times (Mazzella 2006, 2009, 2011).

3 For further information, please refer to Camau (2006).

4 Tunisia currently has 63 private higher education institutes, with a total enrolment of 30,000 (4,600 foreign nationals), representing 10% on the total student population there (Tunisia. Ministry of Higher Education, November 2015).

widely within the Maghreb region), since the year 2000 three types of private higher education have been established and are analysed in this chapter. First, institutions that are formed on market principles of overall profitability in the short term, and which are demanding greater operational freedom; activist institutions whose commercial niche derives from the public sphere, and lastly prestigious foreign public universities that in the Maghreb region have become privatised.

The Public Higher Education Crisis in the Maghreb

Analysis of the higher education crisis in Algeria, Morocco and Tunisia – focusing on the difficulty of finding employment in the public services and also on unemployment among graduates who have not gone abroad – generally describes three phases (Geisser 2000; Gobe 2004). The first few years of independence in each of these countries was a period of economic prosperity in which both high school and university graduates were almost guaranteed to find suitable employment. These job opportunities were due in part to the mass exodus of government administrative and technical support staff working in the colonies, which led to the development of a new national administration and technical activity. The second phase saw the number of students enrolled in higher secondary education in the Maghreb increase from a few thousand to almost two million in the 30 year period following the growth in schools and universities that began in the 1970s.[5] This forced public universities to modify their student recruitment strategies in the late 1970s. Today, graduates in the Maghreb are experiencing a period of crisis due to the saturation of the public sector that neither the state nor private enterprise have known how to or been able to resolve.

One of the sensitive issues related to current public policy in the Maghreb is how to go about convincing national opinion that in the global job market it is no longer economically viable to continue to pursue the idea of 'massification' of higher education in fields that are already saturated, such as medicine, or in areas that do not lead to employment within the private sector. Algeria is no exception, in spite of the initial attempts to reconcile a state-controlled interventionist economic system and egalitarian ideals which place higher

---

5   In 2011 there were approximately 300,000 students enrolled in higher education (not including Tunisians students studying abroad or those undertaking professional training) and a total of 14 universities in Morocco (for a population of 31,478,000). In Tunisia, there were 320,000 students and 13 universities (for a population of 10,102,000) and in Algeria there were 1,100,000 students and 27 universities (for a population of 32,854,000).

education at the heart of the developmentalist nationalist project, namely, to offer uncapped university places for high school graduates, free education, scholarships and subsidised services (Haddab 2008). Thus, in the Maghreb region, where the education system is considered to be instrumental to the development of the state and the upward social mobility of all people, the main challenge of university reforms promoting short and technical studies in both the public and private sector is changing the prevailing idea of social success which, for students and their families, is working in public service or having a degree in medicine. Nowadays we are witnessing a discrepancy between this favourable perception of public university (university as a means of social advancement) and the concrete reality of the lack of job opportunities encountered by the younger generations, which is a source of various forms of resentment; this discrepancy is the main component of the perception of a crisis of the entire system.

In situ Internationalisation of Private Higher Education

Executives in the private sector in the Maghreb are well aware of the importance of dissipating the negative image of being second-rate institutions for wealthy students who have previously failed their studies. Stakeholders involved in the project to establish private higher education institutions in the Maghreb region are not solely concerned with financial gains, e.g. making a return on investment, but also have the political desire to promote the idea of internationalisation at the national level. There are many different forms of private higher education. Courses have been available online since the introduction of e-learning technology in the 2000s. For example, a high school graduate enrolled at the Virtual University of Tunis is now able to pay for and undertake studies online from home, by completing a series of digital teaching modules recognised and certified by the Ministry of Higher Education in their country.

In situ internationalisation of higher education institutions in the Maghreb, whether public or private, can also be in the form of transnational or 'transborder' education (Vincent-Lancrin 2008:67). Courses are taught on-site by professors from reputable overseas universities that grant internationally recognised degrees, such as the Master of Business Administration (MBA) which over a period of one to two years covers everything to do with business (e.g. finance, marketing, management, business strategy). This degree is a form of assurance for businesses seeking local professionals that meet international standards and is a prestigious reference of quality international university education. For example, several higher education institutions (MDI-Algiers Business School, the HEM business school in Morocco, ESPRIT – a Tunisian university specialised in engineering and ICT) offer an MBA International Paris diploma (MBA IP) thanks to a partnership with two French universities: Paris-Dauphine and the Sorbonne.

Another form is that of national (i.e. non-foreign) private higher education institutions established in Tunisia and Morocco since the year 2000. These institutions are able to offer 'LMD' courses (License/Master/Doctorate, which corresponds to Bachelor degree/Masters/PhD) that run from undergraduate study through to masters specialisation (for example in business management, commerce, finance, computer applications for management, law, languages, accounting etc.). These national private higher education institutions confer university degrees, university diplomas of technology, and diplomas of higher education (which are awarded by independent engineering schools e.g. 'diplôme d'ingénieur' and independent architecture schools e.g. 'diplôme d'architecte'). These qualifications are certified by the state and intended to be recognised throughout the national and international jobs market. The certification of awards conferred by these institutions, meaning the recognition by the Ministry of Higher Education of certain minimum standards for degrees or education programmes, is an issue that generates debate.

In situ internationalisation can also be of a more political nature, for example by forming partnerships with the highest authorities in foreign countries and creating private (or public) institutions, self-funded by enrolment fees and subject to Tunisian, Moroccan or Algerian regulation, offering a double degree programme that can lead to two distinct degrees: one from a French university and one from a national university. The most advanced projects in the Maghreb region began in 2009 and have links with France, either by using the name of a French institution or through a consortium of transnational institutions, such as the Institut Tunis Dauphine (ITD). This institution, created through a partnership with the Université Paris-Dauphine, has for the first time in Tunisia brought together local and foreign shareholders: two major Tunisian banks, and the Université Paris-Dauphine (which holds a 33% interest). Similarly, the International University of Rabat was created as an academic consortium, led by the Moroccan ambassador to France and the CEO of Vivendi, who was granted 20 hectares of land in Morocco. The construction of this large campus in the future Technopolis of Rabat is one of the first projects to have been supported by the Union for the Mediterranean (UfM).[6] Algeria

---

6   The Union for the Mediterranean, created in July 2008, brings together the 27 EU member states, the 10 countries involved in the Barcelona Process since its foundation, and Eastern

on the other hand, which is less willing to open markets to privatisation, has chosen instead to create a public institution, the Ecole Supérieure Algérienne des Affaires (ESSA), through an intergovernmental agreement between France and Algeria, which was ratified by presidential decree (no. 05–320) on 12 September 2005. ESSA awards Algerian and French State degrees, Masters in Management, MBAS and high-level professional qualifications. Enrolment fees for these courses vary from about US$9,000 up to US$13,000 for an MBA degree.

It is still too soon to know how selection criteria (educational or financial) will be implemented, or to understand the effects on the national education system in these countries with high and degree hierarchies resulting from these institutions.

Entrepreneurs in the Field of Knowledge – Between Commercial Logic and Public Service

To deepen further the analysis of the hybrid character of the private/public debate in Tunisia, I now turn to an analysis of the experience and career trajectories of the founding presidents of private higher education institutions. In Tunisia, founding presidents, by virtue of their experience and career trajectory, have been able to form privileged links with the government, and the result is the creation of an action plan that blurs the boundaries between public and private. Until recently, most founding presidents of private higher education institutions have been former academics from public universities, or former directors of private secondary schools and professional training institutions. They are actively participating in the 'brain gain' phenomenon, meaning the reinsertion of national migrants who have a degree and have completed their education abroad, for example in France, America or Canada (Michaelis, 1990). Throughout their careers they would have held administrative and political roles within public higher education institutions in their country or managed private consultancy firms. Today, these institutions are calling for the state to join them in providing financial study assistance that would allow them to operate beyond their 'golden ghettos', no longer simply providing education services for the wealthy.

However, the academic and commercial approaches differ from one institution to another, and indeed from one director to another. In this expanding

---

European countries who are candidates for entry into the EU. Its main priorities include civil protection, de-pollution of the Mediterranean, development of solar energy in the Mediterranean and the Euro-Mediterranean University.

sector, which is yet to consider itself as a homogenous and united entity, it is difficult to compare the structures, the interests and the career pathways of the various leaders. Nevertheless, it is possible to distinguish between a few of the more significant differences within the sector. Certain directors (founding presidents) in the national private institutions, who have been trained within the national education system, call for the continuation of their public service role in the national private institutions. These founding presidents, renowned teachers within the Tunisian public higher education system, some of whom have since retired, actively helped to conduct reforms to education in the 1990s. The reforms aimed to create leading university courses, as well as to establish new courses to train high-level technicians and to renew the prestige of public professional training. These advocates of the so-called top level education and training provided by specialist technical schools in the public sector (which are seen as necessary to produce elite professionals to work for the state and also to bring Tunisian companies up to speed) are turning towards the private sector at a time when public higher education, which is overcrowded and more selective, is contributing to the number of young graduates who are being left behind. Most of their students are recent high school graduates who have not been accepted into their chosen course.[7] Alternatively they are students who, having completed undergraduate level studies at a public institution (mostly through short courses taught by higher technical studies institutes), have either not been able to find a job or not passed the entrance exams of the specialist public engineering schools, and therefore find themselves turning to these certified private institutions in order to continue with their engineering studies. Furthermore, the founding presidents hope to somehow attract young people who have not yet studied abroad, or those who have returned disappointed with the experience. Thus they are relying on enrolments from students returning home, as well as enrolments from people who have completed their secondary education at either a French or English speaking high school in Tunisia and experience difficulty adapting due to the 'Arabisation' of courses in the public university system in Tunisia since the 1990s.

One private higher education institution in Tunisia that has been developing a public logic within the private sector since 2000 is the École supérieure privée

---

7   The university application process in Tunisia is very selective: before enrolling, every prospective student must complete paperwork detailing the grades they received in secondary school and also their baccalaureate results, as well as listing a selection of universities where they would like to study in order of preference. Based on this information the enrolment admission service devises a score that will determine the course that the candidate will be placed in.

d'Ingénierie et de Technologies (ESPRIT – Higher Education Institution of Engineering and Technology), a Tunisian institution described by its founding president as "a private engineering school with a public interest" and also as an 'activist school'. Since 2002, this project has brought together three groups of investors. The initial group is composed of 80 universities and Tunisian engineers who live in the country or come from Tunisia (39% interest). The second group is made up of ten private Tunisian companies in the ICT industry (35% interest), and the last group consists of three large Tunisian financial institutions (25% interest). The purported aim is to train engineers who are considered 'operational' and who are in short supply in the current economy. In 2011, 3,000 students were studying at ESPRIT, making up 20% of all students enrolled in private higher education. The school trains specialist technicians (equivalent of three years study post-baccalaureate, e.g. applied degree in telecommunications, computer science, electrical engineering, civil engineering) and engineers (those who complete five years of study post-baccalaureate, thereby qualifying to receive the National Degree in Engineering) and has also created an MBA degree in partnership with the Université Paris-Dauphine.

Tahar Ben Lakhdar is the founding president of ESPRIT. Throughout his career he has worked entirely within the Tunisian higher education sector. He is a recipient of a PhD in physics from the Université de Paris VI (1978) and co-founder of three institutions: École supérieure des postes et télécommunications de Tunis (1990–1993), Institut préparatoire aux études d'ingénieurs de Nabeul, and Institut supérieur technique de Nabeul (1988–1990). From 1990 to 1995 he was actively involved in the reform of higher technical education as well as the creation of leading institutions in the public sector, such as the Preparatory Institute of Scientific and Technical Studies (IPEST). Between 1995 and 1999 he was also CEO and general director of the Tunisian Agency for Vocational Training (ATFP) and was founding director of the Mission Universitaire de Tunisie in France (1993–1995). His presidency at ESPRIT is collegial: he shares the role with three other founding presidents, renowned figures in both France and Tunisia, including the former founding director of IPEST and the Tunisia Polytechnic School (between 1991 and 1995), the founding director of Sup'Com in Tunis, and Elyès Jouini, vice president of the scientific council of the Université Paris-Dauphine.

In September 2009, at ESPRIT in Tunis, the first private classes to prepare students for entrance to specialist engineering schools were created in partnership with Lycée Sainte-Geneviève, which is a renowned high school in France.

Private universities want to work with the state – in partnership with international funding agencies such as the World Bank and the French Development Agency (AFD), Tunisian banks and offshore businesses – towards the reintegration and redeployment into the professional workforce of graduates who are unemployed. In this way, they are participating in a project formed by TACT (Tunisian Association for Communication and Technology) in 2011 following the Jasmine Revolution. With the support of the ministries of higher education and vocational training,[8] the project aims to promote a knowledge-based economy to offshore enterprises that have a division in Tunisia.

Targeting the African Market

Conversely, in Tunisia and Morocco there are also directors of private higher education institutions who have come from a private professional training background, and have joined the ranks of institutions that have found themselves following a quantitative logic of commercial development. They have expanded the facilities of these institutions and increased the range of courses available, now offering up to 80 courses for high school graduates and undergraduates, and also professional training and advanced training for executives of private companies. These limited liability companies can bring together up to 80 shareholders who for the most part are private Tunisian companies. Another distinctive feature lies in the fact that these institutions have the largest number of foreign African students.

Over the past few years, some directors of private universities in Tunisia (and in Morocco) have increased the types of agreements that are made with private and public institutions in francophone countries in Africa. These directors, along with a delegation from the university, regularly travel to African countries (Cameroon, Senegal, Congo, Mali, Guinea, Chad, Ivory Coast and also Algeria and Mauritius). During such visits they organise 'open days' to present the institutions they represent. Such events take place in luxury hotels, or at public universities and private higher education institutions throughout the various countries, and are attended by the Minister for Higher Education and Scientific Research and the Minister for Employment and Professional Training of these countries. Sometimes, as is the case in the Ivory Coast, these meetings take place under the aegis of the Tunisian Ambassador of the host country. More than representing just a university, the members at the meeting

---

8   The objectives of this association are to promote the advantages of Tunisia in terms of human capital (e.g. country with high level of education, good working-knowledge of French, 65,000 graduates per year, including 20,000 graduates in the fields of science and engineering) in order to make recommendations and proposals to the government and to help large global companies located in Tunisia with local training for their skilled workforce.

represent a group; a group of private education institutions (higher education and professional training) that are recognised by the Tunisian Ministry for Higher Education, Scientific Research and Technology.

In these French-speaking African countries, the Tunisian directors of these private institutions (in the same manner as their Moroccan counterparts) have established private 'course advice and information centres' staffed by Tunisian nationals, in order to tap into this market and promote their institutions to sub-Saharan students. Today high school graduates from Gabon or Cameroon can commence the first two years of their course in either a private or public institution in their home country and then complete their studies in Tunisia, thereby obtaining a qualification from one of the private universities located there. The number of students completing such studies in Tunisian private universities has increased threefold since 2001 and continues to grow. The market is so competitive that one particular Tunisian private university attempted to relocate to Gabon. Since early 2000, given the weakness of local demand and the rise in demand in African countries such as Gabon and the Ivory Coast, directors of private universities have increased the number of agreements with public and private high schools in francophone African countries. Foreign African students guarantee that a certain number of places are filled, which at present would not be the case were they to rely on the enrolments of Tunisian students alone.

Annual tuition fees vary, on average ranging from 3,000 to 7,000 Tunisian dinars (TND), approximately US$2,300 to $5,300, with the more expensive studies costing about 8,000 to TND 10,000 (US$6,100 to $7,600). In comparison, the minimum wage in Tunisia is around TND 200 (US$160). Some of the foreign students attending these institutions get a scholarship, either from the African Development Bank Group (AfDB) or the Islamic Development Bank (IDB), or from the government in Gabon and the Ivory Coast. Furthermore, some institutions, with the financial support of private partners (Tunisian businesses and banks) have put in place partial scholarships for high achieving students.

Profiles of International Students Enrolled in Tunisian Private Universities

Over 80% of the international students presently enrolled in private higher education institutions in Tunisia come from sub-Saharan African countries (24 countries represented), 10% come from the Middle and Near East (11 countries represented), 6.4% come from the Maghreb, 0.4% from Asia and 0.2% from Europe (source: Tunisian Ministry of Higher Education). Unlike the public higher education sector in which the three groups of geographic origin are relatively balanced, the number of sub-Saharan students is over-riding in the private sector. Private higher education institutions gather students from 47 different nationalities. Gabonese are the most numerous and represent over 38% of all international students, whereas they are almost absent in the public higher education sector. Inversely, Moroccan students – who represent the highest international nationality in the public sector – are almost absent in the Tunisian private higher education sector. In the private and public sectors, over 60% of migrating students are men. In the public sector, international students divide into four main fields – Arts and Humanities-Languages-Architecture (30%); Health (30%); Sciences (20%), Economics-Law-Management (18%) – whereas over half of international students in private universities specialise in the field of Economics-Law-Management, and more precisely 'Business Administration'. All nationalities considered, 'Business Administration' ranks first, followed by Applied Sciences and Engineering. Legal and Political Sciences come in third place for international sub-Saharan and North African students. Arts and Humanities-Languages-Architecture is very weakly represented in such private institutions, with only 8.7% of international students enrolled in this field. This includes sub-Saharan African and Middle and Near Eastern students enrolled in the 'Information and Communication' field.

A database was established based on the application files of international students enrolled in the first Tunisian private university, called 'Université libre de Tunis', which opened even before the Law 2000, and which, among private higher education institutions, welcomes the highest number of foreign students. Out of 381 international students enrolled in this university, over 90% come from sub-Saharan Africa (including nearly 40% students from Gabon). Students from the Middle and Near East represent 5.5% of the total foreign student population and 4% of the students come from the Maghreb. Undergraduate and graduate students mainly specialise in the fields of Economics-Law-Management and Sciences, including all the sub-Saharan and North African students, whereas students from the Middle and Near East mainly specialise in the field of Arts and Humanities-Languages-Architecture.

The study of a representative, yet not exhaustive, sample of 263 application files filled by international students enrolled in this university reveals the socioeconomic profile of these foreign students, comprising 22 nationalities. In this sample, sub-Saharan African students represent over 95% against 2.7% North African students, 0.8% students from the Middle and Near East, 0.8% students from Europe and 0.4% from America. These international students study in the fields of Economics-Law-Management and Engineering – the most frequently chosen field in this university – as well as Accounting and

Computing sciences applied to Management, Education Sciences, Electronic and Computing Engineering and Computer Engineering.

Before their enrolment in a private university, students most often hold a baccalaureate in their native country (70%), against 30% already enrolled in a public or private university in the country of origin or abroad; they are on average 19 years old. The country in which they get their baccalaureate is their home country in 94% of the cases (i.e. 248 students), while only 3% (i.e. eight students) graduated from their baccalaureate in another African country and just one graduated in a European country. 70% of the students obtained their baccalaureate with an acceptable score. Out of the 263 students, only one obtained his/her baccalaureate with distinction and 15 students with honours. In high school, they specialised in Sciences (43.3%), Literature (22%) and Economics (13%).

Almost two-thirds (64%) of these students do not receive any scholarship. However, amongst the 36% of students with a scholarship, 24% have a scholarship from the Gabonese Government, 5% from the Ivory Coast Government, 5% from the Islamic Development Bank, and 1% received financial support from their parents' employers (just like the African Development Bank employees).

The majority of parents come from a well-off background in their home country. Fathers with executive or highly intellectual jobs represent 44% of the sample. Working class fathers represent only 3.8% and retired fathers 7.6%. Mothers mainly fall in the middle-level category (24.3%) followed by mothers with executive jobs (22%). Unemployed mothers constitute 19%.

To the open question: "How did you hear about our institution?" asked by the administration in one of the personal information forms, the students said they heard about it through alumni (31%), the press or radio (22%), friends or family (16%), the Internet (8%), their embassy (4%), 15% checked the response "other" and 19% did not reply.

More than two-thirds (70%) of the students specify that they do not have a "guardian" in Tunisia (a person morally and financially responsible for the student), but 18% mention a family member residing in Tunisia, 9.5% mention a staff member of the African Development Bank and 2.5% mention their country's embassy (for students with a scholarship).

The five nationalities most represented are Gabon (38.5%), Cameroon (11.4%), Ivory Coast (7.5%), Congo (5.6%) and Mali (4.8%). Except for students from the Ivory Coast, with an equal number of girls and boys, the majority of students were boys (over 60%). The majority of students from Cameroon, the Ivory Coast and the Congo specialised in the scientific field in high school (Literature is in second position); students from Mali and Gabon specialised in Economics. All 81 students from Gabon in the statistical database received a scholarship, either from their Government (79%) or from the Islamic Development Bank (21%). Out of the 39 students from the Ivory Coast, 36% received a scholarship from their Government and 5% received one from the Islamic Development Bank. Out of the 28 students from the Congo, 36% received a scholarship from the Islamic Development Bank and 7% received financial support from their parent's employer. Most students from Cameroon and Mali did not receive a scholarship. Instead they had the highest percentage of fathers in executive positions, respectively 62% and 63%, against 36% for students from Gabon, 40% for students from the Ivory Coast and 28% for students from the Congo.

Mothers with senior executive positions are also more numerous amongst students from Cameroon and Mali: they rank first among all social categories in both cases, representing respectively 30% and 36% of the total against 27% amongst students from Gabon (in second position, after the "retired" category with 28%) and against 15% of mothers from the Ivory Coast with such positions.

Except for students from the Congo who obtained their baccalaureate with an acceptable score or with honours, the majority within the four other groups of foreign students (especially amongst students from Gabon) obtained their baccalaureate with an 'acceptable' score. Amongst students from Gabon, Ivory Coast, Cameroon and the Congo, the highest number of them studied Engineering. In second position, students from Gabon studied Law, students from Cameroon and the Congo studied Economic Sciences and Management and students from the Ivory Coast studied Accounting Sciences. Students from Mali mainly studied Economic Sciences, and Management and Law.

All the foreign students live in popular areas in the outskirts of Tunis. Ibn Khaldoun, an area located close to a big university campus, gathers the highest number of students – foreigners and natives alike. The student population from Gabon, which constitutes the highest number, does not live in the private housing facilities offered by the institution (comfortable, with Internet access in each room, but expensive) unlike students from Cameroon, Mali or the Ivory Coast, for example. We can assume that the Gabonese student population has established a network in the city centre throughout the years, enabling new Gabonese students to rent flats at an affordable price.

Go to the Maghreb... for What Type of Internationalisation?

The following section aims at clarifying why sub-Saharan students enrolled in private higher institutions choose the Maghreb, based on the qualitative analysis of approximately 30 non-directive long interviews (two hours long on average).

Go Anywhere, at Any Price

Students who could have followed equivalent higher education courses in their own country would rather, if they can afford to do so, invest in the 'international label' (especially in Science and Technology), which gives them even more of a lead over others (Niane 1992: 20). This phenomenon establishes a social frontier between them and those who stayed in the home country.

Students clearly state that they are determined to complete their studies. They come to study abroad from the undergraduate level onwards to 'make a difference' between themselves and the high number who stayed in the home country. They try to find fields that do not exist in the country of origin, such as those combining computing and electronic engineering. They also expect to obtain several specialised masters degrees. They are aware of being privileged compared to students from the public sector, either because their family can support them financially or because their Government has granted them a scholarship so that they can benefit from good conditions in which to study.

All these students are also open to a foreign culture. They are open to other men and women and their culture, and have the facility to see certain elements of the language and culture of others as a way of achieving self-improvement. They are open-minded to other cultures, such as a student from the Ivory Coast, who is recognised as a scholar of excellence by his home country, enrolled in a Tunisian private university:

> I triggered my situation. Because I said to myself: 'to only stay in my country, only, may not be enough'. And since a young age I have known that getting the experience of living in another country could always be useful to help my own country to develop. So I say to myself: 'Many things are done in the Ivory Coast but how are things done in Tunisia for example? How are things done in France?' So you come here ... when you get out of your home country and go abroad to study, you are not only here for the intellectual aspect. You study, that's true, Maths and Physics, you can also study in the Ivory Coast. Here, what we come to look for is not really the knowledge in Mathematics or Physics or the practical aspect of the studies. No, it goes much beyond that; it has to do with the cultural aspect.

Most often these students also experience autonomy: handling things by themselves for the first time far from the family unit, finding accommodation or handling administrative proceedings in a foreign country, managing a budget. With time some students, male or female, decide to continue studying and enrol in a specialised master's degree in the same university, with no scholarship or any help from their parents, but through self-financing, i.e. doing undeclared jobs.

A Road Filled with Obstacles

Sometimes they have had to accept a reorientation upon arrival. They have not systematically chosen the course or even in some cases the destination, especially in the case of students receiving a scholarship from their government. Such students often end up criticising the 'international label' put forward by private institutions, which they see more as a 'marketing ploy', benefiting only the most well off:

> It's *marketing.* For example, they establish exchange programmes with Canada. An easy example: a student wishes to go to Canada, what does he do? He pays for his return flight and for his accommodation in Canada. This means that if you enrol in a Tunisian private institution, you already pay 3,000 Euros, then you can go to Canada but once again it's at your expense. In fact, they are looking to attract the super-rich student. But it is written, that's true ... There are some exchange programmes with France but if ... I did something for fun: I checked the schools that have a partnership, I visited their website and looked for 'partnership', I never saw the private university in question. The French principle is that the public school 'makes a deal' with the public school. The Tunisian institution is a private school so in that case, it doesn't work. (Male student from Gabon)

They express a feeling of lack of social and economic recognition of the sub-Saharan student:

> Tunisians think that we come here to beg. But we bring money here. If I were to blame someone, I would blame university leaders. They did not prepare people to welcome new students. (Male student from Cameroon)

Unlike the generally positive image of the skilled European migrant, this type of student migration is exposed to a negative image in the host country. Even before moving to Tunisia, sub-Saharan students were on the defensive, and thought that, in principle, Tunisians were racists. This certainly played a part in the way they experienced their settlement: "We felt we were being watched"; "We were being judged". Some say that they were careful from the beginning and did not intend to initiate any relationships. Others say they were victims of insults and stone throwing in the city's streets. However, despite such obstacles – or partly in reaction to those difficulties – social grouping is strengthening. The oldest students of the private higher institutions share their knowledge of the 'private institutions market' with the newcomers in the host country to help them better rationalise their educational choice.

Conclusion

The social demand for studies abroad has existed for a long time in Africa but it is taking a new turn thanks to the relative democratisation of the means of circulation and communication, a diversification of the scholarship programmes and new educational strategies on behalf of the family. In the Maghreb, it is also taking a new turn with the upsurge of a business strategy by Tunisian and Moroccan private institutions in particular and the sub-Saharan states' will to help the strengthening process of a social group: future African executives graduating from the private sector and trained abroad.

Higher education institutions in Tunisia (and Morocco) are taking advantage of and profiting from the market generated by the rise in the social demand of families of sub-Saharan students, creating genuine 'student corridors' from private or public high schools in their country of origin. The Tunisian state sees in the private national sector a way to develop its higher education services to become an export to the rest of the African continent, both in attracting a pool of sub-Saharan students and, in the mid-term, in foreseeing the opening of private Tunisian higher education institutions elsewhere in Africa.

The high social demand in Africa for studies abroad is taking a new direction. Families of high-level executives in African countries, and even a proportion of the upper middle class, are increasingly opting for private fee-paying courses offered in the Maghreb. This option allows their children to access more diversified higher education programmes which, until recently, has been difficult for those not covered by the quota of scholarships awarded by the Ministry of Higher Public Education. It seems that there is a new trend in the consumption of education services towards the Maghreb by people from the upper and middle classes in the countries of black Africa, for the most part thanks to means of transport and communication becoming more widely accessible, the expansion of scholarship schemes, and a growing interest in all things international. These changes demonstrate the desire of these families and their children to become more competitive in the market of knowledge and of employment by having recourse to and making use of transnational education opportunities, which are far more accessible than those in countries of the western world, yet the cost of which may involve an additional investment.

For over ten years, Tunisia has tried to use private higher education as part of its broader strategic project to compete with Morocco for the status of being a resource for the rest of Africa in terms of the knowledge economy, as well as an economic partner with the North, the place for exchanges between Africa and the Euro-Mediterranean zone. Yet paradoxically, these changes could not be achieved without the support and financial guarantee of the state.

This liberalisation did not occur in the Maghreb region, and in Tunisia in particular, over the last ten years without the influence of the state, which I have referred to in previous works as a 'liberalisation of the State' (Mazzella, 2007, 2009). In the Maghreb, this would not be encountered as a policy to oust the state, rather in the reconfiguration of its functions. At the time of writing, the first elected government of the second Tunisian republic has set as one of its first goals the reform of private higher education, to reinforce its mission of opening up to foreign students coming from the African continent, while establishing a quality control, according to international standards, on these establishments. The success of this reform of the private sector needs to be accompanied by a public policy of teaching, but also by an immigration policy geared toward an amelioration of the conditions of sojourn of foreign students, for example by easing the visa procedures and the actual conditions of lodging. The planned goal is to "offer a public inspired knowledge in the private [sector]", according to the new Ministry of Higher Education in Tunisia.[9] The main challenge is that of offering a realistic and quality alternative to the public system and to global competition. This challenge will be measured notably in terms of the reform of the education system and of the constitutional framework, which will link it to public policy or surrender it, in part, to market forces.

Works Cited

Camau, Michel. 2006. "La globalisation démocratique et l'exception autoritaire arabe". *Critique internationale* 30: 13–27.

Didou, Aupetit S. 2004. "Public et privé dans l'enseignement supérieur au Mexique". *Cahiers de la recherche sur l'éducation et les savoirs* 3: 97–118.

---

9 Communication from the minister, 29 January 2015, to the colloquium *Les migrations de la connaissance dans l'espace francophone : quelle place pour la Tunisie ?*organised in Tunis by France terre d'asile.

Eyebiyi, E. and S. Mazzella. 2014. "Introduction. Observer les mobilités étudiantes Sud-Sud dans l'internationalisation de l'enseignement supérieur". *Cahiers de la recherche sur l'éducation et les savoirs* 13: 7–24.

Garneau, S. and S. Mazzella. 2013. "Présentation du numéro. Transformations des mobilités étudiantes Sud-Nord: approches démographiques et sociologiques". *Cahiers québécois de démographie*, 42 (2): 183–200.

Geisser, V. (ed.). 2000. *Diplômés maghrébins d'ici et d'ailleurs. Trajectoires sociales et itinéraires migratoires*. Paris, CNRS Éditions.

Gérard, É. (ed.). 2008. *Mobilités étudiantes Sud-Nord, trajectoire scolaire des Marocains en France et inscription professionnelle au Maroc*. Paris, Publisud.

Gobe, É. (ed.). 2004. *L'ingénieur moderne au Maghreb (XIXe-XXe siècle)*. Paris, IRMC: Maisonneuve & Larose.

Haddab, M. 2007. "Évolution morphologique et institutionnelle de l'enseignement supérieur en Algérie. Ses effets sur la qualité des formations et sur les stratégies des étudiants". In Sylvie Mazzella (ed.), "L'enseignement supérieur dans la mondialisation libérale", *Alfa. Maghreb et sciences sociales*. Paris, Maisonneuve & Larose / IRMC, 51–60.

Hibou, B. (ed.). 1999. *La privatisation des États*. Paris, Karthala / CERI.

Leclerc-Olive, M., G. Scarfò Ghellab and A.-C. Wagner (eds). 2011. *Les mondes universitaires face au marché. Circulation des savoirs et pratiques des acteurs*. Paris, Karthala.

Longuenesse, É. 2004. "Entre bureaucratie et marché : quelle reconversion pour les ingénieurs ? Remarques à partir du Proche-Orient". In Éric Gobe (ed.), *L'ingénieur moderne au Maghreb*. Paris, Maisonneuve & Larose/Institut de Recherche sur le Maghreb Contemporain, 347–374.

Mazzella, S. 2006. "L'enseignement supérieur privé en Tunisie. La mise en place étatique d'un secteur universitaire privé". *Alfa Maghreb et Sciences Sociales*, Études: 206–217.

Mazzella, S. (ed.). 2009. *La mondialisation étudiante. Le Maghreb entre Nord et Sud*. Paris, Karthala/IRMC.

Niane, B. 1992. "Le transnational, signe d'excellence [Le processus de disqualification de l'Etat sénégalais dans la formation des cadres]". *Actes de la recherche en sciences sociales* 95, décembre: 13–25.

Vincent-Lancrin, S. 2008. "L'enseignement supérieur transnational: un nouvel enjeu stratégiques?" In "L'enseignement supérieur face à l'internationalisation et à la privatisation". *La revue critique internationale*, 2e trim., 39: 67–86.

Vinokur, A. 2004. "Public, privé...ou hybride? L'effacement des frontières de l'éducation". *Cahiers de la recherche sur l'éducation et les savoirs*. 3: 13–33.

CHAPTER 4

Political, Financial and Moral Aspects of Sudan's Private Higher Education

Enrico Ille

In this article, I present some reflections on the categorisation 'private' in reference to Sudan's higher education institutions. This categorisation is treated as merely denoting 'non-governmental' in national legal documents, but many more connotations appear when looking at practices in this sector. Based on the personal experience of 13 months employment as Assistant Professor at the non-governmental and family-owned Ahfad University for Women in Omdurman (October 2013 – October 2014), I point out the varied ways in which work at this institution can be situated. While considering political and financial boundaries in this academic environment, I also engage with some of the categorisations employed by my colleagues that include references to morality. Following these references, I attempt to move beyond the public/private divide by reflecting on my everyday work, which concomitantly covered economic, political and moral aspects.[1]

One of the most important of these categorisations is the distinction between private (Arabic *ḫāṣ*) and communal (Arabic *ahlī*), which, while both being non-governmental, were treated as equivalent to for-profit business and social service, respectively, giving the latter a higher moral value defying lower financial benefits. In the context of Sudan's political landscape, this moral value was often also seen as a political statement for non-partisan civic engagement. While being invoked as 'non-political' in reaction both to external political pressures by the government's security apparatus and international partners' ideals of academic impartiality, this was connected to a deeply sociopolitical agenda – changing society and its organising principles.

I see in these statements and the practices they describe an attempt to combine, in their specific context, protection against being targeted for 'political' activities and civic engagement for societal change. The practical limits of this attempt are indicated through the discussion of admission processes, as well as subsequent modalities of academic teaching. I ultimately suggest that a closer look at practices and speech acts of academicians not fitting dominant models

---

1   I thank Mariam Sharif, Balghis Badri and Daniele Cantini for their critical comments on an earlier draft of this paper.

of privatisation offers, in general, important insights for the research on higher education, especially to understand alternative developments to and resistance against policies formulated on the basis of such models.

The article starts with a short overview of the higher education sector in Sudan, with a focus on northern Sudan for the sake of continuity. This includes a description of the higher education reform of 1990, the subsequent authentisation (*ta'ṣīl*) policies and the categorisation and proliferation of public and private institutions. The rest of the article follows my observations as part of the academic personnel at Ahfad University.

Higher Education in Sudan until the 1990s

In its beginnings, higher education in Sudan, if understood as academic tuition in the frame of a university-based structure, was closely connected to British colonial administration, which was built up from 1898. The early establishment of the Gordon Memorial College in 1902, which was to become the University of Khartoum in 1956, was part of a new education system beyond religious schools, and created a passage into public service. What started as a basic educational institution for professional purposes, with degrees gradually initiated in engineering, law, medicine, accounting, science and education, grew until independence into a full university, including an affiliation with the University of London in 1950. The scope of disciplines expanded further, covering also the humanities, and additional institutions were founded, such as technical colleges that continued the focus on professional training, for instance in agriculture (Shambat Agricultural College). On the level of universities, a few alternatives and disciplinary additions to the University of Khartoum existed, including the Khartoum Branch of Cairo University and the Omdurman Islamic University, but the former remained the focal point of high-quality academic reputation, not least because of an elitist stand that prevented any significant increase in admission numbers (Hassan 1992).

At least since the 1960s, the development of the sector has been criticised for several shortcomings. During the early years after independence, the main problems had been the recruitment of permanent expatriate and other qualified teaching staff, prompting a policy of 'Sudanisation'; the balance between training abroad and research and work in Sudan; constant financial difficulties depending on fluctuating governmental funds; and, connected to this dependency, struggles over academic freedom, leading to tighter control by the presidency under a military regime (1958–1964) determined to curb political criticism. Lack of data collection and planning – constant statistics of student numbers and distribution have only been available since 1972 – added to this set of problems, as well as a substantial over-supply of Arts graduates against low numbers in the Sciences and technical training, and a general problem of unemployment after graduation in all fields (Gizouli 1968: 415–472).

In an assessment published in 1977, during another military regime, the reduction in the number of expatriate staff, especially in leading positions, was still a major issue, as was the lack of technical education, unemployment of graduates and an imbalance of studies abroad and in Sudan, while the underrepresentation of women had just begun to become a concern. The assessment pointed out that the universities, most of all the University of Khartoum, served a limited, protected elite enjoying stable structures through policies of reducing access to universities – by exclusion of technical training and reliance on under-graduate studies abroad. At the same time, they failed to produce the high-skilled technical labour force needed for development programmes, even considering the other post-secondary educational facilities (Thompson et al 1977: 155–177).[2] The latter had grown in numbers during the 1970s amidst large-scale labour migration to the Gulf states, which decreased after the 1980s, causing, together with an extended economic crisis, not just a further spread of unemployment among graduates, but, paradoxically, also an increasing demand for higher education in competition over few better-paid jobs (Hassan 1992).

What made the regulation of universities a constant concern of authoritarian regimes, however, was their central role with regard to political opposition and mobilisation. This had already started in the 1920s with the formation of the Graduates' Club at the Gordon Memorial College, initially focussing on cultural and social activities, but soon a driving force behind the nationalist movement for independence (Sharkey 2003). The foundation of the Graduates' General Congress in 1937 with specific political demands led in 1942 to a memorandum presented to the colonial government. In subsequent decades, students and staff, particularly at the University of Khartoum, were heavily involved in political developments, for instance during the popular uprisings of 1964 and 1985, reacting to and prompting stronger restrictions of academic independence imposed on universities during military rule (1958–1964, 1969–1985).

---

2   The 1977 assessment, although presented as a team effort, was obviously mostly the work of Mohamed Omer Beshir, a known liberal intellectual in deep opposition to authoritarian rule in Sudan and elsewhere (Lewis et al 1992).

Higher Education in Sudan since the 1990s

Revolution or 'Revolution'

In 1989, a military coup in Sudan brought a group of people to power who claimed to be bringing salvation (*inqāz*) to the country, in the beginning as the National Islamic Front, formed later into the National Congress Party. In sweeping declarations, which were to last for over two decades, most of the previous political history of Sudan was devalued, dismissed as a deviation from the righteous path leading to an Islamic state, an Islamic world and ultimately a unified believers' community (*'umma*) at the end of times. It was claimed that this 'salvation' would put Sudan on this path and deeply ingrain it in its future.

In many policies, this was rhetorically augmented by speaking of 'revolutions'. The so-called revolution of higher education (*tawrat al-taʿlīm al-ʿālī*) was officially directed against difficulties in gaining access to universities, including lack of gender balance, lack of geographical distribution, lack of technical education and applied sciences, as well as an increasing number of Sudanese studying and working abroad (MHESR nd-a: 19; Imam 2005: 19). In consequence, a policy was formulated (Strategic Plan 1992–2002) to initiate the foundation of universities and other higher education institutions across the country, with a stronger role for communal efforts (see below), the incorporation and enhancement of technical training in universities and an overall encouragement of scientific research and publication (Imam 2005: 24–25).

In a second strategic plan (2002–2027), these measures were confirmed and extended to include scientific and technological innovation for economic and social development as well as quality control (Imam 2005: 25). Communal presence now also encompassed social responsibility in scientific research, while the importance of international cooperation for the sake of domestic education and employment was stressed (Imam 2005: 26).

This was underpinned by a legal framework, starting in 1990 with the Organisation of Higher Education and Scientific Research Act (*qānūn tanzīm al-taʿlīm al-ʿālī wa al-baht al-ʿilmī*), which completely abolished the previous law of 1975.[3] It placed the president at the top of the hierarchy of higher education, represented by the National Council of Higher Education (since 1993: and Scientific Research, NCHESR), whose mandate was closely connected to state policies and established close control of the sector, from admission and employment policies to the evaluation of higher education institutions' compliance with their aims as defined by the law. These aims (§12), leaving aside

---

3   The post-1989 laws and statutes can be found on the website of the Ministry of Higher Education and Scientific Research (http://www.mohe.gov.sd).

the culturalist elements for the moment, put these institutions in the service of the general public through support for governmental efforts to find feasible solutions to obstacles for progress and the extension of educational opportunities, especially in rural areas.

In a 1993 amendment, the National Council was drawn even closer to governmental policies and organs by making the Minister of Higher Education and Scientific Research (MHESR) automatically its chairman, and members of other ministries and the directors (vice-chancellors) of the government universities regular members – all on the recommendation of the chairman. The appointment of the vice-chancellors, again, was put in the hands of the president. In 1995, the vice-chancellors and board chairmen of the non-governmental universities were made regular members of the National Council as well.

In general, this extended a process that was intended to streamline the education system through the policy of empowerment (tamkīn) of the supporters of the new regime. This included the exchange of personnel, especially in higher positions, with such supporters, masked as a service for the public good (al-sāliḥ al-ᶜām). Control of educational institutions was thus one of the basic ways by which the government tried to establish overall political control. Bearing in mind the great importance of universities, especially the University of Khartoum, in the political history of Sudan, this attempt to stabilise the regime's grip on power can be seen to be even more significant than those of previous authoritarian regimes (Bishai 2008: 5). The attempt failed to stabilise the political climate, although the regime stayed in power, and instead violent clashes have continued inside the University of Khartoum and other universities, right up to the present day.[4]

The aspect of 'alienated' students spending most of their higher educational career abroad became centre-stage after 1989 as well, as the policies of the 'revolution' aimed at much more than just remedying the technical shortcomings of higher education, and added, through its programme of authentisation (ta'ṣīl), a new quality to government intervention in academic institutions.

Sudanisation or Islamisation
A distance between 'Sudanese society' and higher education in general was one of the ills diagnosed by the proponents of the 'revolution' (MHESR

---

4   In September 2014, the University of Khartoum reopened its doors for regular teaching after having being closed in reaction to violent clashes following the killing of a student by militias during a demonstration for peace in Darfur in March 2014 and fruitless negotiations for an independent investigation during the following months (Shibeika 2014).

nd-a: 19). The process that was claimed to be able to 'cure' this ill was *ta'ṣīl* or authentisation, which could be understood as 'return to the origins', but was used as a modernist notion for moving towards a future that contains an authentic way of doing things. It was thus intended to communicate the need for an effort to give the way things go an 'authentic' direction. The legal translation of this 'cure' was inscribed into the 1990 law under §12 as the first aim of higher education institutions. Here it was the connectedness to the specific characteristics of Sudanese society with its roots in Islamic, Arabic and African heritages (§12A), and the education of a generation of intellectual and professional leaders who are believers in God, and adhere and commit to their traditions in their behaviour and their service for the country (§12B).[5]

This culturalist qualification of higher education's function in society, namely to reproduce pre-defined cultural norms, was juxtaposed to only one sentence on academic freedom (§14), merely stating its existence 'in the frame of existing laws', immediately followed by a paragraph on the guardianship of the president to ensure compliance with aforementioned aims and duties (§15).

The topic of indigenising education is, of course, not one limited to Sudan and is ultimately connected to post-colonial discourses of emancipation. However, in the case of authentisation as promoted by the present regime, 'authenticity' was not basically connected to anything African, or Sudanese for that matter, but drew a line to God through the Qur'ān and Sunnah towards Islamic epistemology (*islāmīyat al-maʿārif*). In fact, the subsequent policies meant a strong focus in primary and secondary education on Islam, Qur'ān studies and Arabic language, promoting a picture of cultural homogeneity in contradiction with the plurality of cultural practices existing in Sudan, arguably supporting the intensification of conflicts (Breidlid 2013).

Similarly, the review of university curricula and scientific methods was argued to be oriented towards the future, in the sense of moving forward in a way agreeable to God (*sabīl Allah*), based on Islamic principles (Ḥayr 2008: 14–15). Students appeared as a resource of the believers' community (*raṣīd al-ʿumma*; Ḥayr 2008: 19) and education steered towards affirmation and strengthening of this community's cultural and intellectual identity (Imam 2005: 24). Government positions and organs were created to implement respective policies, such as the Presidential Advisor on Affairs of Authentisation (*mustašār raʾīs al-jamhurīya al-sūdān li-shuʾūn al-taʾṣīl*), the Administration for Authentisation of

---

5   El Tom (2006: 21) noted that "none of the eight goals addresses the needs of students as individuals".

Knowledge (*idāra li-taʾṣīl al-maᶜrifa*) and the Higher Authority for Arabicisation (*hīʾat al-ᶜulīyā lil-taᶜrīb*) at the Ministry of Higher Education and Scientific Research (El Tom 2006: 23).

The argument for pursuing this course was based on the claim that majority opinion in Sudan was in favour of such a policy (Ḥayr 2008: 16–17), implying that the government legitimately represented the majority, and that minorities were largely irrelevant. In critical readings of this process, this not only marginalised liberal Muslims and people of other belief systems in general by imposing a specific understanding of Islam and its importance in social, economic and scientific life. The stress on the "ontological superiority of the Muslim and Arab mind" (Breilid 2013: 38) also devalued the diversity of standpoints and approaches to knowledge, and thereby implicitly devalued the free exchange of thoughts independent from pre-defined authoritarian sources and authorities. This, it was argued, led under the present regime to a lack of critical thinking and intellectual flexibility among the majority of students, who were instead tuned to adopt enough pre-determined knowledge to pass exams and receive certification (Bishai 2008: 7).

The historical accuracy of this reading of post-1989 developments cannot be discussed here, although it may be noted that the criticism of authoritarian 'traditional' education has a longer history, as well as the criticism of 'modern', 'Westernised' education (Khaleefa, Erdos and Ashria 1997). But there is no lack of critical assessments of the resulting landscape of academic teaching and production (see Hassan 1992 for an early critical assessment; Gasim 2010). During the last decade, the 'revolution' was blamed for having

> created generations of students, unable to communicate efficiently in any language; ... [l]ecturers and students developed the bad habit of depending on so called 'hand-outs' or 'sheets' – ... short summarised notes, containing the necessary minimum to pass examinations. ... The typical Sudanese student today ... is thus educated to remain politically, socially and mentally 'illiterate' and hence objectively obedient ....
> ELGIZOULI 2005: 9–10

In the context of several shifts in political and economic development, such as the political side-lining of the Muslim Brotherhood and the start of large-scale oil production in the 2000s, the formulation or at least pervasiveness of central ideological programmes has slightly waned in recent years. Already the higher education strategic plan for 2002–2027 stepped back from some of the exclusionary aims, including now support for scientific languages other than Arabic, a culture of peace, justice and individual rights, as well as an unspecified support for the development of students' mental and skills development (Imam 2005: 25–26).

This did not mean the disappearance of authentisation and restrictive policies at academic institutions.[6] Rather the increasing focus on the privatisation and marketisation of higher education has brought new aspects and arguably further complications into their workings, and it has been a central matter of debate whether this development represents a general improvement in the direction of academic freedom and educational quality.[7]

Privatisation or Outsourcing

Apart from authentisation, the quantitative increase and distribution of universities and admitted students has been a prominent element of the positive self-assessment of the proponents of the 'revolution' (MHESR nd-a, MHESR nd-b). The intake numbers grew continually – 6,000 in 1989/1990; 38,623 in 1999/2000; 117,983 in 2009/2010[8] – with a respective growth in total enrolment – 204,114 in 2000/2001; 290,640 in 2005/2006; 526,894 in 2011/2012 (Watson *et al* 2011, 142; official statistics of the MHESR).[9]

6　One example is the requirement to have succeeded in the subject Religious Education in order to gain entrance. Religious instruction in other countries than Sudan is also permitted if proven either from the foreign curriculum or in a pre-entry exam (MHESR 2012: 13); Christian education is recognized as well (MHESR 2012: 16). This shows a continuation of fusing compliance or at least acquaintance with religious doctrines with access to higher education.

7　Zaki El Hassan (1992) cited the case of Prof. Mamoun Homeida, who was removed in 1992 from his position as vice-chancellor of the University of Khartoum after criticising the 'revolution' as destructive. He subsequently founded a private university in 1996, the University of Medical Sciences & Technology, where he was followed by some of the equally disgruntled staff of the University of Khartoum. Today, his university is a symbol of exclusiveness, with entrance fees beyond the reach of most income levels in Sudan, and he himself became a beacon of aggressive commercialization of the health sector when he ordered – as Khartoum State Minister of Health – the dismantling of public hospitals with low treatment costs, not least to the benefit of the expensive private hospitals he owned. The basic circumstances of this development can be assessed here: http://www.aljazeera.com/indepth/features/2014/01/sudan-hospitals-ravaged-privatisation-2014111212854618o.html.

8　The last number is only for Sudanese Bachelor students. The introduction of an intermediate diploma increased the number of newly admitted students again by about 50%.

9　All official statistical data have been accessed from the website of the Ministry of Higher Education and Scientific Research (http://www.mohe.gov.sd/index.php?option=com_cont ent&view=category&id=4&Itemid=18). Data were published only up to the academic year 2011/2012. The published records are also full of gaps (years 2008/2009 and 2006/2007 are

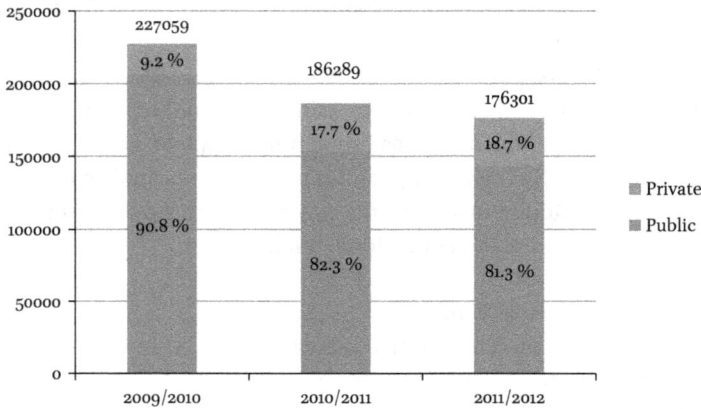

FIGURE 4.1   *Overall admission numbers at Sudanese universities 2009–2011,*
             showing percentages of public and private institutions.

Although admission numbers in the 2000s continued the trend, this seems to have changed during recent years, with a higher absolute and relative intake by private institutions (see Figure 4.1):[10]

Similarly, the number of higher education institutions increased immensely. Before 1990, there were five public universities, ten public colleges and institutes, as well as two private institutions. This rose by 2006 to 27 public universities and nine public technical colleges, plus five private universities and 46 private colleges (Watson *et al* 2011: 142; see slightly different numbers in El Tom 2006: 26). For registration in the year 2012/2013, the Ministry listed 31 public universities and 51 private providers (MHESR 2012).

What counters this success in numbers, however, is constant criticism of a decrease in educational and research quality, which resulted from the imbalance of increasing admission and declining financial and administrative support, effectively reducing equity in access to high-quality academia (Elhadary 2010: 80) and, at the other end of the cycle, causing "lack of

---

missing) and uneven (up to 2009 no distinction between public and private, up to 2006 only overall registered students in B.A. programmes at public universities).

10   Probably the decrease has something to do with the independence of South Sudan in 2011, but admission numbers also failed to rise to the 2011/2012 level in the following years – in 2014/2015 first-round admissions reached 173,952 students (http://news.sudanvisiondaily .com/details.html?rsnpid=240576). However, the existence of second-round and irregular admission limits the reliability of these numbers in general.

employment opportunities for graduates, the low quality of graduates and research outputs, and a deteriorating research environment" (Ibid.: 88).

The 'revolution' was accompanied by a sharp decrease of government funding for universities; the reduction of spending on students' and staffs' accommodation and expenses was an explicit measure of the first decade, stipulated in the 1990 law, and connected to a clear demarcation of parents' and local authorities' future contributions (§6 I). In the context of this change in funding policies, another organ, the National Fund for Students' Welfare (*al-sundūq al-qawmī li-raᶜāyat al-ṭulāb*), was founded in 1991. Government support for students was also redefined in the strategic plan for 2002–2027, where it appeared as a potential positive outcome of a diversification of financial resources (Imam 2005: 25–26).[11]

Whatever the institutional arrangements, however, overall public spending on education in general and on higher education specifically remained low throughout the 1990s, in spite of higher demand and a huge increase in the number of universities (see World Bank 2010 for similar trends all over Africa). This corresponds to the statement that "new and old universities alike were simply too poor to function, lacked basic infrastructure and suffered the weight of a by far too large student load" (Elgizouli 2005: 9).[12]

This somewhat changed in the 2000s, according to World Bank numbers (World Bank & GoNU 2012: 161, 166), but most of the budgets went into salaries (69%), while goods and services only received 16%, and student subsidies were at 14% (World Bank & GoNU 2012: 168). This focus on the basic running costs shows a continuation from the 1990s, as "[t]he politicisation of higher education has relegated research to a secondary requirement for promotion purposes" and "research output during the 1990s decreased by about 22% from its level in the 1980s for the country" (Bloom, Canning and Chan 2006: 66).

This led inevitably to the diversification of finances, and shifted the financial burden onto students (tuition fees) and investors, while maintenance and development, for example of libraries, was deprioritised (for details, see El Tom 2006: 48–51). This paved the ground for private higher education:

---

11   Countering the impression that this grew from an Islamic 'salvation', El Tom (2006: 48) pointed out that this "must be seen as an element in the government's IMF-inspired 3-year (1990–1992) program of 'economic salvation', which withdrew the government's support from social services". As noted below (footnote 21), this World Bank / IMF link still exists today.

12   Elhadary (2010: 90) quotes student/staff ratios at public and private institutions of 85:1 and 117:1, respectively, in the latter ranging from 96:1 at Ahfad University for Women to 939:1 at the Aviation College.

The perception of society at large of education as the gateway to opportunity, low enrolment rates, and a stagnant job market for the educated
have combined to fuel the 'diploma disease'. The ensuing intense competition for education at all levels coupled with the deterioration of its quality have helped create a situation in which private tuition has become
almost a necessary condition for advancement and has encouraged the
mushrooming of for-profit education institutions, especially at the secondary and tertiary levels.

EL TOM 2006: 54

But reasons to be discontent with work in private higher education in Sudan
were numerous as well, and mostly not only very similar to public higher education, but often experienced by the same people:

Private institutions experience a serious shortage of permanent staff,
and mostly depend on part-time staff recruited from public universities. ... Most academic staff are involved in moonlighting (part-timing in
several universities) and change their place of work several times a day.
A lecturer may teach undergraduate studies in the morning, diploma or
even secondary students in the afternoon, and conduct evening classes
at night.

ELHADARY 2010: 89–90

In other words, individual academics represented less and less the 'human
capital' of either the public or the private sector, but constantly shifted between both, making them rather a pool of human resources that was shared
to varying degrees by different employers, in many cases including other than
academic institutions.

This strongly reduced the opportunities to engage in long-term, concentrated research. In spite of a general legal provision that "research is one of the major mandates of universities" (Ibid.: 97), this was not followed up by adequate
budgets and a salary structure that would allow academics to engage in serious
research, including the condition to be free of constant worries about income
(Ibid.: 97). The strained labour market also meant, not just in academia, a dis-
connection between the educational and professional background, and the
job opportunities fitting economic needs (Assal 2010: 5).[13]

---

13   See Mann 2013 for documentation on how the oversupply of engineering graduates led to
      non-professional selection criteria in one of the major private companies in Sudan.

Both dynamics also encouraged people to move away from higher education institutions, or even Sudan, which were not attractive in labour market terms in comparison with job opportunities in other fields or abroad. The 'flight' from hardships or at least limitations in Sudan through emigration is a well-documented issue.[14] Assal 2010 provides one of the most detailed accounts of the emigration of high-skilled labourers with tertiary education, extending the argument that this cannot be invariably regarded as brain drain:

> In effect, a mismatch was created between education and employment and therefore one could talk about 'brain waste' instead of 'brain drain'. Given the fact that higher-educational institutions in Sudan are poorly equipped, in terms of staff and other facilities, it could be said that the education exported abroad through skilled migrants does not constitute a loss for Sudan. (Ibid.: 5)

This is not true for rare specialisations, however, as Assal showed for the case of medicine graduates and medical doctors, 60% of whom worked abroad in 2010, while thousands remained unemployed in Sudan and over 350 specialists per year were lacking (Ibid.: 5–6).[15] In contradictory policies, state organs answered this crisis with coercion and attempted to outlaw emigration of specific professionals or punish it with high fees, but also "seem[ed] to encourage migration, particularly to the Gulf countries as international migration is one source of foreign currency" (Ibid.: 8).[16]

So the issues in higher education since independence were not solved, but only slightly re-routed towards private institutions and, paradoxically, studying and working outside Sudan. Still only 30% of qualified students were admitted to higher education in 2005 and only 6.2% of the relevant age group qualified

---

14   Numbers for 2008 from the Secretariat for Sudanese Working Abroad (quoted in Assal 2010: 4) suggest that there were 451,443 so-called semi-skilled migrant workers, most of them university graduates, against 44,079 bachelor and 11,550 high diploma graduates in the same year. Most of this migration is directed towards the Gulf countries, since the 1990s increasingly also North America and Europe. Assal (2010: 3) noted, however, that "[d]atabases on skilled Sudanese migrants working abroad are inadequate".

15   Here a gender aspect comes in, as the nursing profession is predominantly taken up by women, whose emigration can more easily be prevented through existing laws (Assal 2010: 6).

16   One of the projects trying to tap into the wealth of human resources outside the country, UNDP's Transfer of Knowledge through Expatriate Nationals (TOKTEN), was built on the presumption that the Comprehensive Peace Agreement in 2005 would set off a period of peace and prosperity.

(Elhadary 2010: 81); still unemployment, or employment in jobs not connected with the subjects studied, prevailed among graduates; still, where possible, solutions were sought abroad. Rather than tackling the 'problem' of academic studies and work abroad, the 'revolution' reinforced the process by adding political to economic motivations to emigrate (Ibid.: 96). Ali (2010: 6) pointed out a subsequent contradiction, as "the issue between the conventional national spirit of 'Higher education for development' and the individual aspiration of 'Higher education for emigration' emerged strikingly ...".

A Third 'Revolution'?

It was not least to counter an obvious deterioration of the public sector that in 2013 several attempts at improvements were made. Internal assessments of the M H E S R noted increasing financial difficulties, rising fees, increasing teaching loads, and the emigration of teachers; accordingly, a major shift to increase the attractiveness of employment at Sudanese universities was suggested. This aim was translated by a ministerial conference into an additional budget demand for 2013, wherein unspecified 'improvement of the staff's situation' was costed at 473.5 of an overall 634.3 million SDG (74.6%).[17]

The 'courting' of the teaching staff also took institutional form in a 2013 amendment of the Higher Education Law which introduced a new representative function of the teaching staff (*hi'at al-tadrīs*). It was stipulated that they would have the right to formulate administrative policies, to be affirmed by the Minister of Higher Education, and to name candidates for vice-chancellor and deputy vice-chancellor, still ultimately appointed by the president (§15, §17). Although still based on the 1990 law, this and related documents of recent years did not only stay clear of references to authentisation, but also other culturalist elements in the definition of these institutions' aims (§7).[18] The teaching staff and students now appear as central actors whose academic freedom, however, is limited by law and deferred to inside the campus (*dāḥil ḥaram al-mu'asasa*), suggesting that it is something to be kept within bound(arie)s (§8). In short,

---

17   In the same document – that does not show an approved budget – Arabicization and *ta'ṣīl* appeared with 10 million SDG (see http://www.mohe.gov.sd/index.php?option=com _content&view=article&id=257:----2013&catid=19:2012-02-21-10-27-00&Itemid=54).

18   Already in 2003, Zakariyya Imam, who still wrote advertisements for the 'revolution' in 2005, stayed clear of its culturalist elements and concentrated on things to be improved in the face of international standards. The change of focus did not mean the complete abolition of the culturalist programme. In 2008, Ḥayr still evaluated compliance with *ta'ṣīl* at Sudanese universities (Ḥayr 2008).

the introduction of new power from below, as can be seen by the stipulations, only amounts to suggestion-making, not decision-making.

In the field of private higher education, the line was also made looser, but not cut. The private fees, even at public universities, were now defined by the universities themselves, removing this part of the public sector from government control, but at the same time strengthening it at other points. So it would be misleading to measure academic life in Sudan solely based on budgets, employment and quality standards. A basic mode of operation in Sudan's higher education is the assessment of and dealing with threats by state organs, especially national security. During the present regime, the intrusion of violent security agents into the inner life of universities and the lives of students and academicians is a constant that merits a central point in any approach to higher education in Sudan, be it public or private.

A line can be drawn from earlier events (Africa Watch 1991; El Tom 2006: 27) straight through to today's harassment, arrests, beating and torture, which has occurred untouched by the recent declaration of a 'national dialogue'. Far from being a development towards cultural revival and guided social transformation, the oppressive character of rule from 1989 through to today has fostered and strengthened violent confrontation through means of religious bigotry and legitimisation of threats of violence and death for perceived disobedience and (by claiming it to be the same) apostasy. Student and staff memories of the past two decades are full of cries of *Allahu akbar* from pro-government student bodies as they aggressively confront the appearance of alternative points of views and suggestions.[19]

In the meantime, the political and economic environment of higher education has changed little. Government investment has diminished, but government control has been maintained through the National Council and the national security apparatus, supported by the regime's Islamist and capitalist groundwork. Harassment of students and academic staff by security agents continues, critical voices in the political arena are still answered by censorship and arrest, while the costs of living rise steadily due to high inflation and reduced government subsidies.

The previous sections showed higher education vis-à-vis intricate boundaries: boundaries of access and remuneration, boundaries of political and

---

19   The potential to voice criticism found a rare window of opportunity during the period of the Comprehensive Peace Agreement of 2005; in the field of academia for instance, represented by the conference "Academic freedom and university autonomy in the Sudan", 26–27 February 2007 in Khartoum, organized by the Council for the Development of Social Science Research in Africa (CODESRIA).

cultural orientation, boundaries of academic freedom. People working in the sector come to terms with these boundaries, which influence how they perceive their options in academic work, as, in fact, jobs are constantly filled in Sudan's higher education and many places can be found where academic life and production has not stopped. A closer look at individual perspectives can show how different people actively arrange themselves with the boundaries they experience.

Personal Perspectives

The following case study is based on my own experiences at Ahfad University for Women in Omdurman, where I worked from October 2013 to October 2014 as Assistant Professor and coordinator of the Masters programme 'Gender and Governance'.[20]

Ahfad University for Women was acknowledged as a full university in 1995; its origin is connected to non-governmental schools established by Babiker Badri from 1907, starting with a secular school for girls (Badri 1961/1980: 109–170), and, more directly, to the Ahfad University College founded by Yusuf Babiker Badri in 1966 (Badri 1997). Since the very beginning, these interconnected schools were perceived as a distinctive effort to create an alternative both to schools founded by the colonial administration and to the older system of religious schools (ḫalwa). The schools were also central in advancing girls' education in Sudan, which was not actively supported or was even actively discouraged in the other institutions. This background of distinction can be traced up to the present time and is a crucial resource for the self-definition of the university's supporters as vanguards of values that give a distinctive quality to work at and for the university.

It is important to note that what follows is an initial exploration of the issues put forward here, not the result of systematic research, whose potential benefit will thus be merely indicated. This exploration starts with statements relating positively to this institution, often depicted as an attempt to supersede social, economic and political boundaries by challenging them through an alternative.

---

20   The option to anonymise the institution was not available, since it would have been too obvious given it is the only university for women in the country; but staff members, whose reflective statements this case study discusses, have been anonymised in name, as well as time and place of the conversation. A similar reflection based on personal experiences can be found in Bedri 2013, concerning Ahfad University for Women and girls' education in Sudan.

Distinctions

The early legal language of the 'revolution' denoted all domestic private institutions as communal (*ahlī*, 1990 Law, §11) or non-governmental (*ğayr ḥakūmīya*), which obscured differences between institutions and their financial bases. In other contexts, these differences were marked by a distinction of private (*ḥāṣ*) and communal (*ahlī*), separating profit-seeking and community service, or not-for-profit, as primary respective goals, the latter sometimes strengthened as philanthropic, *ḥayrī*, if based on a charitable foundation. The World Bank's 2012 report on education in Sudan, in cooperation with the Sudanese government, identified five types of higher education institutions: public universities, public technical colleges, private universities, philanthropic universities, private colleges (World Bank & GoNU 2012: 33).[21]

Beyond the organisational distinction concerning financial sources,[22] however, the distinction between private and communal marked, in statements by academic personnel at Ahfad, a moral difference and a point whereby the specific conduct of a private higher education institution is scrutinised and values are seen beyond the level of income. One Assistant Professor clarified this by pointing out his alternatives: a single short-term consultancy for a company or an international organisation brings an income equivalent to a whole year's salary in his full-time position at the university. Even more, just loaning a private car for transportation – without any active role – could generate the same profit each month as three to four months of his regular salary. In addition, there is the time invested in coming to work, involving at least a one hour drive, and the lack of useful health insurance or other social services, in spite of the 25% of salaries given to the National Social Insurance Fund.

The continuation of work at the university did thus not stem from economic or, as he called it, 'rational' considerations, but rather contradicted these, and his continuous chances for consultancy contracts also excluded the argument of lacking alternatives, even if academic institutional affiliation can be an important asset for one's credentials. For him, this work, given the many associated sacrifices he perceived, was a service, an expression of duty towards the country (*waṭanīya*). This also surpassed the perceived illegitimacy of the

---

21 The fact that the only comprehensive study of the education sector in northern Sudan has been conducted under the aegis of the World Bank – the study was explicitly prepared to inform an education sector strategic plan for 2012–2016 (World Bank & GoNU 2012: xiii) – indicates the continuing influence of the organization on government policies (see footnote 11).

22 A relatively new sector is the Open University, which operates based on distance learning, whereby modules and contact hours with tutors are paid for. In Sudan, a branch of the Arab Open University (AOU) exists, as well as the Open University of Sudan, founded, like AOU, in 2002.

present government and stark violations of the social contract, as exemplified, in his view, by the social insurance system, which engaged in private investments rather than in the provision of services.

This kind of reciprocity towards a social environment was a constant element in similar statements. A personal assistant covered the distance between a previous salary of over US$6,000 at the African Union and the fraction of it received in her present work in reference to her own studies at the university and the wish to give back to her *alma mater*, to reciprocate. One of the department heads at the university drew a similar comparison between World Bank commissions bringing up to US$12,000 per month and the more than two years' regular salary this represents by saying, "we don't work here because we have to, we work here because we like Ahfad".

So on the one hand, low base salaries nurtured a system of calculated academic production, where 'usual' academic activities, such as writing papers or organising conferences, were transformed into units of monetary value. On the other hand, what constituted here a 'good' job encompassed a moral or also emotional component that could foster commitment through constituting or continuing a social connection, which made private higher education appear as a communal effort that potentially surpasses the attraction of another, 'better' (paid) full-time job. In how far this good job was allowed to hinder access to a better-paid job remained, however, a strained and constantly negotiable question and heavily influenced how much time and energy were actually committed to the work.

Although only one of several social aspects relevant for working relations, social connections arising from the university's origin in family structures seem to have a special importance in this negotiation. These social connections can, for instance, be found in self-descriptions of members of the Babiker Badri family about how Ahfad University was established. Amna Badri, for instance, described the foundation of the Ahfad University College in the 1960s as

> mobilising the whole family in a mass effort of fund raising. A number of activities were organized for this cause, for example, Gala Nights were held and we performed in entertaining shows, and also an annual charity bazaar was organised […]. We still cherish memories from these events as it was equally fun and enjoyable in spite of the huge efforts and time that went into its planning and implementation.
>
> BEDRI 2013: 27

At the same time, this foundation was not merely a family or communal matter, but connected to a larger societal cause. Indeed, Amna Badri's depiction was challenged by another member of the family, not only concerning its character as family occasion, but also regarding the presence and role of non-family members of Ahfad schools' Boards of Trustees, i.e. an institutional frame beyond family. In any case, the college was created in reflection of a socio-cultural gap in Sudan's education, namely higher education for women, especially women not coming from higher education's mainland in Khartoum. Bedri's argumentative effort, heavily supported by quotes from Sondra Hale (2009), thus directly related the personal experience of civic engagement at the university as a feminist one with its societal position as symbol and active exercise of women's rights to higher education.[23] As both authors pointed out (Hale 2009: 147; Bedri 2013: 30–31), this was valued the more during the harsh public morality regime developing after 1989, represented by the notorious Public Order Law of 1997, which was perceived as threatening women's rights, turning the very existence of the university into a political cause to be supported.[24]

At the same time, the presence of women at institutions of higher education continued to show a similar asymmetry between quantity and quality as the overall development of student numbers. It was only the lower hierarchy of the academic system that experienced an increase in numbers, while the disparity in higher ranks was reduced only slightly, increasing the male leadership of women in higher education rather than moving towards a balance (Badri 2008).[25] Elhadary (2010: 80) diagnosed that this supported "the creation of an elite group (state of male) leading to skewed stratification among the Sudanese population".

Here, the cultural element of the 'revolution' also took hold with numerous training institutions for women with Islamic culture, educational and domestic work skills as primary subjects (Imam 2005: 56).[26] While the complex link between gender roles and perceptions of gender-appropriate professions

---

23   The field of academic civic engagement in Sudan has been assessed in Watson *et al* 2011: 141–149, with Ahfad University for Women as case study by Susan E. Stroud.

24   This does not mean the absence of sexual politics on the grounds of the university. In spite of its general character as protective space for the female students, many of whom are unmarried, incidents of sexual harassment and abuse have taken place, and, not least in reaction to them, appropriateness, for instance of mixed events late in the evening, are frequently part of discussions in and outside administrative meetings.

25   A look at the statistics for the year 2011/2012 shows no change in this regard: total staff 12,463 with 3,887 female (31.2%), the bulk of whom were in lower academic positions; the numbers at the level of full professor were 743 male to 35 female (4.7%). Out of an overall total of 526,894, there were 278,802 female registered students (52.9%).

26   See Badri 2008 for a more differentiated discussion of the relation between disciplines and the gender of students.

cannot be discussed here, the claim has to be noted, as in Elhadary (2010: 83), that "women prefer to enrol for studies in education because it secures them employment in a field that is considered as culturally acceptable profession for women by Sudanese communities".[27]

Ahfad University for Women, on the other hand, was based on the principle of affirmative action, not aiming for internal gender balance, but positive discrimination in favour of female students as a means to influence the external gender balance. This concerned not only women in general, but also "places and scholarships for women from disadvantaged areas of the south, Darfur, Nuba, Red Sea, and Blue Nile states" (Elhadary 2010: 86; Badri 2008), in addition to women from neighbouring countries, such as Ethiopia, Somalia and Eritrea.

Beyond aspirations to be a beacon of women's education, Ahfad's foundation as a university was also closely connected to attempts at creating an alternative to politically or commercially charged universities. The movement between risky political circumstances in Sudan and the cooperation with international partners tacitly addressing these circumstances is thereby the clearest case of dealing proactively with economic and political boundaries. In a memorandum of understanding signed by Ahfad University and a US-American partner for technical assistance on building leadership skills, the university is described as

> committed to a world-class education for women in a non-political environment and seek[ing] to prepare women from all parts of Sudan to become change agents in their families and communities and to assume leadership positions in society.

While 'non-political' reflects external political pressures and the partners' ideals of academic neutrality, the project itself is connected to an essentially socio-political goal, namely enabling leaders of societal change.

This shows an act of balancing, whose practical limits are constantly negotiated. While security agents have an office on the campus, on some occasions even demanding to see the content of courses or 'sitting in', many politically sensitive issues found a venue here as well, as, for instance, debates on the formulation of a new constitution. The moving back and forth between more

---

27   Some of these perceptions are translated into legal regulations, such as the prohibition of female oil engineers from field trips or, in case of the University of Khartoum, even the prohibition from studying subjects such as mechanical, oil and mining engineering (Elhadary 2010: 83). These prohibitions were still in place in 2013 (MHESR 2013: 15) and have been contextualised in Hale 2000.

or less risky public exposure demarcated here, as outside the campus, the relation between citizens and a potentially oppressive police state, a constant
hide-and-seek. This was the experience of a group of university staff who were
chided by the university's president for showing too little political courage by
proposing to protest inside the campus against police violence towards demonstrators in September 2013, partially inside Ahfad University itself.[28] This
was also the experience of a group of university staff who were arrested by
security in late October 2013, when they discussed how to take a stand outside
the campus.[29]

It has therefore to be noted that experienced boundaries, with their economic, political and moral aspects, can be translated into rational, categori-
cal distinctions, which qualify the protagonists' own actions as a challenge
to those boundaries, but vary in their actual effect on these boundaries. If, in
this context, the demarcation of a moral difference as being a community and
being for community is such an important symbolic boundary distinguishing
an institution from the commercialisation of higher education and from state
politics, where can this boundary be found in the everyday workings of such
institutions and how does it translate into an actual alternative beyond the
economic and political boundaries at work throughout the higher education
sector?

The following two sections follow these questions into the fields of admission policies and subsequent teacher-student relations.

Being Admitted

Admission at Sudanese higher education institutions is marked by the tension
between centralisation of the process through bureaucratic rules and the ability of private circumstances independent from academic performance to heavily influence the probability of getting access.

The overall process is tightly controlled by the Ministry of Higher Education,
also with a recent shift to an internet-based system, especially through the
annual admission maximum centrally planned by the National Council (El Tom
2006: 33). Admission is generally built on the competitive results of the Sudan
Secondary School Certificate (al-šihāda al-sūdānīya), or other recognised certificates, and preferences for universities given through the application forms.

---

28   See   http://www.aljazeera.com/news/africa/2013/10/sudan-defends-crackdown-amid
      -more-protests-20131015534486705.html.
29   See   http://www.reuters.com/article/2013/10/29/sudan-arrests-idUSL5N0IJ33E20131029;
      http://english.alarabiya.net/en/News/africa/2013/10/29/Nine-professors-held-in-swoop
      -on-Khartoum-campus-lawyer.html.

At the level of Bachelor, the school results in four subjects, Arabic language, English language, Religious Education and Mathematics are also taken into account during the merit-based placing. At this level, a certificate from Qur'an schools (*šihāda ahlīya wa qarā'āt*), which consists only of Islamic religious subjects (MHESR 2012: 8–11, 16), is recognised as well.

Apart from exclusionary circumstances, however, there are also myriads of special inclusionary circumstances influencing the options and conditions to get admitted, left out of most descriptions of Sudan's higher education system (e.g. UNESCO 2011) and representing, in a sense, 'privatisation' of the overall system, or at least a blurring of lines between 'public' and 'private', enhanced by the linguistic circumstance that the term used in Arabic, *ḫāṣ*, means both 'private' and 'special'.

Regulations distinguish between the general admission (*al-qubūl al-ᶜām*), special admission (*al-qubūl al-ḫāṣ*), direct admission (*al-qubūl al-mubāšir*), transfer from other universities after the first year or other kinds of 'late' admission (i.e. not in the same year as the certificate), admission from distance learning and other unspecified ways from additional regulations (MHESR 2012: 9–10).

But the overall extent of 'special admission' was much wider than indicated in the regulations (Elhadary 2010: 87–88). Admission under special circumstances (*qubūl ᶜala al-nafaqa al-ḫāṣa*) extended the centrally defined admission numbers and allowed students able to pay full tuition fees to enter with up to 12% below the average marks required for general admission (El Tom 2006: 33). In this way, money superseded the performance principle, but was only one aspect of a category with wide spaces for discretion, the door for the multiplication of legitimate ways to enrol, only partly formulated into written, legalised stipulations. In the sense that *ᶜām* denoted the merit-based system, which was the only regular one up to 1989, the widening category 'special admission' was the means by which the distinction of public and private was corroded. El Tom (Ibid.: 34) went so far as to claim that

> [t]hese exceptions demonstrate that MHESR's admission policy for higher education institutions is decidedly biased against the poor and, in view of the membership of NCHESR [...], reflects the interests of members of NCHESR.

There were stipulations that could be read as attempts to merely support institutional reproduction. So the children and spouses of staff and pensioners in higher education and scientific research, including the respective governmental organs, were subject to the private admission rule, but exempted from

50–75% of the tuition fees (Ibid.: 33).[30] But once again, remembering the aggressive policy of empowerment (*tamkīn*) in the 1990s, this institutional reproduction has a link to the authoritarian political environment, even if new rules in 2013 extended this special admission to the staff of non-governmental institutions (MHESR 2013: 8–10).[31]

Other stipulations can be seen as attempts to support access to higher education in so-called underdeveloped regions. Regulations distinguish a group of students as coming from less-developed federal states (*abnā' al-wilāyāt al-'aqalla numwan*), for whom 50% of the places at universities in those states were reserved, plus an unspecified number of places at national universities in subjects not covered in the regional universities. The conditions for this access were permanent residence of the student's family in the state, primary and secondary education had to have been obtained there, the studies had to be used to work in the state for the first five years after graduation, and the student was fixed to the university and subject originally chosen (MHESR 2012: 13; El Tom 2006: 33, Elhadary 2010: 85).

These details show a difficulty built into the provisions, which exclude the large number of internally displaced persons (IDPs) and refugees by presuming residential permanency and continuity in the educational career, a condition highly unfair for the targeted regions, which in most cases have also been the most war-affected.[32] This is even more of a central issue as the Comprehensive Peace Agreement of 2005, on which the present constitution was based,

---

30   Disabled students were exempted from fees as well, but compete for places with all other students (MHESR 2012: 14).

31   At the same time, the admission of foreign students was limited to 5% of general admission.

32   An example of exemption from tuition fees being used to try to address this issue was the stipulation of the 2011 Doha Document for Peace in Darfur that "15% of admissible seats in national universities shall be allocated for students from Darfur" as well as "50% of admissible seats in national universities in Darfur" (Article 14), while "a mechanism or committee shall be constituted to examine the conditions of those affected by war to be exempted from university fees [*maṣārīf al-jāmiᶜa*] for 5 years [and] the offspring of IDPs and refugees from Darfur States [...] exempted from educational fees [*al-maṣārīf al-dirāsīya*]" (http://www.smallarmssurveysudan.org/fileadmin/docs/documents/Peace _Process_Chronology-DDPD.pdf; Arabic inserted from original http://unamid.unmissions .org/Portals/UNAMID/DDPD%20Arabic.pdf). The unclear terminology, and the exploitation of this lack of clarity against students' demands, led to violent conflicts, such as in 2012 at the University of Gezira (https://www.radiodabanga.org/node/39529; http:// www.sudantribune.com/spip.php?article44782) and in December 2014 at the University of Bahri.

stipulated better educational access for war-affected regions as a condition for lasting peace (article 2.6.1.6).

Along the same line, the absence of systematic stipend programmes has been noted as aggravating inequality in access, in spite of higher numbers of institutions, as the political and educational elites have favourable access to high-quality schools and universities:

> Consequently, few poor Sudanese have the option to join a 'good university', and this leads to a situation where the poor are destined to become poorer, not only in terms of material resources but also intellectually.
>
> EL HADARY 2010: 81

This inequality from school education continued at the universities, where not just the places for general admission but also the special places were filled with better-off urban students, who do not have to face the complications of managing the admission process – which includes interviews at the prospective university – when coming from rural or suburban areas (Ibid.: 86).

While this concerns the consequences of written regulations, non-written rules went beyond these and introduced links to religious knowledge, the military and political loyalty. Especially students and staff of the University of Khartoum speak of the admission of students just because they memorised the Qur'ān completely, while, as a general rule,

> the so-called *dabbabeen* (derived from the word *dabbaba* = tank) and *mujahideen* (those who participated on at least two occasions in the war between the Sudan People's Liberation Army and the Government as part of the latter's military forces) got special admission and exemption from fees.
>
> EL TOM 2006: 33–34[33]

The social and political relations reflected in these circumstances of admission also form the background of the initially low status of private institutions which do not have the category 'general admission', so that the performance-based access at public universities still counted for a certain reputation of higher quality, especially for 'old' universities such as the University of Khartoum, although this reputation increasingly wore thin.

---

33   An additional link to military service was created by the stipulation that "[t]he award of degrees to students who successfully complete their degree programs is conditional on their completion of one year compulsory national service" (El Tom 2006: 25). Given the ideological drill – including exclusionary Islamic doctrines – being part of such a service, this introduced another level of political and religious discrimination.

The existence of special circumstances for admission, vis-à-vis inability to pay the full fees, can also be seen not just as recognition of academic performance, as well as assurance and regulation of academic self-reproduction, but also as an element of social responsibility or, in the language used above, of a communal quality. It also means that the increasing importance of the monetary principle for access can lead to a perceived loss of such a quality.

Ahfad University for Women is a good example of this potential tension between principles, as it represents the negotiation of a line between commercial and communal approaches to private higher education. In terms of regular fees, Ahfad University is in the middle field, as shown in Figure 4.2 with tuition fees at major private universities (academic year 2014/2015):

A recent strong campaign to increase compliance with payment of fees stressed their importance, but also corresponded with demands from the Ministry of Higher Education (MHESR 2013: 12). Posters were hung on the walls, asking 'Did you register?', entrance to exams was forbidden with non-paid fees and, in order to sensitise to the problem, calls for raising salaries in general staff assemblies were answered with reference to a budget over 90% reliant on fees, which a majority of students did not pay on time.

At the same time, exemption from fees was a regular part of the admission policies. The 'affirmative action' was channelled into interviews before

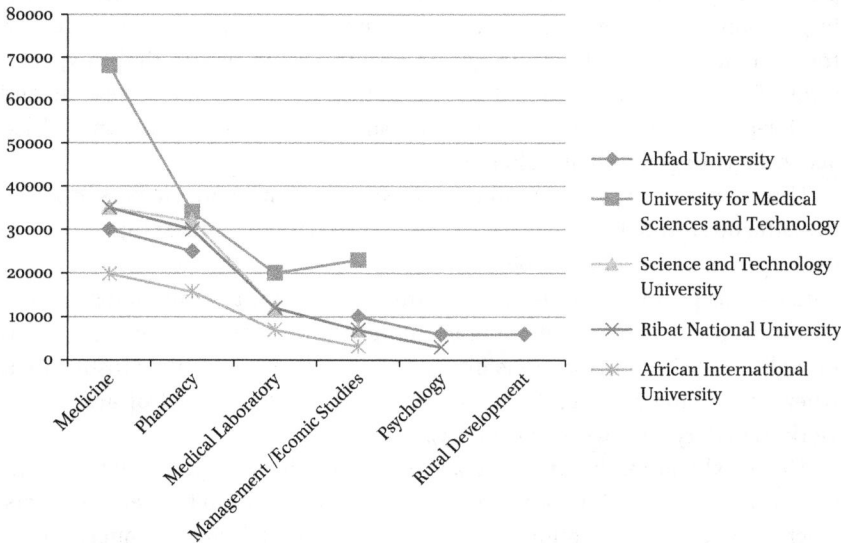

FIGURE 4.2 *Undergraduate tuition fees at Sudanese private universities, academic year 2014/2015, in* SDG.
SOURCE: HTTP://DALEEL.ADMISSION.GOV.SD/AHLI_FEES/DEFAULT.ASPX

admission, at which the prospective student's narrative and the admission board's impression would result in her being placed in one of the categories 'full payment', 'partial' or 'full scholarship'. Some implications of this process in respect of donor-based scholarships will be briefly discussed below, but it is also important to point to the oral, situational character of this negotiation, which is in contradiction with a move to document-based bureaucratisation that recently took place as well.

While these situational adjustments at Ahfad University maintain a component of its civic cause, changes towards a monetary basis of interaction in higher education institutions can cause shifts from their categorisation as 'communal' (*ahlī*). One of the lecturers going back and forth between public and private higher education therefore regarded the Omdurman Ahlīya University as the only real communal university, as it functioned as a cooperative. As well as the mixture of categories associated with 'special admission', she perceived a general trend towards commercialisation that decreased educational and research quality for several reasons, often triggering conflicts between academics joining private institutions out of economic necessity for their own income aspirations and university owners focusing on profits, not performance.

This concerned not only reluctance to offer additional courses for basic skills, which present school graduates often lack, be it language and computer skills or more general skills to read and write critically. It also influenced policies of grading, whereby the marketisation of the university created the impression of a direct link between the payment of fees and the success of the student. She and other colleagues were often confronted with the expectations of parents to have 'bought' a right to high grades for their children, and the for-profit logic of the private owner supported this expectation and led accordingly to grades being altered.

This represents a power symmetry between students and teachers in which the latter often find themselves facing the administration using or threatening to use its power to fire non-compliant staff, in order to maintain students – or their parents – as paying customers. Furthermore, the priority given to institution-customer relations in terms of translating tuition fees into certificates has brought the private institutions into a situation similar to public institutions, where dwindling research budgets have dried out this aspect of academics' work (Elhadary 2010: 92; Assal 2010: 9).

This is why admission policies are not just about granting or denying access, but about the principles according to which a relation between students, teachers and administration is initiated. The specific circumstances under which admission took place in my immediate working environment involved the insertion of several additional complications into the process. A huge part of my academic activities was closely entangled with a donor-funded project which provided Masters students with scholarships for study and research. In the Masters programmes in which I was involved, the requirement for account-ability and performance for annual reports and budgets drove many decisions, connected to overall reputation in the world of international donors.

The funding of scholarships is generally based on the presumption that there is a potential to succeed, wasted by difficulties in funding admission. But in the processes I witnessed, admission to scholarships funded by donors was not simply a decision over individual socio-economic neediness. The process also applied a regional principle targeting federal states outside Khartoum categorised as marginalised areas (e.g. South Kordofan, Darfur, Blue Nile), in addition to South Sudan, and was linked to cooperation with the University of Addis Ababa, Ethiopia, and Makerere University, Uganda. This regional prin-ciple also included an ethnic dimension, as secondary priority was given to students belonging to ethnic groups prevalent in the federal states, but actually living in Khartoum.

In the context of this principle, the written requirement of very good scores in the previous degree and a sound basis of English were deprioritised, in order to fill the places. This was intended to provide opportunities for students oth-erwise in no position to study a Masters degree in English, especially those coming from a situation of marginalisation and poverty, in addition to Sudan's forcibly Arabicised education system. The tension between affirmative action and the aim of quality education, especially in a situation in which applicant numbers were below or close to the available number of scholarships, cre-ated not only a taxing teaching situation with vastly different levels of skills and knowledge among the students, but also required teachers to apply an intricate system of grading. So relative performance within the frame of a specific academic year influenced grading immensely, and the targeted avoid-ance of failure, influenced by both the civic cause and donors' expectations, created a tendency to adjust the frame of reference to this type of relative performance.

The contradiction of principles – quality standards vs. support of those left behind – could not be solved on a general basis, i.e. based on bureaucratic rules that apply to everybody in the same way. The subsequent case-by-case solutions were worked out by shifting the content of distinctions: the grading system allowed for putting students in categories A (80–100%) or B (70–79%) to qualify for a Masters degree, while C (60–69%) would qualify for a Higher Diploma. Upon failure or the student's unwillingness to settle for a diploma, delegation to other Masters programmes at the university was considered. Far from being a standardised process, this demanded the situational negotiation of distinctions, both in individual grading practices of teachers and in discussions at departmental meetings.

The complexity of this struggle was heightened by the social responsibilities the self-ascribed moral quality of this form of higher education brought with it. In the final section, I put my personal experience of this struggle as teacher into the form of reflective questions, arguing that empirical research on academics' practical answers to these questions can make a significant contribution to debates on economic, political and moral aspects of private higher education.

Being Committed

The specific reasons holding students back from concentrating on their studies were among those that held women back in general: no release from duties at home, time limits imposed by restrictive parents, pregnancy without a supportive infrastructure, pre-natal or ante-natal, etc. How could the performance of a student in this situation be critically judged against her potential, in spite of structural challenges? Bearing in mind the categories of performance sought after in the search for international recognition, where would considerations of these circumstances have a place in teaching and grading?

Taking into account other limitations – occasional power cuts, low maintenance and re-supply of reproductive equipment, short library opening hours etc. – these foundations of a teacher-student relation created numerous complications. All this would demand the investment of a great deal of time interacting with students, but in many cases, especially in undergraduate education, class sizes and the subsequent workload prevented such an investment, apart from the shaky grounds of commitment of time and energy outlined above.

The obstacles of upholding strict quality control during admission led not only to huge disparities in the classes, but required engagement with a huge proportion of the students in basic negotiations regarding organisational technologies: information in English had to be repeated several times – or supported by one-to-one explanations in Arabic outside the classroom – course outlines had to be repeatedly pointed out as sources of basic information, time discipline had to be established. Such negotiation also surfaced between the students, for instance in the form of scolding latecomers, and in one case prevented the implementation of an alternative form of teaching. So a self-organised workshop which was supposed to last a whole day was limited to the usual three hour session because the timing had not been picked up from either the course outlines, the announcement in class or the emails sent by the organisers, a group of European students visiting the university in the framework of an international Masters programme. The latter, indeed, supposed that written information would suffice, and had therefore not backed up the flow of information by telephone calls. Since the right balance of oral and written communication did not exist, the additional requirement of putting presentations of those students who had to work during the first half of the day into the afternoon sessions, and vice-versa, could not be implemented as well. The result was a series of rushed presentations, making the grading an intricate task of assigning responsibility for failure to communicate.

This anecdote also points to another challenge: given the many structural obstacles to being on time – including an inadequate public transportation system – what kinds of reasons for coming late are acceptable and credible? Can control of attendance be treated leniently, given the broad range of basic skills that cannot be taken for granted? Do subsequent sanctions help the learning process or do they address the wrong persons, punishing those already punished by their circumstances?

The argument of hardship seems to indicate a clear direction towards leniency and unconditional support, and the choices of socially critical research topics by students emerged directly from shared everyday problems, suggesting an immediate relevance of such studies to discrimination and violence experienced in their lives. But this touches another complication which relates to individual and societal dimensions of hardship. So a family background in one of the marginalised areas served repeatedly as an argument in the negotiation of grades with me, posing the dilemma of having to weigh 'affirmative action' versus the impartial assessment of actual performance. In addition, it required assessment of individual situations which did not follow the simple model of regional marginalisation. Thus a student openly complaining about a grade highlighted 'what she had suffered', in implicit reference to her belonging to a social group the majority of which lives in one of the most war-affected areas of Sudan. At the same time, she actually spent her life in the capital and, in spite of having received a scholarship, took the first chance to follow her husband to Australia without finishing her studies.

In a different way, the consideration of socialisation was problematic because of the widespread existence of plagiarism, which also had to do with an educational system based on memorisation, the widespread usage of PowerPoint presentations as the only course material required for exams, and the orientation towards Google searches as the primary way to find information. Teaching mostly on the basis of reading and writing academic texts, I still had to ultimately subject myself to a practice of distinguishing degrees of plagiarism, since the dismissal of more than 50% of students was not really feasible, especially given the structural conditions of admission I pointed out. But when a student was suspended for a year for cheating in an exam – by copying from a prepared written answer to an expected exam question – the contradiction between ensuring the graduation of students and ethical principles, taught in Research Methodology courses, became apparent, as well as its situationally different treatment.

This student's case also unravels more aspects that concern the influence of identification on teacher-student and student-student relations. Being, as academic coordinator, responsible for following up teacher-student conflicts, I was confronted with an allegation of prejudice against her shown by a professor, who, she claimed, showed favouritism towards southern Sudanese students, being himself southern Sudanese, and openly calling her 'one of those rich Arab girls', based on the conception that she, as a former employee of a UN agency, was far from any kind of hardships. While the specific situation also related to more general questions, such as how much effort a student has to make to access relevant study materials, and the allegations were ultimately denied by the professor and rendered secondary by the student's suspension, the conflict implied 'hardship' based on social grouping as a category of evaluation, a direction supported both by an 'affirmative action' approach in general, and the specific admission practices in particular.

The obvious targeting of a labour market outside the university, mostly in organisations dealing with advocacy, made the choice of focus a delicate task. In Masters programmes teaching 'Development', 'Good Governance' and 'Peace-Building', how much weight should be given to research skills which would not be of much use outside an academic setting? How to deal with the vast differences in disciplinary backgrounds, encompassing medicine, pre-school education, social and management studies? What kind of professional language should be taught, what so-called soft skills, and when and how should I insist on neutral observation against or at least before the formulation of standpoints, the basis of policy recommendations so often called for? How to position towards strong religious beliefs that underpinned most of the previous curricula, when trying to develop academic scrutiny that is underpinned by doubts? How much to insist on not using the generalised jargons of the colloquial and of advocacy through which English language was often acquired, not just in the service of academic quality standards, but as a reflection of the possibility of keeping an open mind amidst wide-spread political polarisation?

During the aforementioned workshop, the complexity of this negotiation appeared when discussing orientalism and the present regime's cultural policies. Being critical in both respects, presentations decried both distorted representation of 'Arabs' and 'Muslims' in 'Western media' as expressions of an orientalist mind set, and the lack of respect for cultural diversity in present school curricula in northern Sudan. The felt urgency of these matters was certainly reflected in the confrontational and activist style of these presentations, but the lack of investigative distance also indicated a lack of differentiation between negative criticism and critical assessment. The underlying tensions around social identification then 'escalated' in a rare display of annoyance through a student vehemently addressing another during statements on ethnic reconciliation, feeling targeted, as a northern Sudanese Arab Muslim, by the latter's critical statements on government Arabicisation and Islamisation policies, as a southern Sudanese Christian. Not at all expressing support for these policies, instead she showed discomfort at discussing contradictions and differences that originated far outside the classroom.

A huge number of other aspects, certainly not confined to this specific environment, could be added. This is an indication that the study of the everyday negotiation of how these questions are to be answered serves more than a purely documentary function. If the avoidance of certain answers is regarded as arising from the influence of economic and political boundaries on the everyday workings of private higher education and beyond, then the opposite, resistance to those boundaries, may be a possibility as well.

The study of individual ideas and practices, as pursued by ethnographic research, can thus not just serve 'small' insights, but can also lead to the acknowledgment of enduring or emerging struggles that may not appear as relevant in macro-structural approaches.

Conclusion

The situation of Sudan's higher education sector invites a sharp focus on its shortcomings, not just economic but also political ones. In a situation in which academic freedom, or critical thinking more generally, is treated as dangerous, the steps taken outside the campus can have serious consequences, and instead of focusing on questions of translating between scientific languages, the governmental policies of the 1990s concentrated forcefully on demanding conformity and ad-hoc changes, which led to a lack of communicative bridges essential for scientific collaboration. In spite of the more extensive and collaborative Arabicisation programmes of recent years, the consequences of this shortcut haunt the quality of higher education up to today.

The rather gloomy picture of the academic environment given in this chapter prompts one to ask what motivates people to engage in higher education in Sudan at all. What has been indicated throughout the case study is an intrinsic value seen in higher education, beyond its immediate function in society, as a civic cause which can challenge existing economic and political boundaries while being challenged by them. In my case study of work at Ahfad University, a Sudanese non-governmental higher education institution, it was these constant challenges that were seen to give it a continuous quality of relevance, both as education for women and as education to steady critical thinking.

The last section of this chapter put forward practical questions that appeared relevant to me while working for Ahfad University. I suggested through the reflective reformulation of these questions that economic and political boundaries of higher education and society at large, outlined in the introductory sections, not only influence the conditions in which everyday work at Sudan's universities and similar institutions takes place. The position taken towards those boundaries through decisions made during everyday work also involves empowerment or resistance to them, a process which, it is argued, imparts a substantial moral quality in the framework of an institution with a self-ascribed social responsibility for disadvantaged parts of the population.

Rather than providing an empirical follow-up to this argument, the chapter aimed at pointing out the relevance of such a follow-up, going beyond this far from idiosyncratic case, especially for ongoing debates on both 'the engaged university' (Watson *et al* 2011) and on the privatisation of higher education and the values empowered or suppressed by it.

Works Cited

Africa Watch. 1991. *Academic Freedom and Human Rights Abuses in Africa*. New York, Washington, DC, London: Human Rights Watch.

Ali, Amna Omer Mohamed. 2010. *Highly-skilled Migration: Sudan*. Florence: Consortium for Applied Research on International Migration (CARIM), Robert Schuman Centre for Advanced Studies, European University Institute.

Assal, Munzoul. 2010. *Highly-skilled Sudanese Migrants: Gain or Drain?* Florence: Consortium for Applied Research on International Migration (CARIM), Robert Schuman Centre for Advanced Studies, European University Institute.

Badri, Babiker. 1961/1980. *The Memoirs of Babiker Badri. Vol. 2*. Translated by Yusif Badri and Peter Hogg. London: Oxford University Press.

Badri, Balghis. 2008. *Gender Mainstreaming in Sudanese universities*. Omdurman: Ahfad University for Women, Institute of Women, Gender and Development Studies.

Badri, Yusuf. 1997. *Qadr al-jīl. Muḏakkarāt al-camīd Yūsif Badrī*. Omdurman: n.p.

Bedri, Amna Mohamed. 2013. "Reflections on the struggle for girls' education in Sudan". In H.B. Holmarsdottir *et al* (eds). *Gendered Voices: Reflections on Gender and Education in South Africa and Sudan*. Rotterdam/Taipei: Sense Publishers, 25–40.

Bishai, Linda S. 2008. *Sudanese Universities as Sites of Social Transformation*. Washington, DC: United States Institute of Peace.

Bloom, David, David Canning and Kevin Chan. 2006. *Higher Education and Economic Development in Africa*. Washington, DC: World Bank, Human Development Section.

Breidlid, Anders. 2013. "The role of education in Sudan's civil war". *Prospects* 43: 35–47.

El Tom, Mohamed El Amin Ahmed. 2006. *Higher Education in Sudan. Towards a New Vision for a New Era*. Khartoum: Sudan Centre for Educational Research & Friedrich Ebert Stiftung.

Elgizouli, M.A. 2005. "'Postcolonial illiteracy': the dilemma of Arabicization and Westernisation". Paper presented at the Conference Across Borders: Benefiting from Cultural Differences, 17–18 2005, University of Nairobi, organised by: DAAD, Goethe Institute, University of Nairobi.

Elhadary, Yasin Abdalla Eltayeb. 2010. "Equity in and access to higher education in Nile Basin countries: the case of Sudan". In Alemu Kassahun Berhanu, Tor Halvorsen and Mary Mwiandi (eds). *Reshaping Research Universities in the Nile Basin Countries. Book II*. Kampala: Fountain Publishers, 79–100.

Gasim, Gamal. 2010. "Reflecting on Sudan's higher education revolution under Al-Bashir's Regime". *Comparative & International Higher Education* 2: 50–53.

Gizouli, El Subki Mohamed El. 1968. "Higher education in the Sudan from its origins to 1966, with special reference to university education". Unpublished doctoral dissertation, University of Durham, Faculty of Arts, Durham, <http://etheses.dur.ac.uk/7976>

Hale, Sondra. 2000. "The Islamic state and gendered citizenship in Sudan". In Suad Joseph (ed.). *Gender and Citizenship in the Middle East*. Syracuse, NY: Syracuse University Press, 88–106.

Hale, Sondra. 2009. "Transnational gender studies and the migrating concept of gender in the Middle East and North Africa". *Cultural Dynamics* 21 (2): 133–152.

Hassan, Zaki El. 1992. "Instability of higher education in the Sudan: the effect of Al-Bashir's higher education policies". *Sudan Update*, July, http://www.sudanupdate.org/REPORTS/education/hi-ed.htm

Ḥayr, Al-Ṭayyib 'Ibrāhīm Muḥammad. 2008. *Masārāt al-ta'ṣīl wa taṭbīqātihi fī al-sūdān*. (Silsila Kitāb Al-Tanwīr 3). Al-Ḥarṭūm: Markiz al-Tanwīr al-Maᶜrīfī.

Imām, Zakarīyā Bašīr. 2003. *Al-taḫṭīṭ al-istrātījī wa al-taᶜlīm al-ᶜālī fī al-waṭan al-ᶜarabī. Išāra ḫāṣa ilā al-sūdān*. Al-Ḥarṭūm: Širka Maṭābiᶜ al-Sūdān lil-ᶜUmla al-Mahdūda.

———— 2005. *Ṭawra al-taᶜlīm al-ᶜālī fī al-sūdān. Al-ḥaṣād wa al-'injāz*. (Silsila 'Iṣdārāt al-Waᶜd al-Ḥaqq). Al-Ḥarṭūm: Al-Markiz al-Qawmī lil-'Intāj al-'Iᶜlāmī.

Khaleefa, Omar K., George Erdos and Ikhlas H. Ashria. 1997. "Traditional education and creativity in an Afro-Arab Islamic culture: the case of Sudan". *Journal of Creative Behavior* 31 (3): 201–211.

Lewis, Ian M. *et al.* 1992. "Obituary: Mohamed Omer Beshir, 1926–1992". *Africa* 62 (3): 435–438.

Mann, Laura. 2013. "'We do our bit in our own space': DAL Group and the development of a curiously Sudanese enclave economy". *Journal of Modern African Studies* 51 (2): 279–303.

Ministry of Higher Education and Scientific Research (MHESR). nd. Achievements of the higher education revolution 1990–2000. [In Arabic]

Ministry of Higher Education and Scientific Research (MHESR) nd. Achievements of the higher education revolution between 1989 and 2009. [In Arabic], http://www .mohe.gov.sd/index.php?option=com_content&view=article&id=130:-------1989-- 2009&catid=19:2012-02-21-10-27-00&Itemid=54

Ministry of Higher Education and Scientific Research (MHESR) 2012. Directory of the admission to higher education institutions 2011/2012. [In Arabic]

Ministry of Higher Education and Scientific Research (MHESR) 2013. Directory of the private admission to government higher education institutions 2013/2014. [In Arabic]

Sharkey, Heather J. 2003. "Education, acculturation, and nationalist networks". In *Living with Colonialism: Nationalism and Culture in the Anglo-Egyptian Sudan*. Berkeley, CA: University of California Press, 40–66.

Shibeika, Alaa. 2014. "A Sudanese student watches a university grow dark". *Al-Fanar Media*, 4 August, http://www.al-fanarmedia.org/2014/08/sudanese-student-watches -university-grow-dark/

Thompson, Kenneth W., Barbara R. Fogel and Helen E. Danner (eds). 1977. *Higher Education and Social Change: Promising Experiments in Developing Countries. Volume 2: Case Studies*. New York, Washington, DC, London: Praeger.

UNESCO. 2011. "World Data on Education. 7th edition: 2010/11, Sudan", http://www.ibe .unesco.org/fileadmin/user_upload/Publications/WDE/2010/pdf-versions/Sudan .pdf

Watson, David *et al* (eds). 2011. *The Engaged University: International Perspectives on Civic Engagement*. New York: Routledge.

World Bank. 2010. *Financing Higher Education in Africa*. Washington, DC: World Bank.

World Bank. and Government of National Unity, Republic of Sudan. 2012. *The Status of the Education Sector in Sudan*. Washington, DC: World Bank.

CHAPTER 5

Private Universities and the State in Egypt at a Time of Social and Political Change*

Daniele Cantini

In 2008, Egypt celebrated the centenary of its first modern university, what is nowadays known as Cairo University, which was established as a private institution in 1908, became the State University in 1925, was later renamed Fouad the First (after the then king of Egypt), and finally became Cairo University after the revolution of 1952. The resonance this institution has in the Egyptian public imaginary is hard to overstate, for the university campus with its magnificent architecture constitutes, in national historiography as in cinema, in novels and autobiographies, a veritable 'place of memory', and it is usually an actor in – or at least a witness to – the country's historical events (Farag 2006).

Historically, Egypt has had a highly centralised education system, central to the project of nation building and to the possibility of achieving progress (Farag 2009). This is associated with the pivotal role granted to it by the revolutionary power of the 1950s, which put education centre stage in the effort to create a new citizenry; in later years, attention to education resulted from the great number of people directly or indirectly affected by it, in a country that has been witnessing an amazing population growth for decades. In the past two decades, crises of the system and of reform have featured prominently in public discourse in the country, with privatisation being a particularly contested topic, as I will show. More importantly, the throughout interest in the reforms, whether applied or not, shows education's "important influence in building the foundations of legitimacy of the political system" (Farag 2012: 83). Education becomes an arena for playing out societal and political struggles,

* The research on which this article is based has been carried out within the framework of an SSRC (Social Science Research Council) project on Arab Universities – Autonomy and Governance – in 2010 and 2012. The results are now available at: www.arabhighered.org. My thanks go to Seteney Shami, to the Egyptian research team, composed of Iman Farag, Nefissa Dessouqi, and Jasmine Ahmed, as well as to Riham Bahi, Ola Galal and Aya Nasser who took part in the second phase of the project. Previous versions of this paper were presented at the project conferences in Beirut, Cairo and Tunis, as well as in Halle (Saale) and Washington, DC. I am indebted to all those who commented on it or offered their feedback in other ways. In particular I wish to acknowledge the support provided by Sabine Dorpmüller, Ala al-Hamarneh and Florian Kohstall.

and this accrues its relevance in a country where open political debate has been largely repressed.

This relevance became apparent in the events that led to the resignation of former President Hosny Mubarak at the beginning of February 2011. Many commentators pointed to the fact that most protesters were rather young – not surprisingly in a country in which people below 24 years of age represent almost half the population – and educated, at the very least in using new media and in organising spectacular forms of demonstration. Protests have gained stronger recognition in countries with a rather solid educational background:

> spearheaded by educated youth, the Arab uprisings have been brought to fruition by the masses of ordinary people (men, women, Muslim and non-Muslim) who have mobilised at an astonishing scale against authoritarian regimes in pursuit of social justice, democratic governance, and dignity.[1]
>
> BAYAT 2011

Protests in Egypt, as in Tunisia and elsewhere, were fuelled by problems such as lack of political freedom and oppression, but a major factor has been the expansion of higher education without simultaneous growth in job opportunities, leading to graduate joblessness. Moreover, despite being spaces where one could hardly expect to find freedom of assembly or expression, universities are nonetheless spaces where critique emerges, as I have argued elsewhere (Cantini 2016). Despite there being spaces where one could hardly expect to find freedom of assembly or expression, as universities are as constrained as other institutions, they are nonetheless spaces where critique emerges, as I have argued elsewhere (Cantini 2016). There are now studies that clearly show the importance of earlier movements and civic actions (particularly since 2002) in allowing activists to acquire experience, and public universities had a central role in many of these earlier movements (Abdelrahman 2015).

Given the absolute centrality of youth and education in the Egyptian public discourse, as well as its renewed importance in wake of the 2011 revolution, continued in the following years, it is necessary to have a more grounded understanding of the actual meaning of 'private' in a country where state

---

1 "Once the protests broke out in Tahrir Square, many of the cohort of civic-minded active young people that universities raised in the past years were quick to join in. As the protests gathered strength, the protestors soon became highly organized with medical stations, cleaning brigades, security checks to stop anyone bringing a weapon into the square or small stands where people could leave their mobile phones to recharge to give but a few examples" (Warden 2011).

control of the university is quite strong. In this chapter, my aim is to show the complex and uneasy relationship between private universities and state power in Egypt by tracing the multiple ways in which the state retains control over private institutions, which in turn are increasingly shaping the face of the state in a context of reduced public spending. Despite the fact that, at least until 2014, private universities have been spaces of multiple mobilisations, both of students and of workers (Kohstall 2015), these struggles are not the focus of my study, partly because they were largely absent from my case study.[2] My contention is that an analysis of how new private universities concretely work helps in understanding not only changing conditions of knowledge production and of societal differentiation processes, but modes of societal engagements (or their absence) as well. While the political developments of the Egyptian revolution are far from being concluded, and involve contradictory elements, changes in university governance and structure are proving to be interestingly enduring, and in need of analysis (Levy and Sabry 2011).

In particular, I deal with the relationship private universities have with the state, and try to highlight the ways in which the meaning of 'private' has to be understood in this context, even more so in the turbulence of recent years. I begin by putting the object of analysis into its context, by outlining the history of higher education in Egypt and its internal differences. I then turn to a discussion of the main reforms that have been taking place in recent decades, and show the spatial dimension of these reforms. I finally turn to my case study, the October 6 University, the biggest to emerge from the wave of privatisation that began in the 1990s, to show how private, for-profit, low-cost universities manage to keep afloat in perilous times, when internal instability and regional competition threaten their position. Through a brief analysis of its functioning, its structure and organisation, I highlight its decidedly corporate character (Shore and McLauchlan 2012), and how this affects the lives of students and faculty. The aim of my ethnography is to show the multiple ways in which private and state power intersect in contemporary Egypt, leading to new power relations and changing meanings of education and knowledge.

Some Remarks on the History of Higher Education in Egypt

Discourses of crisis notwithstanding, the social value of education, including higher education, has not decreased in Egypt, regardless of the many

---

2 An interesting study that tries to compare political attitudes among students of different universities, private and public, is Sika 2009.

difficulties that new graduates face when trying to enter the labour market – and even before, when struggling to get admitted to the faculties of their choice. Central to discourses of crisis, and of consequent need for reform, is the character of the unemployed graduate. At least since the beginning of the 1990s this has entered the public space (Tourné 2007), and it is indeed at the core of the protests in recent years, with growing evidence of the inability of the state to guarantee public employment for all graduates. In this context, the introduction of private for-profit universities has been seen as a crucial tool in offering more market-oriented education, while its critics maintain that these institutions are an impediment to free and equal access to higher education, besides raising fundamental questions about the social contract that involves education being a driver for social mobility.

When higher education in Egypt was officially launched with the foundation of Cairo University in 1908,[3] the university started out as a private enterprise, the main aim of which was the pursuit of all kinds of knowledge, including fields which were not included in the curricula of the existing public high schools that were forming the administrative elite of the country (Farag 2006). Initial programmes of study included history and the humanities, particularly Western knowledge about Arabs and Islam, taught mainly by foreign professors. It was only in 1925 that the university was nationalised, and that "academia as a new profession" (Reid 1990) became a reality in Egypt. In this process the original philanthropic institution was gradually transformed into a Faculty of Arts, and public high schools, created during the second half of the nineteenth century and specialised in law, medicine and engineering, became faculties.

The transformation of an elite into a mass institution occurred mainly in the 1960s and 1970s (see Eickelmann 1992 for a comparison with other Arab countries). This was the heyday of state socialism in the country, when the principle of free education for all citizens was incorporated in the constitution. This period is marked by the idea that the state is responsible for the bringing up of the 'sons of the revolution', who were considered to be the ideal type, especially in the form of engineers or physicians, able to contribute to the essential modernisation of the country. This social contract was enacted not only by the extension of the right to education to all, but equally importantly by the consolidation of the relationship between education and employment, with the idea that the state was somehow responsible for university graduates' entrance into the labour market (Farag 2006: 698–699).

---

3   Al-Azhar, the religious university, is of course much older, and since the 1960s is incorporated, along with its schools, within the public system.

After the 1952 revolution, the education system became fully integrated into the social and political goals of the new regime. There was a significant growth in enrolment, in an effort to grant access to higher education to the newly created middle class that would become the backbone of the nascent regime, while some professors were expelled due to their political tendencies (Reid 1990).

This concept entered into crisis around the end of the 1970s, with disillusionment arising from the imbalance in wealth distribution starting from the *Infitah* period of the 1970s and early 1980s, during which cuts in public sector work were not adequately replaced by a growing private sector, and the continuous rise in population was placing an overwhelming burden on almost all levels of education and consequently weakening the actual relationship between education and employment (Farag 2006). All this notwithstanding, most people believe that it is a duty of the state to provide education for its citizens, and education is still considered a right in the Egyptian constitution of 2014 (article 19). In this context, private education is regarded with suspicion, to say the least, and state jobs are consistently more appealing than jobs in the informal sector, despite their low pay (Assaad 2014). The university has pretty much continued to be associated with success, social status and social mobility, the best jobs and salaries, self-esteem and dignity, contentious politics and citizenship (Farag 2006), and the vast majority of young people, at least those who have a chance of doing so, are still quite eager to enter universities, despite declining job prospects (Assaad 2014).[4]

The introduction of private universities occurred in the context of what was represented as a crisis of the public sector. While the American University in Cairo (hence AUC) has existed since 1919 as a private, non-profit organisation with roots in missionary activities, it was only in 1992 that Egyptian, for-profit private universities were allowed (Law 101/1992).[5] The first four private universities of this kind opened their doors in 1996 (see below for further details on the case study), generating a storm of polemics mostly linked to a rejection of the wave of privatisations in various sectors (Farag 2006; Kohstall

---

4 The same is true in other contexts as well, for example in Jordan (Cantini 2016, Chapter v).

5 I am following Hanafi's (2011) classification, distinguishing between public, including religious, and private, which are divided into for- and non-profit. This classification is only partially satisfactory, as boundaries between public and private are blurred by, for instance, private programmes within the public university. Moreover, it does not include other kinds of institutions, such as the various *ahliyya* universities (see note 7) or higher education institutes, which in a country like Egypt enrol a huge proportion of students (see Elsayed 2014).

2012). While these institutions were mostly welcomed by Cairo's new middle class, the government hesitated to grant them the autonomy they asked for, largely seeing them as an add-on to the public university sector rather than as new players in the educational landscape. Their programmes were supposed to be limited to those not offered by public universities, but in reality they offered the programmes most in demand on the job market, such as medicine, pharmacy, information and bio technology, engineering, and computer sciences (Ibid.).

In this context, in which effective legislation has largely still to be put in place, the mushrooming of private, for-profit universities (of which there are now 24, mostly concentrated in Cairo and Giza but slowly spreading to other parts of the country as well, particularly Alexandria) changed facts on the ground.[6] Moreover the growing costs and the decreasing state budget available for education persuaded many that there was no alternative to at least a partial privatisation of public universities, under the form of 'parallel' programmes created to offer training in selected disciplines in foreign languages.[7] Thus the phenomenon of privatisation is not restricted to private universities, as tuition fees are charged for these parallel programmes, and since a good and valuable diploma is out of reach without a family's personal financial investment in education. From the kindergarten to high school, private tutoring has become the rule at all stages of the education pyramid (Hartmann 2013; Sobhy 2012).

Despite this impact, however, the public model is still by far the most popular in the country. The landscape of institutions of higher education comprises 27 public universities and their various branches, scattered all over the country, with a total enrolled student population of about 1,431,469. To this number is to be added the students enrolled at the so-called 'institutes' (see note n. 5), which can be both public or private, and offer courses from two to four years for students who failed to access universities, as well as the students enrolled at the newly founded private universities, with a total student population, at a

---

6   To these are to be added another four, the so-called *jamia't al-ahliyya* (while private universities are called *jamia't al-khassa*); ahliyya indicates a mixed character between public and private, but this sector is still in its early days and quite contested.

7   In recent years this 'parallel programme' has expanded greatly, especially in the best faculties of the more prestigious public universities; students are allowed to enter these programmes with grades insufficient for admission onto the regular programmes, in return for paying high fees. This has enabled well-off students to have access to courses designed for fewer students, usually in better environments, that have truly become a parallel system within the public university. In addition, since 1998 there is the Cairo Open University which is devoted to those who were not able to enter university under normal conditions.

higher education level, of about 2.5 million. Of these, private universities enroll only 71,728 students (in 2010), and despite the fact that this figure has been growing since their inception it is still far from being statistically relevant, and even less in terms of providing relief to one of the proclaimed ills of public higher education, namely overcrowding.[8]

Private universities are now solidly part of the higher education landscape in Egypt, despite all the polemics and controversies around their establishment which continued well after their foundation, mostly for political reasons (Farag 2006: 706). Other than fundamental opposition coming from those who believe that education should be provided by the state, as well as a broader critique of the inconsistencies of the system, opposition to private for-profit universities has taken the form of questioning of their practical utility – they are not providing new research and training facilities, nor are they significantly reducing the burden on overcrowded public campuses.[9] Another angle of opposition refers to more mundane problems such as irregularities in admission rates, the actual number of students admitted, exam regulations, and transfer rules from one university to another. Moreover, most private universities tend to be less than transparent when it comes to internal regulations and their financial situation, and I have personally experienced many of these difficulties while doing research – in the impossibility of seeing any regulations or statistics concerning a given university, for example, or in refusal of permission for me to speak with students.

Before turning to my case study, in order to show some of the ways in which private for-profit universities operate it is necessary to go into some of the details of the debate over reforms in the higher education sector in Egypt in the past decade, as this debate reveals the strong link between higher education and statehood. It is in this sense I argue (in a more detailed form in the introduction to this book) that attention to what is private about private universities is crucial in order to account for some of the recent changes in the sector. What seems to be happening now is the failure of the rhetoric of modernisation, and the establishment of a new endeavour in which international organisations and private actors play a greater role in the shaping of this rather central feature of modern states (see the introduction for a thorough discussion of this).

---

8 For an analysis of the impact of private, for-profit universities in attracting foreign students, see Cantini 2014.

9 These critics largely echo the assumption, discussed by Alexander Mitterle in this volume for Germany, that private universities should be different from public universities, or better.

Reforming Universities – Reforms as Political Theatre

The material expansion and reform of Egypt's education system in the 1990s was supported by sizeable funding from international donor institutions. Their involvement in the educational reforms ... signalled the gradual disengagement of the [Ministry] from its own 'socialist' past as it partly adopted neo-liberal development policy strategies devised by international donors, who see investment in education as a means to increase productivity, national income and socio-economic mobility, which would eventually lead to socio-economic transformation and ultimately democratisation. Part and parcel of this strategy is a call for more market and less state ....

FARAG 2012: 82

The reforms that have been implemented in Egypt during the last 20 years tend to present similar characteristics to those in other countries, not only in the Middle East, as the contributions to this volume make clear (as discussed in the introduction).[10] The discourse of a crisis of higher education, prominent in national debate for two decades, has been instrumental in creating the space for reforms (Farag 2009). This global agenda, pushed forward by international agencies such as the World Bank, posits that developing countries should expand higher education as the latest way to leapfrog out of poverty, but that they should do so through privatisation (Wright and Rabo 2010). Higher education worldwide becomes, like other previously largely public endeavours, a marketable commodity, a business, and this raises questions of equity and accessibility, as well as contending the very link between statehood and educational landscapes.

Egypt is no exception to this trend, whereby national governments increasingly adopt the donors' perspective, with "[s]eemingly neutral international standards ... adopted by all parties and propagated through a kind of semi-specialised language ('knowledge economy', 'producing the elite')" (Farag 2012: 84). In this context, higher education reforms, "nothing more than a carbon copy from a single source, were integrated into free trade agreements, assuming 'international competition' as the highest goal for the educational process" (Mousselin 2007, quoted in Farag 2012: 84). Moreover, such reforms have been

---

10   Steiner-Khamsi (2012) discusses 'travelling reforms' in the university sector, resurfacing in different parts of the world; I offer an ethnographic analysis of university reforms for Jordan in Cantini (2016), Chapter 11. For a detailed analysis of reforms at the basic education level, which nonetheless show much affinity to what I am discussing here, see Sayed (2006).

remarkably persistent over time, as an early analysis of privatisation realpolitik shows:

> Increasingly, concerns about the quality and standards of learning pro-vided by mass higher education seem to be disconnected from those about equity, as if these competing goals involved different social groups. According to some, higher education no longer has to address social ex-pectations or the quest for knowledge, but rather the job market. The variable that is supposed to adapt is higher education, rather than the job market, which is a "given". Here too, an "invisible hand" adjusts develop-ment goals to the market, which is no longer national but globalized.
>
> FARAG 1997

Here I briefly deal with two aspects of the reforms, the Higher Education En-hancement Programme (HEEP) and the issue of quality, before pointing to some of the forms of resistance to them. In March 2002, the World Bank ap-proved a loan of US$50 million to support the HEEP, the first tangible overall reform project after years of debating over the crisis of the university – and "an excellent opportunity to draw up an anthropology of educational reform in a globalized world" (Farag 2009). The HEEP consists of six projects that aim at improving the quality of Egyptian higher education; its guiding principle is to prepare students for the labour market and to adapt the higher education system to a global knowledge society. The six projects concentrate on faculty training, the improvement of teaching quality, the diversification of higher ed-ucation institutions, and the modernisation of the administration.[11] The HEEP operates according to two basic principles, the grant approach and quality as-surance. While the first project, the establishment of a fund to administer the grants, was indeed implemented, the rest of the project came to a halt amidst huge controversies (Ibid.; Kohstall 2012).

Public discourse about educational reform abounds with terminology that can hardly be disagreed with, but its exact meaning remains ambiguous (Wright and Rabo 2010). Within this terminology, 'quality' has a paramount im-portance. Quality assurance was first introduced into the educational debate as a necessity in order to be on a par with the global standards, and it soon transformed from a project into a reality – now there is a national independent

---

11   While the HEEP plan did not involve the government directly, as soon as its relevance be-came clear it was exploited by members of the then ruling party, the NDP, and especially by Gamal Mubarak, the son of the former president. For an analysis of one of the plan's predecessors, see Kohstall 2012.

institution for quality assurance, the National Agency for Quality Assurance and Evaluation, whose task is to evaluate the quality of the various institutions of learning in the country, with the goal of establishing competition among them that will ultimately make educational standards better, and nearer to international ones. The National Authority for Quality Assurance and Accreditation of Education, though, was established in 2008, and had a first five-year plan, to be concluded in 2012. Despite the interruption due to the revolution, an EU document of 2012 posits, with bold nonchalance, the same objectives and keywords, "for the post-revolutionary rebuilding context".

Reforms, or plans to reform, seem to indeed have some capacity to navigate hard times, to resurface as soon as there is the chance. In August 2014, the government announced an eight-year plan to reform the higher education sector, to bring it into line with the provisions of the 2014 Constitution (which indicate the level of public spending for education), with the goals of "reforming the educational system to reflect the needs of the marketplace and incorporate the competencies necessary for innovative and entrepreneurial thinking" (Sawahel 2014). More recently, in January 2016, the government announced plans to remedy the 'damage' done to the education system in the past 30 years, which naturally meant not offering education in line with market needs (Bothwell 2016).

Some of the strongest resistance to these reforms has come from the ranks of professors and other people directly involved in academic life, despite the risks associated with taking sides at times of intense political repression. The main critics of this reform project were a small but influential minority of professors, who organised themselves into the 9 March Group for the Autonomy of the University. This group managed to impose itself on the stage and act as an active and visible opposition to the Ministry of Higher Education and Scientific Research – quite an achievement for an oppositional movement in Egypt before the revolution (Aboulghar and Doss 2009; Abdelrahman 2015). 9 March is concerned both by the material conditions under which academics have to work, as well as by the intellectual and political environment which restricts the autonomy of the university, and which hampers professional ethics. Their main criticism of the HEEP projects is that they are disconnected from reality, for they ignore the central structural problems of higher education, namely the scarcity of public expenditure on universities.

While these resistances clearly played a role in organising dissent for over a decade (Ibid.), government support for the reforms has never been wholehearted, but framed with resistance and delays.[12] On the one hand, there was a

---

12   It has been argued that the government has failed to create the necessary consensus around these reforms, particularly before the 2011 uprising (Kohstall 2015). I see the

public waiting (even calling) for some of these reforms, particularly those who had benefited from the economic reforms of the past decades. Largely educated at private schools,[13] and dissatisfied with the state of higher education institutions, they called for more privatisation, while at the same time being on the move to satellite cities, which started to be built in the desert around Cairo, as I discuss in the next section. On the other hand, government support for such endeavours has been mixed, to say the least, and some reforms have been slowed down, at times stopped, while an overall sense of precariousness hangs over the entire privatisation and internationalisation process. To this day, the state keeps a solid grip over private universities in various ways, as I make clear when discussing the case study.

It is precisely in this political context that the actual meaning of 'private' is to be understood, where political participation is hardly encouraged, business is closely tied with political power, and policy makers are hardly accessible. My contention is that an ethnographic understanding of how a private institution works is needed in order to understand how the system works in practice – how often contradictory sets of rules, contentious issues, as well as political and social change, are accommodated in the everyday life of an institution so central to the state apparatus, at least in Egypt.

Privatisation, Internationalisation, and the Restructuring of the City

In recent years quite a number of studies have started to examine the changes in late twentieth century and early twenty-first century Cairo; these changes

> include the emergence of a new spatial economy, where globalization and structural adjustments have led to high unemployment, particularly

---

slowing down of reforms as a part of the grand récit of democratisation in Egypt since the 1990s – while the language of internationalisation and privatisation is the new lingua franca, the government refuses to relinquish shares of power, and actually seeks to expand it. It seems that the current phase will present some elements of continuity with the pre-2011 phase, with some oscillation between the need to make the system sustainable and the necessity of keeping tight control.

13 Private schools of all kinds, religious (belonging to different confessions), foreign or simply for-profit (largely founded in response to new language requirements), have long been part of the educational landscape in the country – unlikely private universities, as said. Some private schools cater to the elite, some to the upper-middle classes, and a newer wave has spread into the poorer districts as well. All private schools are subject to state controls (Farag 2012).

among educated young people, and the selling off of the public patrimo-
ny to enhance the private sector and build exclusive, luxury, gated communities for a phantom luxury class.

AMAR AND SINGERMAN 2006

Since the beginning of the Mubarak era in 1981, urban planners and political
elites have argued that population density was consuming the promises of economic growth, and the government deployed laws, investments, policies and
infrastructures to subsidise and build satellite cities in the desert to facilitate
the "productive redistribution of the population" (Ismail 2006). Cities like 6
October or 10 Ramadan (both established in 1979, but scarcely populated until
the beginning of the 1990s) attract manufacturers, often linked to international companies and government supporters, which benefit from tax deductions
and cheaper rents in these vast satellite cities (see Denis 2011). On the other
hand, workers have to commute daily on minibuses from their homes in the
poorer neighbourhoods of historical Cairo to these cities, which can be 35 to 40
kilometres away in the desert, with long queues at peak times, and this results
in longer days away from home, making it more difficult for women to accept
jobs there (see Wahdan 2012).

It has been argued that this "demonisation of the demographic masses" is
linked to the state's embrace of a neo-liberal order. In this process Egypt's elite
and upper-middle class started to feel safe in walled enclaves in the satellite
cities' industrial zones, largely abandoning the urban core of Cairo on the basis
of what Denis (2006) calls a "security risk" discourse that identifies the city and
its poorer residents with poverty, pollution, disorder, criminality, violence and
terrorism.[14]

Veritable symbols of these last years are shopping malls, more luxurious
than ever, being substituted every few years by yet another bigger and more
modern one – and this is again a well studied phenomenon, with the associated consequences in terms of style, distinction, and taste (Abaza 2006). It's
easy to see, when travelling to either New Cairo or 6 October City, private universities are part of this landscape as well (see figure 5.1). It is not only that
newly built cities need schools – as briefly mentioned before, the process of

---

14   This discussion deserves much more space, as the elites do not abandon proprieties in
      historic neighbourhoods, and there is routine discussion about having them polished and
      made suitable for a proper life. Yet it seems quite clear that this process of "wall[ing] some
      in and keep[ing] others out" (Elsheshtawy 2006) is well advanced in Egypt as elsewhere,
      in a globalised order in which there is a high degree of segmentation in the spheres of
      both production and consumption.

FIGURE 5.1 *Advertising O6U along with other private universities and housing projects on the road from Cairo to Six October City.*
PHOTO TAKEN BY THE AUTHOR

getting away from the 'collapsing' public sector had started long ago, and most elite schools are still located in the historical part of Cairo. The whole idea of segregation resonates well with new conceptions of private, for-profit education. This is one of the ways in which the private character of private universities in Egypt is to be understood – since these satellite cities are an integral part of state resource management, it is not difficult to see how private universities are boosted by public policies, as elsewhere in the world.

The fact that almost all of the new private for-profit universities is located in one of the new settlements around Cairo should not come as a surprise, given the lack of suitable space in the congested historic Cairo. More striking, also for its political significance, has been the relocation of the American University of Cairo (AUC) from its old campus overlooking Tahrir Square to a new campus, partly funded by private investors, in New Cairo. As mentioned, AUC is a non-profit organisation well established in the country and largely respected as a place of knowledge and research; its presence in the ideal centre of the capital was far from accidental, and its library was the most accessible and up-to-date source of scholarship for the vast Cairo-based community of researchers.

The New Campus is more than 30 kilometres away from central Cairo, in a satellite city which is equipped to host a projected population of 2.5 million people, together with various ministries and companies. The 'move' raised several concerns among faculty, staff, workers and students, including the ability of this isolated and highly securised campus to maintain connections with the wider Cairo metropolis, and the increasingly visible corporate presence on campus as exemplified by the naming of gates after commercial labels, such as 'Pepsi gate' (Ahmed and Galal 2014). On the other hand, the university administration insist that the move opens up new possibilities for the university to achieve its mission, that is, to "provide high-quality educational opportunities to students from all segments of Egyptian society, as well as from other countries, and to contribute to Egypt's cultural and intellectual life" (Ibid.).

Recent research has shown that opposition to the 'move' came largely from the most vulnerable categories of the AUC community, namely junior faculty on tenure-track, adjunct lecturers, grant-based faculty members, outsourced workers, staff, graduate working students, and LEAD students (Ibid.).[15] The last few years have nonetheless shown that the move has enabled the university to continue functioning, since the old campus has been at the centre of some of the bloodiest confrontations since 2011.

Moreover, the move was understood to be a part of a broader context in which knowledge is increasingly a commodity, research a privilege, and segregation a necessity – or on new reconfigurations of urban space, class reproduction, and critical thinking in education. If the old AUC had a clear missionary background, and its aim of forging the elites was more or less overt, the new trend is still unclear, and fears that the established and recognised 'role model' university will turn into yet another commercial enterprise abound (Ibid.). All this notwithstanding, AUC is still one of the very few places in which faculty and students can study and do research, as well as exercise critical self-reflection.[16]

---

15   LEAD students refer to undergraduates fully funded by USAID through a scholarship scheme, the Leadership for Education and Development Program. They usually belong to a less-privileged social class than standard family-funded AUC students. As for the faculty, different treatment between international and local hires (the former receive housing and other benefits, while the local faculty do not) results in the latter being more affected by the move. As elsewhere, adjunct lecturers are at the lowest level (Ahmed and Galal 2014).

16   For example, in 2012 there were discussions about its landscape (extending to issues such as changing the name of some of its halls), on its relationship with the state, and on how to link with broader societal movements. Worth mentioning is the initiative

O6U

Located in the homonymous city on the edge of the desert west of Cairo, 6 October University (O6U) was among the first Egyptian private universities, the biggest, and particularly relevant for a number of reasons. It was established in 1996 as a consequence of Presidential Decree No. 245/1996 in accordance with Law No. 101/1992, which enabled the first Egyptian private universities to be created (Misr International University, Modern Sciences and Arts University, Misr University for Sciences and Technology, and 6 October University). It was the first to open its gates to students, with the first buildings completed in 1999/2000, and represents one of the better examples to illustrate conditions and the changes that private universities in Egypt are currently undergoing. The O6U is part of the current trend that involves an increasingly corporate character, even within private universities, that has many consequences for university governance and academic freedom, as well as for students' life on campus and the possibility of doing research.[17] Considering the O6U as an entirely private institution would be misleading; it started as a private enterprise, owned by one individual, but it soon became a far more complex reality, governed by a board of trustees that is composed of the stakeholders, the vast majority of which are companies and banks, other than a few individuals whose shares are a tiny minority. Some of these companies and banks are public, or semi-public, so the private character of the O6U has to be understood in this context.

The university, built on 40 *feddan* in the 'new city' of 6 October, on desert land, consists of three main buildings each constructed on a square model with an inner courtyard. These buildings house classrooms, offices, and the majority of the university's 14 faculties as well as the university hospital (located on campus, with external access for patients), the university hotel (which serves

---

'The University on the Square: Documenting History in Real Time', launched by the Egyptian National Archive and headed by Khaled Fahmy, Chair of AUC's history department, with participation from AUC, Cairo and Helwan universities members. The goal of the initiative is to collect and preserve an exhaustive collection on the revolution, including government documents and demonstrators' narratives, many of whom came from the AUC ranks. http://digitalcollections.aucegypt.edu/cdm/landingpage/collection/p15795coll7.

17   The fieldwork was conducted as part of an SSRC (Social Science Research Council) project on Arab Universities – Autonomy and Governance, in 2010 and 2012. The 2012 fieldwork was considerably shorter, as it was intended as a follow-up phase to account for the first changes after the 2011 revolution, and unless otherwise stated the data presented here refer to that year. For a more comprehensive introduction to the O6U, see Cantini (2015).

as a residence for girls and as a training facility for students in the Faculty of Tourism). All O6U buildings are named after martyrs of the wars against Israel or after army heroes, and the very date, October 6, is highly patriotic. The campus also includes a fourth building that in 2012 was under construction; three squares, two of which serve as parking lots, while a third and central one is a garden; a vast playground, and another garden, which is not yet completed, but hosts nevertheless an obelisk, a series of sphinxes, and other contemporary imitations of pharaonic heritage pieces. As I will elaborate below, the university was clearly an integral part of the development project for the whole 6 October area, which is similar to other private universities that have been established in the last ten years.

O6U is foremost among Egyptian private universities not only because of its relatively early foundation but, more importantly, because of its numbers. Even now, after a few years of slow decline it continues to attract the largest proportion of students: from the total of 56,802 students enrolled in private universities in Egypt in the 2008/2009 academic year, around 14,000 were enrolled at O6U (CAPMAS 2009, Statistical Yearbook). Around 40% of these students are female and they come from different countries, mainly from the Arab world (especially from Saudi Arabia and other Gulf countries), while South Asia is markedly less represented. The international dimension of O6U is further demonstrated, as almost all administrators I spoke with were eager to emphasise, by its agreements with foreign institutions, for example, universities in the United States and in Europe, but mostly in the Arab world, and by the existence of exchange programmes, mostly for visiting professors and, to a lesser extent, for students.

O6U is also considered among the most important private universities in Egypt because of its range of faculties, which are more numerous than in any other for-profit, private university in the country. There are 14 faculties at O6U, five of which are in the medical field: medicine, applied medical sciences (members of the administration claimed that this faculty is completely new in the country, both in private and public universities), dentistry, pharmacy, and physical therapy. Among the scientific programmes are engineering, information systems, and computer sciences. The others are part of the humanities and social sciences: applied arts, media and mass communication, economics and management, languages and translation, education, social sciences, and hotel management and tourism. The only fields of study not covered are agriculture (which is supposedly already well-covered in public universities) and law (which presents an interesting case to be studied further for its relative irrelevance in the context of private universities). The medical faculties are housed in a building attached to the university hospital, while the

Faculty of Hotel Management and Tourism has responsibility of the university hotel – both these institutions, along with the university library, are cited by top administrators as being among O6U's main positive aspects.

The more common scientific and market-oriented disciplines such as pharmacy, computer science, information technology, engineering, and media studies experience greater competition for students also due in part to the amazing rate with which new universities, all of which offer similar courses, are opening in the country. On the other hand, O6U also has faculties that are rare, and in some cases unique, for private universities in Egypt, such as economics, social science, education, medicine, and languages. These disciplines are underrepresented in private universities because of the prevailing negative view of social science and humanities graduates as presumably less employable.[18] The presence of humanities faculties at O6U constitutes a major strength, and this is usually considered, by administrators and professors alike, to be one of the main proofs that O6U is an all-round university and not simply one of the many private institutions of higher education mushrooming all over the country. On the other hand, it also shows that the initial principle by which private for-profit universities would offer different options than the public ones is not necessarily the case. The case of Medicine is quite different, as it has to operate in the context that post-graduate studies are not allowed in private universities, and graduates of this faculty are among those who are more affected by this. O6U managed to establish this faculty not only as a part of its services to the broader 6 October community, especially for its hospital, but also due to its privileged relationship with Cairo University and its University Hospital of Qasr el-Aini (in central Cairo), where graduates of O6U can pursue their post-graduation studies.

Lastly, O6U is an appropriate subject for study because of its special relations with the local government and the community of the new city of 6 October, and while this might be considered to be a problem more typical of public universities, it is quite telling in terms of the controversial nature of the private character of O6U. The university is at the same time a private, profit-oriented

---

18   Finding a job more easily after graduation is cited as one of the main advantages of private university education by those who either teach or study there; other advantages are the freedom to choose the programme one prefers, less bureaucracy, good relations between professors and students due to small class sizes, the (presumably) more flexible character of courses, better interfaculty communication, and better conditions for classes, exams, and the like. Given that employability is an important criteria for private universities, they tend to focus on programmes such as computer science, information technology, and engineering, which are considered to provide students with the skills better suited for today's labour market.

company which operates in the field of higher education, but also an instrument of state planning with regard to new areas to be built around the overcrowded capital city. This was often highlighted by the administrators with whom I spoke and who recommended that I look at O6U from the point of view of the local community for whom it is one of the main sources of revenue, helping the local economy in many ways.[19] I was even told to consider the university as a form of cultural tourism where 'tourists' (i.e. students) do not limit their stay to two weeks or one month, but stay for years – consuming, eating, sleeping, and so on.

O6U as a Company

It is O6U itself (and this also seems to be the norm in other private universities) that employs its workers and faculty, and so its premises are treated like those of a private firm, with an opening hour and a closing one, fixed at 4pm. At least half an hour before that time, the employees begin packing their things and walking to their private cars or the buses provided by the university to bring them back to Cairo where the vast majority of them live. Students, faculty, staff, and even heads of departments and deans are not allowed to stay on the O6U premises after 4pm except if they have official permission from the president himself or on special occasions. The general atmosphere is that most people at O6U consider themselves as employees and behave as such, while students are customers to be treated with care (see Cantini forthcoming). The closing time is particularly striking, especially when compared with other, mainly public, universities in Egypt, which are crowded until late in the evening, since the students generally see the campus as a gathering place, its green areas offering them space to wander at their leisure.

The campus space is organised quite rigidly. The buildings in which most of the academic life takes place are quite distinct among each other, even internally, with most faculties occupying one of the four storeys, and this encourages separation among students. Air conditioning is present almost everywhere, and is quite necessary since the weather can be quite hot for most months of the year. This is one of the first things that students and professors alike are likely to point out when talking about the advantages of studying at

---

19   As acknowledged by a recent analysis of the urban fabrics of 6 October. Until the recent inflow of refugees from Iraq and particularly from Syria, the students of private universities were the main inhabitant of this new settlement (Nagi 2014). In addition to O6U, the city of 6th of October is the location for a number of other recent Egyptian private universities: the Egyptian University for Science and Technology, the Ahram Canadian University, the Egyptian International University, and the Academy of Akbar al-yawm.

O6U, especially when they want to mark the distinction between the private sector and the public one, which is depicted as being overcrowded and almost unbearable.

Students' activities are quite structured, and little if any space is left for free activities outside those planned for and within the different courses. Conversely, the latter are quite well organised and most students consider them to be among the main advantages of studying at O6U, again especially if compared to experiences within public universities. From admission procedures to the presence of faculty advisors, from trips to post-graduation assistance especially in finding a job, everything seems to be designed to make life easier for the students enrolled in the university.[20] Admission is quite easy, and the fact that students pay for the education that they receive allows them to have the freedom of choice which is normally not to be found within the public sector, due to the strict admission quotas for the most in-demand faculties.

Any form of political or similar activity is formally banned, and the formation of unions is not among the possibilities offered by O6U. This is particularly striking if we take into consideration the relevance, also on a national level, of students' movements throughout Egyptian history, and given the fact that other private universities, the AUC and others, have seen massive demonstrations in the 2011–2014 period. The avoidance of any political activity is explained differently according to who is being questioned; some administrators will point to the fact that students themselves are not interested in politics, and since they pay for the time that they spend within the university organised activities should be related to their field of education. Others mention that the presence of many different nationalities (more than 40 at the time of my research), most of which are Arab, is likely to foster hatred between different communities, and as such it is even more important to keep students away from political activity, as well as to ensure the respectable image of O6U in the eyes of foreign families who may enrol their offspring there. Beyond these partial explanations, it seems that the absence of politics pertains to the very essence of the neo-liberal attire, that of gaining 'neutral', 'scientific', 'objective' knowledge with little if any concern for possible different points of view, not to mention for the reflexive nature of knowledge.

The internal structure of the university is hierarchical and centralised, with almost all major decisions made at the administrative level while minor ones have to be reported by the heads of departments to the relevant superiors. From an academic point of view, participation of the lower echelons of the hierarchy

---

20   For a recent critique of this attitude, not limited to O6U, see Barsoum 2016

(junior members of staff) is not encouraged, apart from a few individual cases, and participation in crucial decisions is not extended to senior professors. The same complaints could be heard at the senior level; it is claimed that the state imposes on almost all daily decisions in university life, including the academic curriculum.[21]

Staff Composition – Where Profit Meets Control

The composition of the staff is quite typical for this kind of low-quality for-profit university, for there are few full professors, normally on leave from public universities and who are given the biggest organisational burden within each department, which they actually shape in many cases. The category of associated professor is limited, and the biggest share of teaching is done by junior professors, usually selected from among young PhDs from public universities, but some of them are selected among students of the O6U itself and are hired while they are still studying for master's degrees or PhDs at public universities. Their contracts are normally renewed every year upon satisfactory performance, and this arguably affects their autonomy and freedom within the university (the casualisation of junior academic staff is far from being an Egyptian peculiarity).

The procedures for evaluating the teaching, presented by the administrators and the senior staff as one of the biggest achievements in the struggle for quality, is seen by junior professors as essentially threatening them, both when carried out by senior staff and by students, in the latter case through questionnaires. Most contracts, in some cases also for senior staff, are renewed every year, and therefore the administration retains its position of privilege toward employees. This control is not only put into practice once a year through the contract, but for junior staff is a constant source of worry, especially the evaluation procedures, some of which are internal to O6U but others are

---

21   State control over universities is not the sole prerogative of private ones, as is widely
      known; see for example the website of Munufiyya University, a public institution, in which
      it is plainly stated that the university coordinates with the security services to ensure that
      academic appointments and activities are agreed upon by the services (quoted in Fahmy
      2016). In the case of O6U, at the time of my fieldwork there was an 'academic consultant'
      whose task was to check all activities within the university, to make them compatible
      with the expectations of the Ministry of Higher Education. At the time of writing, the
      person then responsible for that task sits on the board of the university, and the position
      is now occupied by another person, under the title of 'Adviser to the Ministry of Higher
      Education for O6U affairs'. In the second phase of the fieldwork, in 2012, few professors
      were euphoric about being finally able to held seminars and conferences without burden-
      some control being imposed (see Cantini forthcoming).

designed to respond to the need to assess 'quality'. This has led to the creation of a 'quality commission' which is present in each of the 14 faculties, headed of course by one of the senior staff. The main criteria for having a good evaluation are being cooperative, having success in teaching, and being able to raise students' participation levels, both inside and outside classes. It is the senior person responsible for the junior who watches him/her, and then reports to the dean, who in turn reports to the vice-president for post-graduate affairs, who in turn goes to the president in order to decide which contracts will be renewed.

The condition of the junior staff is made more difficult still by the private character of the university, and by the fact that most students have a quite different attitude toward professors from those in the public sector. This leads to a strange relationship, in which students feel that they are the employers of professors, especially junior ones, and they behave accordingly. This is rather too schematic, but in general terms it is possible to say that students tend to treat professors, especially junior professors, as if they were their employees, paid by their own fees. In this respect, the condition of junior academic staff is rather hard, squeezed between control from the upper echelons of the hierarchy and widespread disrespect from students.

The Necessity of Being Profitable

In the early years of its existence O6U witnessed an impressive rise in numbers, both of students enrolled in the different faculties and of professors hired. This trend, especially the enrolment rate, reached its peak in 2002/03, with almost 16,500 students being enrolled (compared to 568 in the first year); subsequently it has continuously declined at a very slow pace, while there has been a tremendous rise in the number of private universities in Egypt and elsewhere in the Arab world. Some of these universities have benefited from the decrease in student numbers at O6U. This is the case, for instance, of the October Modern Sciences and Arts University located not far from O6U. The number of students in 2009/10 academic year was only about 12,000,[22] while the administrators calculated that O6U facilities could accommodate up to 20–21,000 students. The government was blamed for this, as it limits the number of student admissions in some faculties, usually those that are most in demand such as medicine, where 300 students can be admitted, while the faculty could accommodate up to 500. In other faculties, such as social sciences, the increased competition

---

22   I was not able to obtain official statistics from the university, with officials citing increased competition as a reason for lack of transparency; this figure was published on the university website.

between private universities in the country is to blame; while in the peak year 2002/03 almost 300 first-year students were enrolled, in the year 2009/10 this figure dropped to 40, according to the dean of the Department of Political Science.

As a consequence, there has been and still is increased pressure on the administration to keep the university profitable without severely cutting services in order not to lose too many students. This is one of the main challenges for the coming years at O6U and at private Egyptian universities in general. This is not the case for all disciplines; each year the number of students applying to study medicine and engineering exceeds the maximum capacity per faculty, which is fixed by the ministry. According to the head of the Faculty of Medicine, O6U is more than willing to accept more students, but the ministry is concerned about saturation of graduates from these disciplines.[23]

It is interesting to consider the segment of the market that O6U and similar universities in Egypt and in the Arab world (understood as a region with good internal mobility of people, including university students) are targeting. For students from affluent families, studying abroad, or at least at the AUC, is their best bet. In recent years, some 'foreign' for-profit universities (such as the German University in Cairo and the British University of Egypt) have emerged as less expensive alternatives to the AUC. With its comparatively inexpensive tuition fees, O6U is seeking to enlarge the platform of potential customers, since it is a for-profit organisation, in order to pull ahead of the increasing number of competitors. The aggregate numbers suggest, however, that this attempt is failing, since the total number of students whose families can afford private education is not growing. Moreover, the competition is also increasing on a regional level. During my interviews, top administrators expressed their worries about the growing number of universities in Saudi Arabia, the home country of many of the international students studying in Egypt.

The composition of the student body is particularly telling. Almost 40 per cent of the total student population come from Arab countries, and as a group they are more profitable for the university because they pay higher fees in addition to accommodation and living expenses, but the competition is strong at the regional level (Cantini 2014). Some faculties have had to decrease their tuition fees, by more than half in some cases, including the Department of

---

23   As mentioned earlier, the Faculty of Medicine needs a cooperation agreement with the public system in order to allow its students to do the compulsory practical year. This dependency might explain the reluctance of the ministry to grant additional seats.

Computer Science (of which there are now around 25 across Egypt alone, while at the beginning of the 2000s there were only two) and the Faculty of Education. Following the typical commercial logic of such an enterprise, the most desirable faculties have increased their fees by 5 or 10 per cent. Moreover, O6U is seeking to expand its collaborations with universities in the developing world, especially with Eastern Asian countries such as Thailand, and also with few universities in Europe and the United States, in order to become more attractive by offering 'international experience', which seems to be increasingly in demand by those willing to pay for education.

Conclusion – What is Private about Private Universities?

The private for-profit sector at the university level remains almost irrelevant in terms of percentages, despite the undeniable growth it has enjoyed in the past two decades. This notwithstanding, my contention has been that looking ethnographically at the concrete functioning of a private university helps in understanding not just changing conditions of knowledge production and of societal differentiation processes, but modes of societal engagement (or their absence) as well. In this article I initiated an analysis of the logic and practices of privatisation in Egypt by discussing some general aspects, such as the main reforms, variously implemented (if at all), and the link with other phenomena such as urban restructuring. I went on to focus on a particular case study, the for-profit private university O6U, introducing its structure and functioning, and its position in the broader market of private higher education.

This analysis if far from being conclusive, since the higher education sector is still in turmoil, and developing fast. In Egypt, public universities have always been a security issue for the regime. With over 2.5 million students, mostly concentrated in the main public universities, campuses have the size of medium-scale cities (Farag 2006). Students and professors are more politicised than the rest of the population. Since the 1970s, when mass education began to reshape the university landscape, campuses have been a battleground for Marxist, liberal and Islamist groups. Indeed it was on campuses that those factions would fight out arguments for which there was no space in the official political arena, which was monopolised by a one-party system (Abdalla 1985). Following the crackdown of security forces on political activists in the 1980s and 1990s, their attention turned away from internal political issues to the foreign intervention in Iraq or to Palestine. The demonstrations in solidarity with the second intifada mark the beginning of the decade-long series of civic activism that ultimately led to Tahrir, according to one analysis of the pre-2011 social movements in Egypt (Abdelrahman 2015). More recently the reforms, and in particular the Higher Education Enhancement Programme, triggered debates on higher education related issues such as autonomy, the promotion system for professors, and external evaluation.

Despite the vicissitudes of the years following the ousting of Mubarak, which are far from being concluded, the overall stability of the system is quite remarkable, as well as the persistence of a direction for reforms, despite governmental hesitations and (partial) societal opposition. In particular, the process of privatisation is still ongoing, and it has not been challenged by any ministry, of whatever political inclination, on the contrary private universities have been largely free from violent confrontations. Despite the absence of data for the past few years, it seems safe to conclude that private universities, with their internal differences of prestige and standing, are likely to profit from the quest for stability and tranquility that seems to be currently prevailing in Egypt (as well as in the donor community). Far away from the city centre, they are also easier to control, as my case study shows, while being less expensive for the state (or being 'cost-sharing' institutions, in the language of the reforms).

Yet the confrontations over the role of knowledge and that of the state are hardly over, and are likely to resurface in the coming years, as the problems that affect Egyptian universities – massification, chronic lack of funds, over-crowding, lack of quality, and the like – are unlikely to disappear. More fundamentally, it is the role of the state that seems to be precisely what is at stake. It has been widely noted that while the original meaning of reforms such as privatisation and decentralisation was to empower local stakeholders in the educational process and thus make the system more accommodating and effective, this has been confined to "technical dimensions" (Farag 2012: 84). The roles of political censorship and security were hardly touched, and are unlikely to be challenged in the coming future. As noted elsewhere (Mazzella 2007 for instance), the liberalisation of the economy and of education is proceeding in combination with persistent political authoritarianism, and thus it is hardly serving its original purposes. At the same time, these policies have also been a reflection of a "lowering of expectations and ambitions by the State, which thereby basically gave up on its agenda of modernisation and development through education" (Farag 2012: 92). If "the 1990s saw the return to the variety of educational paths along regional and class lines" (Ibid.), it becomes more apparent how the new, for-profit private universities suit the needs of an increasingly polarised society.

Works Cited

Abaza, Mona. 2006. *The Changing Consumer Culture of Modern Egypt, Cairo's Urban Reshaping.* Leiden/Cairo: Brill/AUC Press.

Abdalla, Ahmed. 1985. *The Student Movement and National Politics in Egypt (1923–1973).* London: Al-Saqi Books.

Abdelrahman, Maha. 2015. *Egypt's Long Revolution: Protest Movements and Uprisings.* London: Routledge.

Aboulghar, Mohamed and Madiha Doss. 2009. "Min Ajl Jami'a Afdal: Majmu'at 9 Maris" (For a better university: the 9 March Group). *Alif: Journal of Comparative Poetics* 29: 89–100.

Ahmed, Yasmine and Ola Galal. 2014. Higher Education in the Arab region. http://arabhighered.org/wp-content/uploads/2015/11/Galal-and-Ahmed-Protest-Forms.pdf

Amar, Paul and Diane Singerman (eds). 2006. *Cairo Cosmopolitan: Politics, Culture, and Urban Space in the New Globalized Middle East.* Cairo: American University of Cairo Press.

Bayat, Asef. 2011. "Arab revolutions and the study of Middle Eastern societies". *International Journal of Middle East Studies.* 43 (03): 386.

Bothwell, Ellie. 2016. "Egypt government seeking to fix 'damage' to education system". *Times Higher Education,* 28 January, https://www.timeshighereducation.com/news/egypt-government-seeking-fix-damage-education-system.

Cantini, Daniele. 2014. "Une université privée égyptienne dans le nouveau marché international de l'enseignement supérieur". *Cahiers de la Recherce sur l'Education et les Savoirs* 13: 167–179.

Cantini, Daniele 2015. "October 6 University – the First Egyptian Private University". Higher Education in the Arab Region, http://arabhighered.org/wp-content/uploads/2015/11/Cantini-October-6.pdf.

Cantini, Daniele 2016. *Youth and Education in the Middle East. Shaping Identity and Politics in Jordan.* London: I.B. Tauris.

Cantini, Daniele Forthcoming. "We take care of our students: private universities and politics of care in Egypt".

Denis, Eric. 2006. "Cairo as neo-liberal capital? From walled city to gated communities". In Paul Amar and Diane Singerman (eds). *Cairo Cosmopolitan.* Cairo: American University of Cairo Press, 47–71.

Denis, Eric 2011. "Transformations du territoire, urbanisation et libéralisme autoritaire". In Vincent Battesti and François Ireton (eds). *L'Égypte au présent: inventaire d'une société avant révolution.* Paris: Sindbad-Actes Sud, 75–110.

Eickelman, Dale F. 1992. "Mass higher education and the religious imagination in contemporary Arab societies". *American Ethnologist* 19 (4): 643–655.

Elsayed, Hanaa Ibrahim. 2014. "Reform of Higher Education Institutes in Egypt". *Comparative & International Higher Education* 6: 12–15.

Elsheshtawi, Yasser. 2006. "From Dubai to Cairo: competing global cities, models, and shifting centers of influence?" In Paul Amar and Diane Singerman (eds). *Cairo Cosmopolitan*. Cairo: American University of Cairo Press, 235–249.

Fahmy, Khaled. 2016. "Muqatil Giulio Regeni wa Ma'sa'a al-Baht al-Ilmi fi Masr (the killing of Giulio Regeni and the tragedy of scientific research in Egypt)". *Al-Bedaiah* 5 February, http://albedaiah.com/articles/2016/02/06/106473.

Farag, Iman. 1997. "Higher Education in Egypt: The Realpolitik of Privatization". *International Higher Education* 18: 16–17.

Farag, Iman 2006. "Egypt". In James J.F. Forest and Philip G Altbach (eds). *International Handbook of Higher Education*. Dordrecht: Springer, 693–709.

Farag, Iman 2009. "Going international: the politics of educational reform in Egypt". In André Mazawi and Roald Sultana (eds). *Education and the Arab World: Political Projects, Struggles and Geometrics of Power*. London: Routledge [World Year Book of Education], 283–299.

Farag, Iman 2012. "Major trends of educational reform in Egypt". In Samira Alayan, Achim Rohde and Sarhan Dhouib (eds). *The Politics of Education Reform in the Middle East: Self and Other in Textbooks and Curricula*. Oxford & New York: Berghahn, 80–96.

Hanafi, Sari. 2011. "University systems in the Arab east: publish globally and perish locally vs. publish locally and perish globally". *Current Sociology* 59 (3): 291–309.

Hartmann, Sarah. 2013. "Education 'home delivery' in Egypt: private tutoring and social stratification". In Mark Bray, André E. Mazawi and Ronald G. Sultana (eds). *Private Tutoring across the Mediterranean*. Rotterdam: Sense Publishers, 57–66.

Ismail, Salwa. 2006. *Political Life in Cairo's New Quarters: Encountering the Everyday State*. Minneapolis, MN: University of Minnesota Press.

Kohstall, Kohstall. 2012. "Free transfer, limited mobility: a decade of higher education reform in Egypt and Morocco". *Revue des mondes musulmans et de la Méditerranée*. 131: 91–109.

Kohstall, Kohstall. 2015. "From reform to resistance: universities and student mobilisation in Egypt and Morocco before and after the Arab Uprisings". *British Journal of Middle Eastern Studies*. 42 (1): 59–73.

Levy, Daniel and Manar Sabry. 2011. "Egyptian private higher education at a crossroads". *International Higher Education*. 65: 13–15.

Mazzella, Sylvie (ed.). 2007. *L'enseignement supérieur dans la mondialisation libérale*. Paris: Khartala.

Musselin, Christine. 2008. "Vers un marché international de l'enseignement supérieur?" *Critique internationale* 39: 1–23.

Nagi, Ahmed. 2014. "6 October: Madina al-A'ir al-Muqaim" (City of transient residents). *Cairobserver*, http://cairobserver.com/post/72305652767/6-october-city-of-transi ent-residents#.VrykNFJjVNU.

Reid, Donald M. 1990. *Cairo University and the Making of Modern Egypt*. Cambridge: Cambridge University Press.

Sawahel, Wagdy. 2014. "Eight-year Egyptian plan for higher education". *University World News* 29 August, http://www.universityworldnews.com/article.php?story =20140829120505683.

Sayed, Fatma H. 2006. *Transforming Education in Egypt: Western Influence and Domestic Policy Reform*. Cairo & New York: American University of Cairo Press.

Shore, C. and L. McLauchlan. 2012. "'Third mission' activities, commercialisation and academic entrepreneurs". *Social Anthropology* 20 (3): 267–286.

Sika, Nadine. 2009. "Private universities in Egypt: are they venues for democratic attitudes and behavior? Towards an Arab Higher Education space: International challenges and social responsibilities: proceedings of the Arab regional conference on Higher Education, Cairo, 31 May, 1–2 June 2009", http://search.shamaa.org/ PDF/41452/SikaEn41559.pdf.

Sobhy, Hania. 2012. "The de-facto privatization of secondary education in Egypt: a study of private tutoring in technical and general schools". *Compare: A Journal of Comparative and International Education* 42 (1): 47–67.

Steiner-Khamsi, Gita. 2012. "Understanding policy borrowing and lending: building comparative policy studies". In Gina Steiner-Khamsi and Florian Waldow (eds). *World Yearbook of Education 2012: Policy Borrowing and Lending in Education*. London/New York: Routledge.

Tourné, Karine. 2007. "'Devenez votre patron'. La mise en scène du chômage et la figure du jeune entrepreneur". In Mounia Benani-Chraïbi and Iman Farag (eds). *Construtions sociales de la jeunesse dans le monde arabe*. Cairo/Paris: CEDEJ/Aux Lieux d'Etre, 165–194.

Wahdan, Dalia. 2012. "Transport thugs: spatial marginalization in a Cairo suburb". In Ray Bush and Habib Ayeb (eds). *Marginality and Exclusion in Egypt*. Cairo: American University in Cairo Press, 112–132.

Warden, Rebecca. 2011. "Egypt: Universities incubators for the revolution". *University World News* 176, 19 June, http://www.universityworldnews.com/article .php?story=20110618183237325.

Wright, Susan and Annika Rabo. 2010. "Introduction: anthropology of university reform". *Social Anthropology* 18: 1.

CHAPTER 6

University is a Private Matter: Higher Education in Saudi Arabia

Annemarie Profanter

Using a broader definition of the concept of 'university', it could be stated that higher education in the Arab countries was born about 200 years earlier than in Europe, especially in the field of medicine (Denman and Hilal 2011: 305). With the advent of Islam about 1400 years ago Mecca and Medina became the main centres from which knowledge diffused particularly to the Islamic world (Saleh 1986). However, that being said, to date the university landscape presents itself very heterogeneously, and in the case of Saudi Arabia the higher-education system has not kept pace with the breakneck speed of development since the end of World War II, when oil production transformed this country into one of the richest in the world.[1]

To use the country's wealth to build a 'Knowledge Society' was the declared aim of King Abdullah, who died aged 90 in January 2015. Especially since his takeover at the beginning of 1996, remarkable reforms have been initiated. In line with this aim, the ninth Five-Year Development Plan claims that 50.6% of the budget goes to human resource development including education and training. This has been interpreted as one important step to further realise the Kingdom's goal (Saudi Arabia. Ministry of Higher Education [n.d.](a)).

Another important step towards achieving this objective was the encouragement of private participation in higher education. While this trend in the MENA region dates from the 1980s and accelerated in the early 1990s (Willoughby (2008: 25) describes this phenomenon as "an explosion of higher education institutions in the small GCC countries"), Saudi Arabia began to gradually follow suit only two decades later. In contrast to other nations of the MENA region where the World Bank often sponsors educational reforms (World Bank 2014), policy makers in KSA have adopted other strategies of working in partnerships and affiliations with universities and colleges abroad, establishing so-called private, transplant-universities (Tétreault 2003), foreign affiliated universities/institutions, branch campuses or, in other words, satellite and offshore campuses (Miller-Idriss and Hanauer 2011). The vast and sometimes

---

1 When Saudi Arabia formally became a nation in 1932, education was largely limited to instruction for a select few in Islamic Madrassas.

confusing terminology mirrors the relatively recent explosion of transnational educational relationships in the Middle East (Miller-Idriss and Hanauer 2011).[2] In Saudi Arabia these transplant-universities are financed by private businessmen or members of the royal family.

For years there were just a handful of government universities catering to a minority of high-school graduates, the number of private universities is now helping to take up the slack. The inefficiency of public educational institutions in the preparation of young people for working in a modern economy, as outlined in the Arab Human Development Report 2013,[3] coupled with a growing youth population looking for educational and employment opportunities, continue to create demand for private participation in the higher education sector in Saudi Arabia. The Saudi government "has set a target for the private sector to achieve a 30% share of the total enrolments" (Parthenon Perspectives n.d.: 10). Thus,

> private higher education enrolment in Saudi Arabia has grown at ~33% p.a. making it one of the fastest growing private education segments worldwide. Between 2007 and 2011 revenue has grown by over 40% per annum and is estimated at ~USD 300M. ... Similar to India, China and Malaysia, the majority of private higher education enrolment in the KSA can be found in undergraduate courses.
>
> Parthenon Perspectives n.d.: 9

Training institutions are not only growing at a national level, as international collaborations and programmes are also being intensified. The number of educational opportunities for Saudis is therefore expanding, even beyond the borders of the country. Moreover, for decades government and private institutions alike have strived to join the international league table of the world's top universities. King Salman bin Abdulaziz Al Saud is determined to continue these diverse programmes and initiatives, to pursue his predecessor's strategy to use the country's wealth in the development of a 'Knowledge Society'.

The mission of private educational initiatives in the kingdom is strictly tied to the government's key goals of re-nationalisation of its work force and the

---

2 "At least a third of existing branch campuses (34 of approximately 100 worldwide) are located in the Middle East, and there are an additional 23 institutions or programmes in the Middle East region that fall under the category of transnational educational arrangements, such as turnkey institutions or replica offshore institutions" (Miller-Idriss and Hanauer 2011: 186).

3 "Despite relatively high levels of educational attainment, employers frequently cite the lack of employable skills among the region's youth as a barrier to employment" (Mirkin 2013: 24).

development of tertiary and specialist education to fill existing key skills short-ages and curb dependency on foreign labour[4] (The Observatory on Borderless Higher Education 2006). The government tries to solve the problem of unem-ployment among Saudi nationals through 'Saudisation' (Fakeeh 2009): "Among Saudis, unemployment rates have risen from 10.5 percent at end-2009 to 12.1 percent at end-2012, especially for youth and women" (International Monetary Fund 2013: 14). Through promoting private higher education the authorities try to tackle the problems associated with unemployment, such as the rise of po-litical and religious radicalism (Lidstone 2005). Thus educational policy pack-ages foster school-to-work transition and aim to enable graduates to function in the local economy and society.[5]

> In 2012, significant numbers of men and women with tertiary education were unemployed, pointing to a potential skills mismatch between the education system and the labor market. In particular, women with uni-versity degrees accounted for over 70 percent of female unemployment.
> International Monetary Fund 2013: 14

Moreover, "going forward, addressing weaknesses in the education system and barriers faced by women in accessing employment could help support a knowledge-based economy" (Ibid.: 20).[6] Thus, major challenges for private educational institutions in Saudi Arabia which themselves are constrained by their legal, structural and cultural domains lie in the difficulty of balancing international academic standards with national (economic) needs.

This article examines the rise and development of private higher education, focusing on the ways in which transplant universities operate in Saudi Arabia. In line with the overall goal of the volume, the intersection of private and pub-lic and the principle of internationalisation are analysed. The discussion of different 'forms' of private (transplant-) universities and their (not for) prof-it orientation is based on a thorough review of the literature, governmental

---

4 In mid-2013, the number of non-Saudis stood at 9,723,214, or 32.4% of the total resident population of 29,994,272 (De Bel-Air 2014).

5 Research has indicated that young graduates consider themselves poorly prepared for the world of work and that their training was not appropriate for the labour market: only 27% of unemployed graduates regarded their education as having been useful (Bosbait and Wilson 2005).

6 "Options that could help increase FLFP [female labour force participation] include improving access to transportation, [...] and flexible work arrangements such as teleworking" (Interna-tional Monetary Fund 2013: 14). However these measures seem useless if cultural constraints such as male relatives' or husband's consent impedes female labour force participation.

regulations and judicial interpretations. The analysis is complemented by a personal account of teaching and research at a private university in the Eastern Province of the Kingdom of Saudi Arabia, Prince Mohammad bin Fahd University (PMU). This case study explores how the model of transplant-universities is implemented adopting the national (and global) function of education[7] within cultural and religious constraints.

Methodological Note

The methodologies adopted are interview techniques and participant observation. In my role as visiting professor at PMU I participated at numerous planning and progress meetings and community events, and although conversations at these events were not recorded they were drawn upon for general impressions. A research diary provided the scaffolding for me to construct my research knowledge. Data were also gathered through interview techniques: I taught study courses such as 'Critical thinking', 'Written communication', 'Professional Development', 'DYNED – Computer based IELTS preparation' in the summer semester of 2008 and was a visiting research scholar at PMU in 2007 and 2009. This provided me with access to independent information, and to people who would not be easily available to any researcher in the region who was not infiltrating the system. Key interviewees were identified through a purposive sampling strategy, with snowball sampling drawing on information gained from interviews. Following the oral tradition in Arab culture, potential informants were approached personally or by phone, without prior contact through email or mail. By adopting this strategy it was possible to integrate both knowledge and experience into the narrative. Thus the informants interviewed were judged to be people with the best knowledge and insight into the university landscape: academics, administrative personnel, senior management and students. The use of several data sources, triangulation, supported the reliability of the interpretations. The validation provided by the interviewees upon receipt of the researcher's interpretational framework supported its appropriateness. One of the reasons for the limited geographical focus of this study is the single status and female gender of the researcher, which in Saudi Arabia limits freedom of movement both geographically and societally. Although I am not the first to make this point, it is important to recognise that Saudi society does restrict the free movement of people and communication

---

7   All education in Saudi Arabia is tied to its Islamic roots, curricula at all level – whether in
    public or private institutions – must conform to the Islamic Sharia laws and the Qur'an.

of ideas. The fact that my research had the blessing of the Prince Governor of the Eastern Province considerably smoothed my path, but did not completely neutralise societal imperatives.

Origins and Development of Saudi Higher Education

The Ministry of Higher Education was not established until 1975; however, the first 'real' public university,[8] King Saud Bin Abdul Aziz University, opened its doors to the public in 1957. While in the 1950s only the elite could take advantage of educational opportunities, with the foundation of the University of Medina in 1961, the University of Riyadh in 1957 and the 'Abd al-'Aziz University in Jiddah in 1967, the educational movement was initiated. The Saudi government approved the first two private universities in collaboration with US institutions, and has since been actively encouraging the expansion of the private sector (Observatory on Borderless Higher Education 2006).

In terms of higher education, the information on the total number of universities in Saudi Arabia and their classification as public or private differs from source to source.[9] There are both colleges (which generally offer undergraduate degrees) and universities (which generally offer both undergraduate and advanced degrees including Master's and PhD programmes) in Saudi Arabia.[10] The Ministry of Higher Education reports nine private universities[11] and 36 private colleges.[12] Other sources suggest that there are currently 52 universities, of which 24 are public (46%), eight are private (15%) and 20 are private colleges (39%) (Denman and Hilal 2011: 306). The Royal Embassy of Saudi Arabia reports that

---

8   While the first University in Saudi Arabia was King Saud University in Riyadh, est. 1957 with 22 students and 7 faculty, Saudi Aramco (previously known as ARAMCO) has served as a 'de facto university' setting for thousands of Saudis from all over the kingdom; from the southern heights of Najran to the northern plains of Hail and all parts in between since 1963. This multinational entity has made itself a force to be reckoned with in the kingdom for the last three generations.

9   It is surprising that even on Ministry websites and publications there seem to be no consistency in percentages and total numbers.

10   http://collegelife.about.com/od/glossary/a/The-Difference-Between-A-College-And-A-University.htm.

11   http://www.mohe.gov.sa/en/studyinside/privateedu/Pages/Universities-Higher-Education-Eligibility.aspx.

12   http://www.mohe.gov.sa/en/studyinside/privateedu/Pages/Higher-education-colleges-eligibility.aspx.

today, Saudi Arabia's education system includes 25 public and 27 private universities, with more planned; some 30,000 schools and a large number of colleges and other institutions.[13]

Between 2003 and 2013, the total number of higher education students more than doubled, with 1.2 million students enrolled in 25 public universities and 30 private universities and colleges.[14] The Ministry of Higher Education (2009) reports over a quarter of a million students attending an ever increasing number of private and government funded universities in the kingdom.

King Abdul Aziz University (KAAU) in Jeddah originally opened its doors as a private university in 1967; thus, it was the first private institution in the kingdom. But it lasted only four years, and then it became a public university. Inspired by an article in Al-Madina Saudi newspapers in 1964, a well-known businessman donated land and infrastructure for the establishment of a campus, despite the opposition of important citizens and the government itself. The endeavour was launched on the basis of the enthusiasm of its local supporters, and the commitment of local and Western experts (Batarfy 2005). However, financial sustainability was soon an issue, as tuition was free and the demands on this start-up university were substantial. Though initially the government granted financial support, in 1971 the university board officially requested that it should be made a public university (Ibid.).

Of course, the failure of this private initiative had negative effects on the development of the private educational sector as a whole for decades. Only after the publication of the Sixth Development Plan 1995–2000 did the idea of private higher education reappear on the agenda. This meshes with global trends in education policy associated with patterns of globalisation and attendant trends of neo-liberalism.

> Studies were conducted, and the Council of Ministers approved the reestablishment of private higher education in 1998. This was only the second time the Government authorised the development of private higher education in the Kingdom of Saudi Arabia (KSA), and it is thus considered a very new phenomenon.
>
> JAMJOOM 2012: 15–16

---

13   http://www.saudiembassy.net/about/country-information/education/.

14   These numbers do not include the 163,000 students enrolled in undergraduate and postgraduate programmes in international universities in many countries throughout the world (Aljubaili 2014).

Thus the first institutions opened only in 2000, and Jamjoom[15] reports on critical responses from educators who claim that private higher education remains
an experiment until this very day (Ibid.: 15–16).

However, to date

> the General Directorate for Private Higher Education endeavours to en-
> able the private sector in the Kingdom of Saudi Arabia to offer higher
> education in accordance with international standards of quality and
> academic accreditation in a manner which realises the kingdom's higher
> education policy.
>
> Saudi Arabia. Ministry of Higher Education n.d.(b): 9

In October 2005, Mohamed Al-Saleh, secretary-general of the Higher Education Council, announced that preliminary licenses had been issued to approximately 60 additional investors in Saudi Arabia to establish private colleges
across the kingdom (Observatory on Borderless Higher Education 2006). Later,
in 2006, an announcement was made by the Ministry of Higher Education that
foreign universities would for the first time be allowed to set up campuses in
the kingdom. Saudi Arabia is certainly opening up foreign collaboration and
is looking to private and foreign provision as a source of additional capacity.

> The mission of the Directorate is to plan, organise and supervise institu-
> tions of private higher education in accordance with a vision and goals
> which it shares with them, and the policy of higher education in the
> Kingdom of Saudi Arabia.
>
> Saudi Arabia. Ministry of Higher Education [n.d.](b): 9

Saad al Haqqan, Director of Public Relations at the Ministry, indicated that
"we hope that foreign universities will help us meet the demands of higher
education for Saudi students" (Observatory on Borderless Higher Education
2006). In general, foreign interest in higher education remains high; in a report published in 2006, the MoHE reported that 38 UK institutions and other
universities from Australia and Singapore had made inquiries to the Saudi government about the possibility of opening branch campuses in the kingdom.
In contrast to other Gulf states this form of internationalisation is, on the one
hand, viewed with scepticism by the authorities, and therefore may not seem

---

15   Dr Yussra Jamjoom is the Vice Dean of Academic Affairs at the private Univer-
      sity of Business and Technology in Saudi Arabia, see: http://sa.linkedin.com/pub/
      yussra-jamjoom-phd-mpm/3/b92/7b3.

directly applicable to this closed environment. On the other hand, cooperation is fostered, as we shall see. It also becomes apparent that sending students
overseas is only one aspect of the Saudi plan for tertiary education, while developing a strong private sector is certainly another (Ibid.), as demonstrated
by the following overview of private initiatives in the kingdom (Saudi Arabia.
Ministry of Higher Education [n.d.](b): 18–19). The task of creating a comprehensive map was, however, made difficult by the paucity of data available and
the often conflicting information on the ministerial and university websites.

Prince Sultan University (PSU) in Riyadh was originally founded in 1999 as
Prince Sultan Private College, but in 2003 the Ministry of Higher Education
declared it to be a university.[16] Bachelor degrees are offered in: Information
Systems; Business Administration; Finance; Accounting; Marketing; and Computer Science;[17] its governance works on a non-profit basis.

Another private university is Effat University located in Jeddah. It is a leading private non-profit institution for women, which started offering its academic programmes in 1419 AH (corresponding to 1999) under the name Effat
College.[18] Effat University fosters academic partnerships with several international universities, such as the University of Miami, the University of Southern
California, Boston University, Duke University and the Sorbonne.[19] Its governance works on a non-profit basis.

The Arab Open University (AOU) located in Jeddah and Riyadh is another
non-profit institution.[20] It also has branches in other Arab countries, including Jordan, Lebanon, Kuwait, Oman and Bahrain. It was founded in 1996 as

---

16   http://www.psu.edu.sa/AtAGlance.aspx.
17   http://www.psu.edu.sa/DegreesOffered.aspx.
      Undergraduate programmes on the Men's Campus are: Computer Science, Account-
      ing, Communication Engineering with Digital Media Track, Finance, Network Engineer-
      ing, Information Systems, Marketing, Construction Engineering with E-Commerce Track,
      Aviation Management, Production Engineering.
      Undergraduate programmes on the Women's Campus are: Computer Science,
      Accounting, Architecture, Digital Media, Finance, Interior Design, Information Systems,
      Marketing, Graphic Design, E-Commerce, Translation, Law, Applied Linguistics, Compu-
      tational Linguistics.
      http://www.sacm.org/article/042913.aspx.
18   Operating under the umbrella of King Faisal's Charitable Foundation, its founder, Queen
      Effat Al-Thunayyan Al-Saud, is the wife of the late King Faisal Bin Abdal-Aziz.
      http://www.effatuniversity.edu.sa/About/Pages/History_And_Heritage.aspx.
19   http://www.effatuniversity.edu.sa/About/Pages/Academic-Partnerships.aspx.
20   AOU has more than 30,000 students in seven countries and has celebrated the gradua-
      tion of more than 12,000 students, over half of them women. http://www.arabnews.com/
      aou-open-new-campus-riyadh.

a non-conventional academic institution,[21] and contains the following faculties: Business Studies, Computer Studies, Education, General Studies, and Language Studies.[22]

Al Yamamah University (YC) is also located in Riyadh. It was established in 2001 by the Al-Khudair family.[23] In December 2008 it was promoted from Al Yamamah College to university status. Now Al Yamamah is a comprehensive university pioneering in offering a wide variety of specialisms for men and women on separate campuses, in the fields of Business Administration and Computer & Information Systems.[24] Collaborations are maintained with several international universities, for example Washington State University, the University of Canterbury, Ludwig Maximilian University (Germany), Valparaiso University (USA), and Steinbeis University (Berlin). Its governance works on a non-profit basis.

Another university open to both male and female students is the University of Business and Technology (UBT) located in Jeddah, which has grown gradually from a Junior College to a fully-fledged Four Year College (CBA), and was officially named the University of Business and Technology in 2012.[25] Men and women are separated onto two campuses, while the third, the MBA Campus, is accessible to both.[26]

The Prince Fahad Bin Sultan University (FBSU) was established in 1424 H (corresponding to 2003) in the city of Tabuk, with one college, the College of Computing. In the academic year 1427–28 a branch for girls was added.[27]

Alfaisal University was founded in Riyadh in 2002 as one of the first private non-profit, research and teaching universities in the kingdom. It is made up of four faculties, Business, Engineering, Medicine, Science and General Studies, offering its programmes to male and female students.[28] Its governance works on a non-profit basis.

Dar Al Uloom University (DAU) in Riyadh was initially founded as a college in 2008 and received its university status in 2009. It offers a Department of Computer Engineering and Information Technology, Department of Business

---

21   http://www.arabou.org.sa/.

22   https://www.arabou.edu.kw/index.php?option=com_content&view=article&id=515&Ite
        mid=666&lang=en.

23   The Al-Khudair family also established the first private school in Riyadh in 1957.

24   http://yu.edu.sa/about-yu/.

25   http://www.ubt.edu.sa/Home/UBT-History/Governing-Body.

26   http://www.ubt.edu.sa/Campuses/MBA-Campus.

27   http://www.fbsu.edu.sa/about-us-1/about-university-4/university-background-2.

28   http://web.alfaisal.edu/about/.

Administration, Department of Architectural Engineering and Digital Design, Department of Law and a Department of Education for women.[29] The campus is divided between men and women.[30]

To conclude there is Prince Mohammed bin Fahd University, a for-profit institution in Al Khobar in the Eastern Province, which was established in 2008 and will be described in further detail later on.

This chronology of the establishment of private universities in the kingdom highlights a crucial pattern. Cooperation is sought with lucrative and prestigious institutions in the West, focusing on employment-based education programmes with a valorisation of subjects such as economy, ICT, engineering and business. This "hegemonic sweep of capitalism and the logic of the market" are educational trends that are not restricted to the Kingdom of Saudi Arabia but reflect a global neo-liberal agenda (cf. Altorki 2013).

Enabling Legislation, Regulations and Judicial Interpretations

In 1997 the Council of Ministers issued decree no. 33 and later approved the regulations "granting the private sector the right to establish non-profit educational institutions based on sound administrative, scientific, economic and financial foundations" (Saudi Arabia. Ministry of Higher Education [n.d.](b)). While some suggest that the development of the private sector was largely unplanned and experimental,

> this may indicate that policymaking toward private higher education was procreative. At first, the Ministry's approval and regulations were only for non-profit higher education institutions, limiting the establishment of private higher education to charity foundations.
>
> JAMJOOM 2012: 211

In 2000, however, these limitations were abolished, and the principle of for-profit higher education institutions was approved (Decree No. 212). Since then profit oriented institutions have been mushrooming in the kingdom, although there is a paucity of information regarding to which category a university belongs, as shown above. Al-Eassa (cited in Jamjoom 2012: 211–212) notes that the rules and regulations put forward by the Saudi Government on the

---

29   http://whatwhere.me/riyadh/university/dar_al_uloom_university_143772448977602.
30   http://uniandi.com/?p=university_home&univid=221.

establishment of profit oriented or non-profit oriented private institutions were basically identical. There was no significant incentive that would encourage providers to opt for the not-for-profit model despite its being tax-free; this is of minor importance as there is a fixed tax rate of 2.5% which doesn't significantly affect the profits of private institutions. On the other hand, donors can be more easily attracted to non-profit higher education institutions.

A decree of April 2001 issued by the Ministry of Higher Education regulates administrative procedures and technical regulations of all private initiatives in this area.

> Investors wishing to establish a private non-profit institution are required to undertake a feasibility study that examines the academic/training specialties proposed, the extent to which those specialties are understood and agreed with by other experts to be necessary and the potential for developing a particular academic market. Should the study be accepted by the Ministry, the prospective owners are granted a preliminary license to proceed further.
>
> AL-DALI, FNAIS and NEWBOULD 2013: 133

Since every nation has its own criteria by which to define private institutions, and the boundaries between private and public sector are increasingly ambiguous, it is necessary to understand how the private higher education sector and the concept of privatisation are related to each other in the kingdom. Forms of privatisation could be, for example, 'function shifting' and 'cost-shifting'. Here, an analysis of private higher education in the kingdom shall be undertaken according to the following categories: 'funding'; 'ownership'; 'orientation'; 'functions and roles'; and 'governance'. These represent the complexity of the definition of private higher education in the kingdom, and show that the ambiguity in the available official statistics is a result of unclear classifications for both sectors, public and private.

a. The category of 'funding' can be considered the clearest category by which to distinguish public and private institutions.
   The first financial incentive the Government offered to the private sector was the leasing of government lands, which are owned by the Ministry of Municipal and Rural Affairs, as well as other government authorities. This was approved by the Council of Ministers Decree No. 87, released on the 6th of April 2002.
   MOHE, cited in JAMJOOM 2012: 223

In Saudi Arabia most of the public educational institutions are tuition-free.[31] Moreover students receive a monthly stipend (Jamjoom 2012: 28), but also private universities and colleges are heavily subsidised (Aljubaili 2014).

> In September 2006, a Royal Decree was issued establishing Ministerial grants to pay for the fees of approximately one-third of the students at each private higher education institution.
> AL-DALI, FNAIS, and NEWBOULD 2013: 129

The Ministry of Education also provides scholarships to "selected students to study in private universities or abroad" (Marcucci, and Usher 2012: 54). In order to achieve the goal of increasing enrolment in the private sector to 30% of the total,

> the government offers preferential funding to set up private universities. Students in private higher education receive ~90% of the government scholarships provided to students enrolled in all tertiary education institutes.
> Parthenon Perspectives [n.d.]: 10

b. In terms of the category 'ownership', private institutions are owned by local private investors or non-profit organisations; however,
   in Saudi Arabia, no transnational institutions exist yet, as no foreign ownership is allowed – unlike in many countries where ownership by foreign individuals is permitted, Saudi Arabian law requires that there be at least five partners acting jointly as owners. A company may also be an owner.
   JAMJOOM 2012: 32

Foreign institutions encounter many challenges in their attempt to establish collaborations with the Saudi education market. The Saudi government permits foreign providers to operate vocational training institutes, but it is not possible to gain licenses to run higher education institutes. The only way

---

31   However, according to official sources not one third but 50% of the students have the privilege of studying tuition-free based on their individual merits. Council of Ministers resolution no. 29 dated 3/2/AH 1431 (18/1/2010) ordained payment of fees for 50% of students studying in private colleges and universities in the specialisations of their choice if they have not been accommodated in government universities (Saudi Arabia. Ministry of Higher Education, [n.d.](b): 14).

to operate in the private higher education sector in the kingdom is through management contracts with Saudi education providers. "There are examples of large global higher education companies entering into management contracts with local Saudi education providers".

Parthenon Perspectives [n.d.]: 10

c. In terms of orientation, private institutions are more concerned with teaching rather than research or vocational training, and most academic personnel have to be 'imported'. For example, it was announced in *Arab News* on 5 January 2015 that 25,000 teachers and employees are to be trained abroad (United States, UK, Canada, Australia, New Zealand, Finland and Singapore) as part of the King Abdullah Public Education Development Project (Arab News 2015).

d. In terms of religious affiliations, Western education is perceived by most Arabs as being liberal – not bound to any religious conviction – and most private universities are affiliated with Western institutions. On paper there is no discrimination based on Islamic religious affiliation, in other words sunni or shi'a; however in practice this is a very important factor which is never openly discussed or admitted. Religious or clerical police, referred to as muttawwa'in, are highly influential in the kingdom. The Wahhabi tradition dominates Saudi education, and religious affiliation within Islam is the determinant factor in securing jobs and admission to educational institutions.[32] Examples of how this is influential also in the educational arena of the private sector are in the hiring of personnel and in student admissions and grading with reference to their family names and tribal affiliations.[33] It is relevant to this point that strict gender segregation is applied in all educational institutions; few institutions are established primarily for females, for example King Fahd University of Petroleum and Minerals (KFUPM) has separate colleges, which offer traditional, 'female-specific majors' such as Medicine and Interior Design.

e. Education, while having a global function, also fulfills a national function. Jamjoom (2012: 42) analyses three assumptions often raised with regard to

---

32   The majority of the population in the kingdom is sunni, estimates of the shi'a population range from 10 to 15%. Shi'a are concentrated primarily in the Eastern Province (33% of the population there) where the case study reported here is located.

33   The dynamics of sunni-shia relationships in KSA do not stop at the university gates. Drawing from my personal experience I have witnessed discrimination on the basis of religious affiliation at PMU.

private higher education: (a) more educational opportunities; (b) differ-ent forms of education; and (c) higher quality. The private higher educa-tion sector is supposed to respond to the high demand for higher education when public institutions cannot meet them anymore because of their small size or their restrictive admission policies. Although the u.s. Saudi Arabia Business Council states that

> the 2015 national plan is an extension of previous developmental plans, education and healthcare remain the priority of the kingdom's budget, representing 44% of total spending. Education continues to receive the largest share of the budget at 25% of the total allotment, among the high-est in the world.
>
> US-Saudi Arabian Business Council 2015

audi Arabia publishes few details of its budgetary assumptions in line with the generally low level of data releases (Middle East Monitor 2006: 2). Saudi is often perceived as a land of unlimited wealth due to its reputation as pe-troleum king; however, "an estimated 20% of the population lives in crippling poverty" (English Islam Times 2014). The government has only recently begun to acknowledge this problem, and poverty is largely hidden from the public eye. "The Saudi authorities are [...] concerned about the potentially flammable mix of unemployment and political and religious radicalism" (Lidstone 2005, 50). Sponsoring private higher education has been a strategy to keep the young generation busy for a couple of years and off the streets.

Private institutions respond to special needs of, for example, minor-ity groups and may provide higher quality education even in remote areas (Jamjoom 2012). In terms of functions and roles the kingdom's 1978 education policy defines higher education as

> the stage of specialisation in all its types and levels, which nurture those with competence and intelligence, develop their talents, and meet the various current and future needs of society, to maintain useful develop-ment which realises the nation's goals and noble objective.
>
> Saudi Arabia. Ministry of Higher Education 2011

The definition suggests that opportunities are open, with full equity, to men and women (this issue shall be addressed later),[34] indeed to all citizens who

---

34   The concept of 'equal opportunity' is limited by laws requiring gender segregation and censorship, and by educational and social limitations on females that are institutional as much as cultural. Education "remained under the Department of Religious Guidance until 2002 [...]. This was to ensure that women's education did not deviate from the original

are willing and capable of undertaking undergraduate and postgraduate studies (Ibid.).

> The Ministry is convinced that educational reforms helped to transform Saudi universities into 'functional developmental institutes' via a careful balance of international academic standards, national needs, local cultural identity, and careful management of knowledge production, management, dissemination, access, and control.
>
> Saudi Arabia. Ministry of Higher Education 2009

However, the development of a knowledge based society is a long term venture. The mere establishment of private institutions and expansion of collaborations with foreign universities of high standing is a good starting point, but needs to find methods of implementation within the constraints of a very conservative society. So far, governmental discourses on the function of the university have been the centre of my analysis; the following section focuses on my personal experiences at Prince Mohammad bin Fahd University in the Eastern Province.

The Case Study: The Transnational Framework of PMU

Prince Mohammad Bin Fahd University was the first private institution in the Eastern Province, which is considered one of the poorest regions in KSA (Salih 2014: 78).[35] It opened its doors in 2006,[36] and is particularly significant as it was the first 'co-educational', 'high tech' private university in the Eastern Province, delivering its curriculum in English. More precisely, PMU was the first to enrol both male and female students in separate facilities. It has now been going for ten years and is on a steep growth curve in the employment of new personnel

---

purpose of female education, which was to make women good wives and mothers, and to prepare them for 'acceptable' jobs such as teaching and nursing that were believed to suit their nature" (Hamdan 2005: 44).

The Ministry of Higher Education and the Department of Religious Guidance both ensured that the interpretation of freedom would be in line with Wahabi Islam.

35   Although it's the poorest region, the province is also home to Saudi Aramco, which produces and exports most of Saudi's oil and gas.

36   Stages in the growth of PMU: in 2006 both campuses shared one building (Preparation Programme and MIS programme); in 2007 the separation of campuses took place and the startup of three colleges; in 2008 the new auditorium was inaugurated and the official opening of PMU took place, as well as the opening of the LRC building.

as well as in the intake of new students. During the fall semester in 2008/2009, there were 351 students (260 male and 91 female) enrolled, whereas in the fall semester 2010/2011 the number increased to 747 students (567 male and 180 female) (PMU [n.d.]: 17).[37]

(a) Governance: PMU was promoted by a banding together of 52 Saudi busi-
     ness men under the auspices of HRH Prince Mohammad Bin Fahd, gov-
     ernor of the Eastern Province, who donated the land for this project with
     a view to providing education for both male and female students. They
     not only wanted to meet the needs of a growing economy but also aimed
     to establish an institution where female students could reside at home
     and still receive 'Western style education'. The educational concept was
     designed by a group of 22 Texas universities grouped under the Texas In-
     ternational Education Consortium (TIEC). Needless to say, PMU is still
     under close supervision.
         The chief decision-makers at PMU are the members of the board of
     trustees; however all major decisions are taken by the Rector, Dr. Issa Al
     Ansari, who was educated at King Saud University in Riyadh and holds a
     master's degree from the USA and a PhD from the UK. In each college the
     dean is usually male and holds the top position; females are always in as-
     sociate positions and have to answer to the dean. Independent decisions
     by the associate dean are usually not accepted.
(b) Mission Statement: enable graduates to assume leadership roles; link
     academic programmes with the requirements of the surrounding work
     environment; guide research activities to create solutions to persistent
     problems in surrounding communities; and provide community service
     through continuous training and education.
(c) Academic programme: The diagram below (figures 6.1, 6.2, and 6.3) shows
     the structure of the study programme.

The Preparatory Programme provides a bridge between high school and college that primarily emphasises instruction in English, along with Maths and
Study Skills. The inadequacy of English language education throughout the
Gulf is taken into account by the university administration (Tétreault 2011).
The problem arises at middle and high school level, and the university students
struggle to compensate for poor English language instruction throughout their
school career (Kelly 2011). Therefore entry criteria at PMU had to be lowered
in order to ensure a sufficient number of enrolments. Rote learning is still the

---

37   Since 2011, no official statistics have been released.

The Program

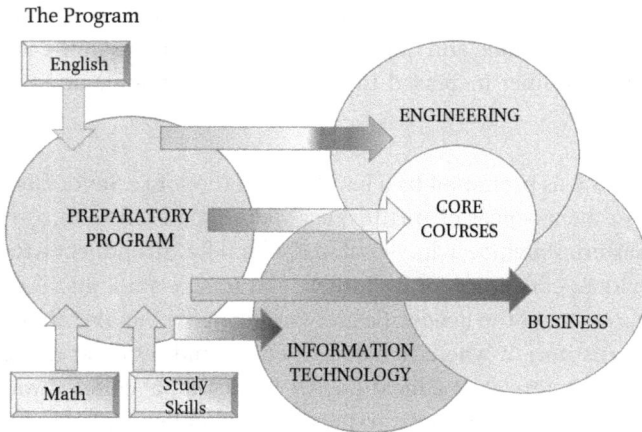

FIGURE 6.1 *PMU – Study Programme*
© 2012 PROFANTER, ANNEMARIE

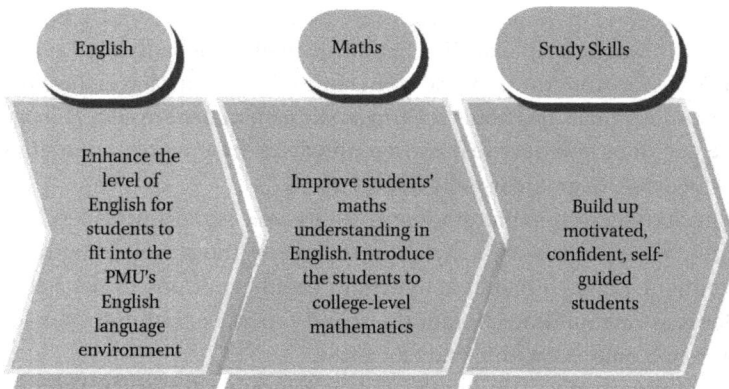

FIGURE 6.2 *PMU – Preparatory Programme*
© 2012 PROFANTER, ANNEMARIE

paramount pedagogical method, and it is not surprising that the weakest output pillar is the dimension of 'creative outputs'. Introducing 'Study Skills' was believed to be necessary because of rote learning being the basis of Qur'anic studies and the method of choice in all government schools. This had to be supplemented by a method which included critical thinking and other specific skills important in the building of a knowledge society and sustainable development (cf. Altorki 2013). This development is attributed to the role of private universities in Saudi Arabia and the MENA region in general, and they claim to train students for careers in the government and business – in other words, to

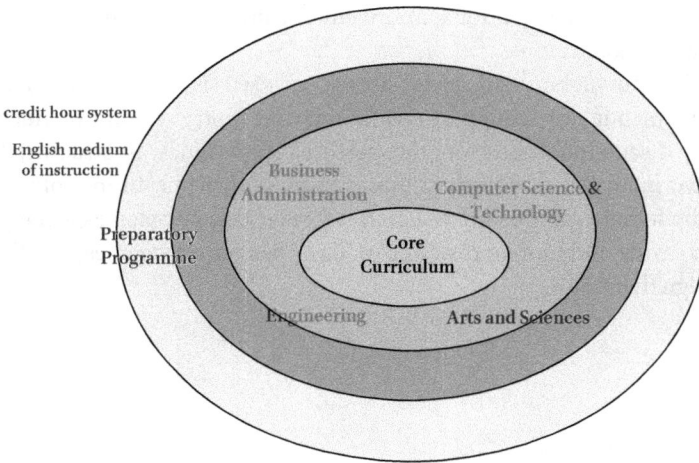

FIGURE 6.3 *PMU – Academic Programme*
© 2012 PROFANTER, ANNEMARIE

educate young people appropriately for them to be able to market their skills. This strategy was adopted as a response to the challenge of unemployment discussed earlier.

In accordance with this strategy the focus of PMU is on technology related subject areas and not so much on humanities. There are three colleges focusing on Engineering, Business and Information Technology. This "failure to establish courses in philosophy of science and the philosophy of social sciences [...] and an excessive deference to the needs of the market in structuring academic programmes, with a consequent stress on market economics, management and business administration at the expense of the social sciences" (Altorki 2013: 237), seems to mirror a trend in educational policies in the MENA region that goes hand in hand with a global neo-liberal domination (cf. Altorki 2013; Miller-Idriss and Hanauer 2011).

The Engineering College is entirely for males, and females are not catered for in this area. Local personnel are particularly hard to find in these fields, and thus the policy of Saudisation is difficult to implement.

> Most of the new foreign institutions offer specialised degree programmes in fields such as business, IT and health sciences. They are therefore offering technical skills which are high in demand, but so far lacking in most university graduates in the region.
>
> MILLER-IDRISS and HANAUER 2011: 193

Thus, these transnational educational arrangements involve a high dependency on an ex-patriot labour force.

To conclude, the higher education system at PMU is challenged in a multitude of ways, but two seem particularly relevant from my point of view. The following discussion based on my personal experience is structured around the two main issues regarding this start-up endeavour. In my role as professor at the female campus my research interests were focused especially on the gender divide and human resource management challenges, especially the local/foreign dynamics.

Discussion

An Ongoing Debate: Gender

Historically it was the hidden agenda of the ruling class to use a strategy of severe segregation (Doumato 1999). In both religious and secular discourse, women represent a figurehead of religious morality which, through easily enforceable representative symbols such as sex-segregation and veiling, reinforces the comfort and stability of cultural continuity. This fusion of gender to definitions of appropriate Islamic behaviour has led to a self-perpetuating paradigm for the status quo (Doumato 1999). Tétreault (2003) claims that Islamic patriarchal politics has been increasing because of the feminisation of higher education. According to my observation there is growing controversy over the role of women in the Islamic patriarchal system which clashes with the growing standing of women in higher education.

Having taught at one, I have personally lived the challenges that are inherent in mushrooming modern educational institutions being forced to grow in line with religious restrictions, conservative mores and political structure. These institutions are surrounded by a conservative Muslim society that presents many challenges, one of which is the waste of female potential for societal development. Domestic and geographic spaces help Arabian women assess class, value, and identity, when moving from one sphere into another, whether that is from being an unmarried tribal member into married status, or from being a university student into a business professional. This is key to the establishment of a new phase of existence for Khaleegy women.

> ... International concerns about the status of woman and non-Saudi academics, even in the Kingdom's most progressive higher education providers will take concerted effort and time to address in a meaningful way. ...
> It seems more likely that such barriers will only slow down the progress

rather than derail it. Because many of their senior staff trained over-seas (primarily the USA, the UK and Australia), most universities in the Kingdom are aware of the concerns and are leading the push to achieve greater parity for all staff.

ONSMAN 2010: 518

Despite the fact that social and religious restrictions persist, women are, with the limitations discussed earlier, included in the educational opportunities that continue to spread, although they experience network limitations in the choice of their course of study.[38] It should also be borne in mind that women's institutions have not yet reached the same level of quality as those for men.

The interpretation of the concept of co-education in Saudi Arabia needs to be further addressed. Specifically, gender segregation, reinforced by law, is strictly applied, with the genders kept segregated on separate campuses with ID control on each side. The exception is Masters' classes, where lecture rooms are divided by a wall and male students enter on one side and females on the other, both being able to see the lecturer but being unable to interact with or see each other.[39] This 'creative solution' was necessary due to a substantial shortage of instructors and professors on both campuses for the higher edu-cation programmes. In the beginning the interpretation of a co-educational institution was different. The academic dean told me of an incident that hap-pened on the very first day at PMU, when classes started in September 2006 – a sample case that will be described in the following section:

> The male and female faculty and students were in the same building, and though classes were set up on opposite sides of the building for male and female students, faculty and administrative personnel were allowed to intermingle in a central area. However, within hours of opening this

---

38   Because of the rules of 'Mahram', women need "a male relative's agreement before seeking work, education or travel" (Vidyasagar and Rea 2004: 266). The number of women who study abroad has increased in recent years, reaching 20% of all Saudi students abroad (Bukhari and Denman 2013). This reflects the emergence of Shehada (2009: 24), i.e. the as-pects of the socio-political context are crucial, in particular the primacy of the concept of family honour (Sharaf), the mutually constitutive relationship between the Shari'a court and the community, and the specificity of court cases.

39   Moreover, PMU has the advantage of the latest IT technology, which includes two-way video conferencing connecting the male campus and the female campus through state of the art wired lecture halls. The fact that they are now able to offer courses across the cur-riculum independent of gender restrictions that apply to face-to-face lecturing begs the question as to why females continue to be excluded from certain career paths.

was noticed by the Muttawa,[40] who came to monitor what was happen-ing on campus and a report was passed on to the governor, saying that this was not permissible. I was in the rector's office when a phone call was received from the governor's office to desist this immediately, and within 45 minutes all the women were cleared out of that section, and within days a wall was set up to prevent intermingling. This was a turning point, it showed how influential the Muttawas are, and the rector was really scared. I still think he could have stood up to them and told them that this is a private institution and we apply Western standards. But the longer I stay here the more I think we have to start at the point where the people are at and feel comfortable within the bounds of their social and religious mores.

RICHARD HOOGEWERF [PSEUD.], interview by author, Saudi Arabia, 12 May 2011

This statement exemplifies the struggle in applying the rules and regulations stipulated by the private partners without crossing boundaries. This gender segregated atmosphere at the university, however, only reflects the societal make-up at large. So currently educational opportunities for women, while be-ing based upon an American or European framework, are being delivered in an idealised 'women's only setting'. Moreover the tools and often the career paths they will need to function effectively in a diversifying capitalist setting with a huge pool of potential employees, both male and female, are not part of their collegiate experience.

Traditional gender segregation is upheld by encouraging social dislocation from one female-only sphere to another, thus reinforcing the female to female transition of knowledge and economic investment. The symbolism is evident in the choice of majors of PMU students, such as Interior Design as it is within the circumference of the home, Mechanical Engineering being forbidden due to the masculine arena within which it is applied, i.e. outside the home, and Computer Engineering, which again encourages spatial segregation although allowing for economic participation. During my stay at PMU the Department of Interior Design was under the umbrella of Engineering and for women only.

---

40   The religious or clerical police arm of the Ministry, referred to in general as the Muttawah, is used to implement these interpretations in line with Wahaibi Islam, "a revivalist move-ment that has for two centuries dominated Najd, the home of the ruling dynasty, and has shaped government social policies in all the rest of the [Arabian] peninsula that came under Saudi rule in the twentieth century" (Doumato 2000: 28) by providing regular on-site supervision of curriculum, staff and administration.

The home being a sacrosanct female sphere explains the admittance of females to this particular course of study.

Another challenge for students at PMU is the fact that they are "back-seat drivers" (Beg 2006: 21) despite the fact that their right to drive has been campaigned for for years.They must rely on a male relative or a chauffeur/limo engaged by their male relatives for transportation to and from work and school. Even when fairly reliable transportation is arranged, it does not allow them to be as competitive in their various fields due to the limitations involved.

In terms of governance, gender plays no small role. For example, at the beginning of the second year a new chair of department had to be selected; both candidates were expatriates, the male had less experience than the female associate chair. In line with cultural constraints and gender dynamics, the female candidate could not take on the position of chair with the male acting as associate, instead the less experienced person had to be appointed chair on the basis of gender.

The associate department chair who has worked at PMU from the very start, an American woman holding a master's degree, stated that her biggest adjustment was: 'loss of identity'. She explains this by stating:

> I have to wear an *abaya,* I am covered from head to toe whenever I want to go out. Then I can't drive, of course. Decisions at the university are taken by men, it doesn't matter what the women say. When the women need something done, they always have to go through a man, we can talk to the women at HR but this is useless because they themselves have to go through the men at HR. Women experience a loss of identity, a loss of power.
>
> MAYA WATSON [PSEUD.], interview by author, Saudi Arabia, 21 October 2011

Becker (1991: 88) found that women in professional roles of authority were received with respect and were listened to in their jobs. However this was written almost two decades ago, and things have changed.[41] Women no longer occupy public positions of responsibility and, especially in education, the male voice is the one that is heard and respected.

---

41   The presence of females from the USA working for ARAMCO (Arabian American Oil Company) in the Kingdom in Dhahran influenced female movements with their American lifestyle (unveiled, driving): "Saudi women were forbidden to do. Saudi women soon began asking for some of the same rights as their American counterparts. Some discussions took place on a formal level. However, with the Mecca uprising of 1979 such discussions came to a halt" (Hamdan 2011: 43). The Iranian revolution and the Gulf War of 1990 both influenced the women's movement in that same direction.

> In 1980, there were more female graduates in the humanities than male.
> University women could study most of the same subjects as their male
> counterparts except those which might lead to their mixing with men.
>
> HAMDAN 2005: 42

One of the professors at PMU reported complaints directed towards a decision that she had made. The students were very adamant that she acquiesce to their request. Because of her many years of experience working in the Gulf region, and also having been at PMU from the very start, she knew how to deal with this situation, telling the students: "I cannot do anything about this but if you want it changed you will have to talk to the registrar" (Maya Watson [pseud.], interview by author, Saudi Arabia, 21 October 2011). At this point the students stopped their badgering. She had accepted the loss of power and adjusted her thinking and response accordingly by pointing to the male authority.[42]

A whole raft of crucial questions arises in the context of the school to work transition for females. Employment opportunities for women in Saudi Arabia are limited, and in general we see high youth unemployment, since students do not possess the requirements of the knowledge economy. What happens when Princess Noura University's 50,000 women begin to graduate and find themselves in a country where women do not have the independence necessary to pursue a professional career? Will all of the university's graduates be content with limited opportunities (Reizberg 2011)? The same concern also applies to the many female and male students studying on scholarship programmes abroad. How will the future be for the 120,000 scholarship students when they return? After being exposed to so many different cultures and ideas, will women easily re-integrate into this conservative and restrictive society? Will young adults be content to relinquish the freedoms and opportunities that they enjoyed while abroad? What kind of future will a new generation of well-educated Saudis expect? What kinds of limitations will they accept (Reizberg 2011)? Will there be enough job opportunities for this highly specialised elite?

Human Resource Management Challenges: The Local/Foreign Dichotomy

Faculty in educational institutions in Saudi Arabia are generally recruited in the USA, Canada, the UK, continental Europe and Australia, while support staff are recruited in Southeast Asia (India, Pakistan, the Philippines). Accurate

---

42   The few examples given here can only show a slice of my personal experience there. For
      further information, see Profanter 2009; Profanter 2010; Profanter and Cate 2010; Profanter
      and Cate 2011.

statistical information on staff educational and national backgrounds was difficult to procure, although appropriate management programmes were in place. For example, Banner, a management system for universities, had only just been introduced and was yet to be fully implemented when I was working at PMU. PMU seeks international faculty in many ways. Recruitment methods include the Teacher Education Accreditation Council (TAEC), employment agencies, conferences, personal contacts, and even incentives for current faculty to suggest names – if this led to the person being hired, the faculty member received 500 Saudi Rial, equivalent to 130 US Dollars. Wages differ substantially, even within the same employment category, according to origin and family background, and of course educational attainment and the country/university issuing the qualification.

> Faculty, mostly recruited from overseas, are largely non-Muslim. Many have had little experience in majority Muslim societies and may have received little or no cultural sensitivity training about the region or its local, religious, and cultural norms and values.
> MILLER-IDRISS and HANAUER 2011: 189–190

In an interview with the associate department chair at PMU this was addressed:

> I have to wear an *abaya*, I am covered from head to toe whenever I want to go out. Then I can't drive, of course. Decisions at the university are taken by men, it doesn't matter what the women say.
> MAYA WATSON [PSEUD.], interview by author, Saudi Arabia, 21 October 2011

Associated with this is the concept of *wasta* which permeates all aspects of society in the Middle East and involves both the act and the person who mediates or intercedes towards finding middle ground. For expatriate professors socialised in Europe or the US this hidden force is unknown. In Western culture *wasta* is frowned upon by university professors, who feel that when giving grades students should be evaluated on the basis of the actual grades earned. This individualistic approach stands in opposition to the collectivistic make-up of the social groups that hold power in the Middle East.

All (foreign) professors and lecturers at PMU, because it is a for-profit oriented organisation, cannot ignore the importance of *wasta*. The author has direct experience of the implementation of this concept. The failure of certain students was not accepted by the administration because of the strength of the particular *wasta* of her family. Disagreements between students (especially those with strong *wasta*) and instructors have resulted in non-renewal of faculty contracts.

Expatriate teachers and university professors who are not familiar with the concept and have not received any cultural training, impose their cultural mindset on the treatment and evaluation of students and are regarded as "inflexible, hard-headed, arrogant, and stupid" (Cunningham, and Sarayrah 1993: 127). Cunningham and Sarayrah (with reference to Jordan – Ibid.: 120) explain the meaning of *wasta* in the educational realm:

> After being admitted, students socialised in an environment heavily dependent on *wasta* sometimes assume that *wasta* will influence the university professor. They attend class irregularly, do not study for midterm tests, and then appear before the teacher asking to be passed ....Often the father or an important relative visits the professor. The probability of success in this *wasta* attempt depends on the fortitude of the teacher, the hump over which the student wishes to climb, and the strength of the particular *wasta* on the particular faculty member. Occasionally, this plea meets with success; more often, the student faces the rude shock of failure at the end of the semester. That failure is incomprehensible to students socialised to family loyalty as the primary value.

Related to all this, is a high level of frustration due to cultural constraints and a high percentage of termination of faculty. Kelly's (2011: 218) observations at the American University of Kuwait apply directly to PMU: "Expatriates must work under contracts of limited duration and may also be subject to age and health limitations".

Many studies have proved that personality characteristics can be used to predict with accuracy whether expatriates will succeed in their educational assignment (Arthur and Bennet 1995).[43] One director of PMU stated:

> Part of the screening process involves finding out from prospective employees as to the reasons why they would want to come to Saudi Arabia. Several reasons have been postulated as to why expats chose to work in any particular location: some come from money, others just want an

---

43   Arthur and Bennett (1995) focused on the factors expatriates themselves perceive as being crucial for success. Five factors were highlighted: (a) family situation; (b) job knowledge; (c) relational skills; (d) flexibility/adaptability; and (e) extra-cultural openness. Other researchers have related the success of international assignments to three other factors: (a) adjustment; (b) performance; and (c) premature departure decisions. These factors, while theoretically well documented, are treated in a superfluous manner in pre-employment screening in educational institutions in the Gulf.

overseas experience, some to be involved in the opening of a new university, others because they can't get a teaching job back home, some to be exposed to a different culture and others to escape from ordinary life to a place with the aura of mystery.

SOLIMAN WATSON [PSEUD.], interview by author, Saudi Arabia, 18 June 2011

Another challenge at the administrative level is the fact that there is no tenure, and therefore little security for foreigners – job loss is a constant threat, as the unintentional violation of standards can occur even to an experienced foreigner or, in my words, 'transplant junkies', due to a lack of publications. Career development transplant faculty are often caught in these structures across the Gulf, with no possibilities of returning to higher educational institutions outside the MENA region.

The motivation to accept a position at PMU varies; according to one director it can also be a craving for adventure:

Saudi always seemed to be the big mysterious country. Everybody that I knew that had spent any time in the Middle East, had been to Saudi. It's almost like you had to get your ticket punched to come to Saudi Arabia. I do know that this doesn't sound right or good but I do mean this in the best sense.

SOLIMAN WATSON [PSEUD.], interview by author, Saudi Arabia, 18 June 2011

Another reason often cited is the desire to visit and explore new lands and financial packages (Feldman and Thomas 1991). The head of HR gives the following reasons for expats coming to PMU:

Some have come for money, for recreation, for easier loads, for personal prestige, some are putting their heart and soul into making this a success.

AHMED ABAS [PSEUD.], interview by author, Saudi Arabia, 12 June 2011

Another department chair stated:

A lot of our teachers have had considerable experience and authority in other locations. On coming to PMU they find themselves having to follow very explicit rules and regulations and do not have a chance to utilise the expertise that they have brought with them.

ANNE GIBSON [PSEUD.], interview by author, Saudi Arabia, 15 November 2011

This is contrary to findings by Feldman and Thomas (1991: 38), who state:

the reason most frequently given by our participants for accepting their assignments in Saudi Arabia was autonomy. They wanted to be in charge, to run their own operations with minimal interference from head-quarters.

The 'loss of professional identity and power' as well as the chain of command is further explained by one of the directors:

> I was one of six people who were told to start and lead out and my job was to get the academic programme started. I thought the decisions that I made would be carried out and would not be challenged or changed by my superiors. This happened for a while until a new layer of Saudi management was put in place, thus taking away any power or authority previously held.
>
> PAUL GREGSON [PSEUD.], interview by author, Saudi Arabia, 2 May 2011

By adopting the following strategies the relatively high percentage of termination of faculty could be balanced: (a) proper screening prior to their arrival; and (b) appropriate measures to assist with adjustment.

To conclude, other initial start-up concerns include transportation of faculty from and to the university campus. For example, while I was teaching at PMU, female faculty were caught in a maelstrom. Faculty loads is a constant issue due to a lack of professors and the possibility to supplement one's income. Due to the profit-orientation of this private university, the fact that an increase in the load on each instructor offers the possibility of saving on personnel costs is very significant. Additional daily challenges and trials faced by expatriates hired at PMU are: (a) obtaining work visas and Iqamas;[44] (b) housing and medical allowance on local standards; (c) lack of social events and activities; (d) language problems due to a lack of English proficiency (e.g. by locals such as taxi drivers or shop assistants); (e) religious challenges and customs (all shops close regularly at prayer times); (f) safety; and (g) banking.

While remaining sensitive to the needs and desires of this conservative Islamic nation, after reviewing the data, and taking account of my personal and professional experiences, I question whether in today's economic climate the luxury of 'separate but equal' educational institutions, work environments and commercial ventures can be maintained.

---

44   'Iqama' is an employment visa that permits an expatriate to work in Saudi Arabia with the sponsorship of a Saudi company or citizen.

Conclusion

The mushrooming of transnational offshore educational institutions in Saudi Arabia is part of a globalised phenomenon that involves deterritorialization, economic liberalisation, internationalisation and Westernisation (cf Scholte 2005). However, even though academics trained abroad are the hired elite in private higher educational institutions, educational curricula are shaped by local culture and traditional customs. Because of the tremendous socio-religious pressures constantly playing out, education in Saudi Arabia must strictly adhere to religious and cultural mores.[45]

> Of primary concern to many local citizens in the Persian Gulf, for example, are issues of homogenisation and Westernisation. The replacement of Arabic instruction with English-language instruction, the reduction or replacement of religious courses and the introduction of new fields of study which may threaten traditional local beliefs are but a few examples.
>
> MILLER-IDRISS and HANAUER 2011: 189

In a time of cuts for educational institutions in Europe and the US, it is hard to imagine the possibilities that open up when there are virtually no budgetary restrictions hampering the development of higher education. Various strategies are employed: (a) establishing educational institutions around the country, both private and public;[46] (b) recruiting international experts for teaching and research;[47] (c) promoting access for Saudi students to foreign universities

---

45   Why would one not expect it to be this way, because when one looks back at the history of modern civilisation, so much of what is studied and practiced today has its roots deeply entrenched in the Arab world, with Saudi Arabia playing no small part.

46   According to the Ministry of Higher Education (2009), "a number of new facilities will be built, including 25 technology colleges, 28 technical institutes, and 50 industrial training institutes. The government will also expand and diversify the post-graduate programmes offered within the kingdom and seek to increase the amount of post-graduate students to 5% of all university students. The plan also encourages innovation in science and technology by providing US $240 million in grants for research projects each year. Other initiatives include the establishment of 10 research centres, 15 university technological innovation centres in association with King Abdullah City for Science and Technology (KACST), and at least eight technology incubators at KACST and other universities. The government will also continue to promote university collaboration with international companies".

47   Robertson, quoted in Bhattacharjee's article, justifies the behaviour of 'buying' international academics by calling it a simple act of capitalism, "they have the capital and they want to build something out of it" (Bhattacharjee 2011: 1344).

through scholarship programmes which enable them to study in specialised areas (Reizberg 2011: 5). These efforts have gained formal international appreciation, as "Saudi Arabia was ranked 31 globally with reference to the efficiency of the higher education system" (Saudi Arabia. Ministry of Higher Education 2009). This investment may end up being miniscule in comparison with the ultimate benefits of developing its latent industrial, commercial, business and economic resources. According to the Webometrics of World Universities, as of June 2010 three Saudi universities ranked among the top 200 world universities, and in total six were among the top ten universities in the Arab Gulf states, Arab world and Islamic states.

> In 2009, King Saud University was also admitted to the academic ranking of World universities, known as Shanghai ranking, within the top 500 international universities and the sole Arabic University.
>
> Saudi Arabia. Ministry of Higher Education 2009

Although the weak points of international ranking systems are evident, and in the case of the Gulf states often discussed with regard to their business relations with top universities in Europe and the US and the resulting exchange of faculty, Saudi Arabia's ambitious efforts for higher education reform have clearly borne fruit.

In the light of the developments in the education sector and the research presented here, the following questions are yet to be answered: Can an institution designed to bring together top international scientists to collaborate on research thrive within a walled-off campus in the desert? What does 'private' mean in this context? How long will international scientists be willing to remain in a society that places unaccustomed limitations on their personal lives, and thus how long will such an endeavour be sustainable? How easily will foreign women renounce their right to drive a car or adapt to the gender segregation that defines the society beyond the university campus? Is it possible to create the relaxed collegial camaraderie that often generates new ideas over a glass of apple juice (Reizberg 2011)? How much scientific output can one produce with the limited access that private universities in Saudi Arabia grant to international scientific databases? How will Saudi Arabia benefit from the important and well-prepared human capital?

The educational realm in Saudi Arabia has without doubt undergone huge reforms in recent decades, yet a long road lies ahead. Education cannot be separated from the larger sociopolitical context in which it takes place: Educational models encourage new ideas and new thinking; however the political and social conditions of the whole system need to be taken into account.

In a country deeply entrenched in religious-social culture, one must expect to come across opposing points of view in relation to these changes. Privatisation and internationalisation are highly contested in the kingdom, as Saudi Arabia remains a very traditional, conservative society where new concepts are not easily implemented. The findings, coupled with my first-hand experience as a visiting professor at this private institution in the Eastern Province between 2007 and 2009, nevertheless suggest the need for greater private participation in the Saudi higher education sector and unified norms for its regulation.

However, with reference to the critique concerning the quality of educational institutions and its effects on the school to work transition, private higher education institutions seem to have some assets as compared to the public ones: (a) better academic performance than public schools in the past based on results in national examinations; (b) as opposed to public universities, where no expatriate students are admitted, 25% of enrolments to private universities are expatriate students; (c) better quality English language instruction thanks to more expatriate teachers (37% of all teachers as compared to 5% in public universities). All these factors also highlight the role of private higher education in the context of reform of the labour market. It seems that the government's strategy of promoting the development of private higher education – although implementation has been reluctantly pursued, involving attempts to maintain control at each step of the way – has borne some fruit in terms of raising educational opportunities for all members of society, including in rural areas, and for both male and female. However the strategy they have adopted must be categorised as experimental, involving trial and error.

> From the perspective of regulations alone, Saudi government may have appeared to be pro-active, as the government appears more concerned about controlling the private sector than facilitating its development and integration into the higher education system.
>
> JAMJOOM 2012: 228

As Al-Dali, Fnais and Newbould (2013: 136) claim:

> The more significant and difficult challenge is the development of human expertise at all levels in the private universities and colleges. If the new private institutions are to successfully surmount the criticism that the higher education system as a whole has been unable to meet the needs of Saudi society and industry, the development of more programs and approaches and, above all, the knowledge, skills and understanding of the faculty and students is now the challenge – not bricks and mortar.

There are only a few studies on the phenomenon of private universities in the kingdom, and this case study tries to give insights into the practical challenges of transplant businesses. The impact of social development on tribal and urban life in this region is one that can add depth and texture to the study of human responses to globalisation worldwide. The question remains: Will 'modern' education when separated from a 'modern' culture bring about the same results? The themes of self-definition and creative outputs are taking on ever more importance in the Southern Arabian region as globalisation and its attending ideas slowly leach into this time-bound land and its cultures. Cultural identity as a cognitive, moral and emotional system is morphing in response to the mass global media and influx of Westernised cultural models represented by the large numbers of expatriates now being engaged in the educational processes in the region. Change must come from within, and enlightened change comes from the development of a knowledge-based society holding on to the past with one hand and stretching out to the future with the other.

Works Cited

Al-Dali, W., M. Fnais and I. Newbould. 2013. "Private higher education in the Kingdom of Saudi Arabia: reality, challenges and aspirations". In L. Smith and A. Abouammoh (eds). *Higher Education in Saudi Arabia.* Dordrecht: Springer Science+Business Media, 127–136.

Alamri, M. 2011. "Higher Education in Saudi Arabia". *Journal of Higher Education Theory and Practice* 11 (4): 88–91, http://www.na-businesspress.com/jhetp/alamriweb11-4 .pdf.

Aljubaili, A. 2014. "Saudi Arabia – dramatic developments in higher education". *Showcase Asia, Middle East & Africa* 11 February, http://qsshowcase.com/main/ saudi-arabia-dramatic-developments-in-higher-education/.

Altorki, S. 2013. "Taking stock: wither the social sciences in Gulf universities". *Contemporary Arab Affairs* 6 (2): 237–250.

News Arab. 2015. "25,000 teachers to be trained abroad". *Arab News* 5 January, http:// www.arabnews.com/saudi-arabia/news/684731.

Arthur, W.J. and W.J. Bennett. 1995. "The international assignee: the relative importance of factors perceived to contribute to success". *Personnel Psychology* 48 (1): 99–114.

Batarfy, K. 2005. *Ahmad Salah Jamjoom remembering.* Jeddah, Saudi Arabia: Al-madina press establishment.

Becker, S. 1991. "Treating the American expatriate in Saudi Arabia". *International Journal of Mental Health* 20 (2): 86–93.

Beg, Ambur. 2006. "Back-seat drivers". *New Statesman* 135, no. 4820 (27 November): 21.

Bhattacharjee, Y. 2011. "Saudi universities offer cash in exchange for academic prestige". *Science* 334: 1344–1345.

Bosbait, M. and R. Wilson. 2005. "Education, school to work transitions and unemployment in Saudi Arabia". *Middle Eastern Studies* 41 (4): 533–545.

Bukhari, F. and B. Denman. 2013. "Student scholarships in Saudi Arabia: implications and opportunities for overseas engagement". In L. Smith and A. Abouammoh (eds). *Higher Education in Saudi Arabia*. Dordrecht: Springer Science+Business Media, 1–12.

Cunningham, R.B. and Y.K. Sarayrah. 1993. *Wasta: The Hidden Force in Middle Eastern Society*. London: Praeger.

De Bel-Air, F. 2014. "Demography, migration and labour market in Saudi Arabia". *European University Institute and Gulf Research Centre*, http://cadmus.eui.eu/bitstream/handle/1814/32151/GLMM%20ExpNote_01-2014.pdf?sequence=1.

Denman, B.D., and K.T. Hilal. 2011. "From barriers to bridges: an investigation on Saudi student mobility (2006–2009)". *International Review of Education* 57 (3–4): 299–318.

Doumato, E.A. 1999. "Women and Work in Saudi Arabia: How Flexible are Islamic Margins?" *Middle East Journal* 53 (4): 568–583.

Doumato, E.A. 2000. *Getting God's Ear: Women, Islam, and Healing in Saudi Arabia and the Gulf.* New York: Columbia University Press.

El-Rashidi, Y. 2005. "'Oprah' is attracting young female viewers to TV in Saudi Arabia". *Wall Street Journal – Eastern Edition* 246 (18): B1-B6.

English Islam Times. 2014. "Saudi Arabia richest and poorest". *English Islam Times.* 22 February, http://islamtimes.org/en/doc/article/354261/saudi-arabia-richest-and-poorest.

Fakeeh, M.S. 2009. "Saudization as a solution for unemployment. The case of Jeddah Western Region". Doctorate in Business Administration, University of Glasgow, 2009, http://theses.gla.ac.uk/1454/1/Fakeeh_DBA.pdf.

Feldman, D.C. and D.C. Thomas. 1991. "From Desert Shield to Desert Storm: life as an expatriate in Saudi Arabia during the Persian Gulf Crisis". *Organization Dynamics* 20 (2): 37–46.

Hamdan, A. 2005. "Women and education in Saudi Arabia: challenges and achievements". *International Education Journal,* 6 (1): 42–64.

International Monetary Fund. 2013. *Saudi Arabia. Selected Issues.* IMF Country Report No. 13/230, http://www.imf.org/external/pubs/ft/scr/2013/cr13230.pdf.

Jamjoom, Y. 2012. "Understanding Private Higher Education in Saudi Arabia – Emergence, Development and Perceptions". PhD thesis, Institute of Education, University of London, 2012, http://www.albany.edu/dept/eaps/prophe/Yussra%20Jamjoom%27s%20DISS-PHE%20in%20Saudi%20Arabia.pdf.

Kelly, M. 2011. "Balancing cultures at the American University of Kuwait". *Journal of Arabian Studies: Arabia, the Gulf, and the Red Sea* 1 (2): 201–229.

Le Renard A. 2014. "The politics of 'unveiling Saudi women': between postcolonial fantasies and the surveillance state". *Jadaliyya* 15 December, http://www.jadaliyya.com/pages/index/20259/the-politics-of-unveiling-saudi-women_between-post.

Lidstone, D. 2005. "A clear objective". *MEED: Middle East Economic Digest* 49 (50): 49–52.

Marcucci, P. and Usher A.. 2012. *2011 Year in Review: Global Changes in Tuition Fee Policies and Student Financial Assistance*. Toronto: Higher Education Strategy Associates, http://higheredstrategy.com/wp-content/uploads/2012/03/YIR2012.pdf.

Monitor Middle East. 2006. "Economic Budget". *New Budget* 2 February.

Miller-Idriss, C. and E. Hanauer. 2011. "Transnational higher education: offshore campuses in the Middle East". *Comparative Education,* 47 (2): 181–207.

Mirkin, B. 2013. *Arab Human Development Report. Arab Spring: Demographics in a Region in Transition*. Research Paper Series, United Nations Development Programme.

Moaddel, M. 2006. "The Saudi public speaks: religion, gender, and politics". *International Journal of Middle East Studies* 38 (1): 79–108.

Observatory on Borderless Higher Education. 2006. "Saudi Arabia shifts in glance eastwards for higher education collaborations", http://www.google.com/url?sa=t&rct=j&q=&esrc=s&source=web&cd=1&ved=0CB8QFjAA&url=http%3A%2F%2Fwww.obhe.ac.uk%2Fdocuments%2F2006%2FArticles%2FSaudi_Arabia_shifts_its_glance_eastwards_for_higher_education_collaborations&ei=0D41VNvKLsesPJLtgKgF&usg=AFQjCNEYMCRflP5Od6D2h1CRdqYck6fSwA&sig2=jbY2BNPtzxm316ih-Sy82Q&bvm=bv.76943099,d.ZWU.

Ones, D.S. and C. Viswesvaran. 1997. "Personality determinants in the prediction of aspects of expatriate job success". In Z. Aycan (ed.). *New Approaches to Employee Management, Vol. 4: Expatriate Management: Theory and Research*. Stamford, CT: JAI Press, 63–92.

Onsman, A. 2010. "Dismantling the perceived barriers to the implementation of national higher education accreditation guidelines in the Kingdom of Saudi Arabia". *Journal of Higher Education Policy and Management* 32 (5): 511–519.

Perspectives Parthenon. [n.d.]. "Investment opportunities in K-12 and higher education in UAE and Saudi Arabia", http://www.parthenon.com/GetFile.aspx?u=%2FLists%2FThoughtLeadership%2FAttachments%2F36%2FBFE-MENA.pdf.

PMU. [n.d.]. "Annual report 2009–2011", http://www.pmu.edu.sa/Attachments/About/PDF/Second%20annual%20report%202009-2011-%2006May2013.pdf.

Profanter, A. 2010. "Desert frontiers. The devil of education: a blessing and a curse". *Enseñanza & Teaching* 28 (1): 185–196.

Profanter, A. 2011. "The Middle East at a crossroad: an educational revolution". Paper presented at the 3rd World Conference on Educational Sciences, Istanbul, Turkey, February.

Profanter, A. and S.R. Cate. 2009. "Higher education on the center stage for change in the Middle East". Paper presented at the 3rd Redesigning Pedagogy International Conference June 2009 on Designing New Learning Contexts for a Globalising World. National Institute of Education, Nanyang Technological University, Singapore.

Profanter, A. and S.R. Cate. 2010. "A new dawn for women in higher education in Saudi Arabia: looming changes on the horizon". In V. Piacenti and E. Maestri (eds). *Saudi Arabia and Women in Higher Education and Cultural Dialogue. New Perspectives.* Milan: CRiSSMA-Research Centre on the Southern System and Wider Mediterranean, Università Cattolica del Sacro Cuore, 25–54.

Reizberg, L. 2011. "Saudi Arabia's extravagant investment in higher education: is money enough?" *Inside Higher ED* 10 May, http://www.insidehighered.com/blogs/the_world_view/saudi_arabia_s_extravagant_investment_in_higher_education_is_money_enough.

Rubin, B. 2006. *The Long War for Freedom. The Arab Struggle for Democracy in the Middle East.* New Jersey: John Wiley & Sons.

Saleh, M.S. 1986. "Development of higher education in Saudi Arabia". *Higher Education* 15 (1–2): 17–23, http://link.springer.com/article/10.1007%2FBF00138089.

Salih M. 2014. *Economic Development and Political Action in the Arab World.* New York: Routledge, https://books.google.it/books?id=SYX8AgAAQBAJ&pg=PA78&lpg=PA78&dq=poorest+province+in+KSA&source=bl&ots=O8kfT3iBrK&sig=qsGIdCdw73aXg-7BpIrpZty1UfU&hl=de&sa=X&ei=QDe1VNfhDsy7UaOjg9gN&ved=0CDQQ6AEwBQ#v=onepage&q=poorest%20province%20in%20KSA&f=false.

Saudi Arabia. Ministry of Higher Education. [n.d.](a)a. "Brief report on the Ninth Development Plan (2010–2014)", http://fanack.com/fileadmin/user_upload/Documenten/Links/Saudi_Arabia/Report_Ninth_Development_Plan.pdf.

Saudi Arabia. Ministry of Higher Education. [n.d.](b)b. "Private higher education", http://www.mohe.gov.sa/en/ministry/general-administration-for-public-relations/bookslist/book6eng.pdf.

Saudi Arabia. Ministry of Higher Education.2009. "Saudi's higher education achievements & challenges. Global assessment & international experts' views", http://www.mohe.gov.sa/en/default.aspx.

Saudi Arabia. Ministry of Higher Education.2011. "The current status of higher education in the Kingdom of Saudi Arabia", http://www.mohe.gov.sa/en/Ministry/General-administration-for-Public-relations/BooksList/stat7eng.pdf.

Sawahel, W. 2010. "Saudi Arabia: rapid growth for universities". *University World News* 22 August, http://www.universityworldnews.com/article.php?story=20100820171202577.

Scholte, J.A. 2005. *Globalization: A critical introduction.* 2nd ed. New York: Palgrave Macmillan.

Shehada, N. 2009. "House of obedience: social norms, individual agency, and historical contingency". *Journal of Middle East Women's Studies* 5 (1): 24–49.

Tétreault, M.A. 2003. "Kuwait: sex, violence, and the politics of economic restructuring". In A. Doumato and M. Posusneym (eds). *Women and Globalization in the Arab Middle East: Gender, Economy and Society*. Boulder, CO: Lynne Rienner, 215–238.

U.S-Saudi Arabian Business Council. [n.d.]. "Saudi Arabia's 2015 budget maintains strong spending, diversification initiatives", http://www.us-sabc.org/custom/news/details.cfm?id=1645#.VLQttnvlxko.

Unicef. [n.d.]. *Saudi Arabia Statistics.* http://www.unicef.org/infobycountry/saudiarabia_statistics.html.

United Nations Development Programme. [n.d.]. "Human development data for the Arab states. Saudi Arabia. 2012", http://www.arab-hdr.org/data/profiles/SAU.aspx.

Vidyasagar, G. and D.M. Rea. 2004. "Saudi women doctors: gender and careers within Wahhabic Islam and a 'westernised' work culture". *Women's Studies International Forum* 27 (3): 261–280.

World Bank. [n.d.]. "World Bank and Islamic Development Bank join forces to improve quality and relevance of education", http://www.worldbank.org/en/news/press-release/2014/10/12/world-bank-and-islamic-development-bank-join-forces-to-improve-quality-and-relevance-of-education.

CHAPTER 7

In Search of the Private: On the Specificities of Private Higher Education in Germany*

Alexander Mitterle

Introduction

Private higher education in Germany is considerably under-studied. As Roger Geiger (1985, 385) put it decades ago, the few who raised "the issue of private higher education were voices crying in the wilderness". This was for a simple reason: in 1995 only about 2,700 freshmen took up their studies at a private university, amounting to around 16,000 enrolled students in the sector during the same year. This was less than 1% of the overall student population. Until recently the private sector did not play any relevant role in higher education. Within the context of the overall expansion of higher education during the last decade, private higher education's share has increased considerably: in 2012 the number of freshmen was – with around 35,000 students – nearly 13 times as many, and the number of enrolled students amounted to 138,000, nearly nine times as much. Today private higher education accounts for 6% of the total student body enrolled at German universities (Stat. Bundesamt 2014c).

This expansion is not reflected in the literature. Recent publications either discuss the potential for elite reproduction among a small number of universities in the private sector under the rather distracting title "private higher education in Germany" (Doelle 2013) or concentrate on aspects of management (Frank *et al.* 2010; Sperlich 2006, 2008). The research is either statistical (Stanneken & Ziegele 2005; Darraz *et al.* 2009) or anecdotal from self-experience (Konegen-Grenier 1996). Very often it is conducted by researchers involved in private higher education (Brockhoff 2003, 2011; Müller-Böling & Zürn 2007). The most profound discussion of the private sector universities is rooted in law and addresses the form and the status of private compared to the public universities from a judicial standpoint (Steinkemper 2002; Kämmerer 2003). There is so far no substantial discussion of why private higher education is expanding nor on the structural differences between private and public higher education in Germany.

* The article is based on research conducted in the research project "Elite formation and higher education" as part of the DFG-research group "Mechanisms of elite education" (FOR 1612). I especially thank Jörn Franke for his help with some of the data.

In the following I aim to address both. First I give a broad overview of the German private higher education sector. I use Roger Geiger's typification of private higher education as 'different', 'more' or 'better' to explain what purposes private universities traditionally serve within German higher education. With severe structural change taking place recently I further develop how this impacts on the purposes of private higher education. While several similarities between the public and the private are visible, private universities are primarily student demand-oriented – both with reference to 'different' and to 'more'. In contrast, public universities follow multiple pathways that partially have opposite effects. Aspects of 'better' education are difficult to trace as the German higher education system has only recently started to stratify among same-level degrees. Even though aspiring private universities seem to be among the first to develop specific distinctive arrangements, most can be also found among various public universities. In using on-site experience and interviews from three case studies I show that access, admission and ambassador policies are particularly useful in producing an institutional distinction between public and aspiring private universities. Because of specific regulatory schemes and their size, the latter are more able to use organisational borders to alleviate their standing.

State Accredited Private Higher Education in Germany – The Rise of a Still Unsettled Sector

Despite its small size, private higher education is not a new phenomenon in Germany. In fact the University of Cologne, the Goethe-University in Frankfurt and the University of Mannheim all arose from – to a certain degree – private founding initiatives. Cologne[1] and Mannheim were former German *Handelshochschulen* (business schools) destined to educate local business leaders for the early twentieth century, while Frankfurt arose from an initiative of its mayor and local elites in 1912/1914. Most *Handelshochschulen* and non-state universities were, however, integrated into the public sector during National Socialism and in the reordering of the public sectors after 1945 (Meyer 1998; Pfeiff 2009). Figure 7.1 depicts the cumulated founding dates of still existing state-accredited private universities by period according to reports by the universities themselves. While several of these were founded

---

1   Cologne was originally founded as a full university in 1388 by citizens of the free town Cologne. However, it was closed down by French revolutionary troops in 1798. The re-foundation in the early nineteenth century arose from the *Handelshochschule*.

before 1945, their status and structure have considerably changed. The old-est still existing business school in Germany, the *Handelshochschule Leipzig*, for example, was founded in 1898, subsumed under the *Führer*-principle in National Socialism, integrated into Leipzig University in 1946, retransformed into a semi-autonomous socialist leadership school in 1953, re-merged with the university in 1969 and was re-founded after the fall of the Berlin Wall in 1992 through a concerted initiative of state and private actors (cf. Göschel 2008). The *Hochschule Georg Agricola* on the other hand was founded in 1816 as a mining school but only transformed into an engineering degree granting high-er education institution in 1963 as a response to a regional mining crisis and growing academisation (TFH Georg Agricola 2012).

Both the legal status and the meaning of 'private' through all these years have varied considerably. Overall what counts as private sector in Germany today comprises universities that have been state-accredited and those that are church-aligned. The latter are treated as autonomous due to the specific historical status of the Protestant and Catholic religion in Germany. They have only marginally profited from the expansion in student numbers. Non-accred-ited cross-border private providers exist in Germany (such as the Asklepios Medical School in Hamburg, a branch-campus of the Semmelweis University in Budapest, or the GISMA campus in Hannover), they are however difficult to track. Their degrees are not directly recognised by the German state but indirectly through bilateral agreements between third states and the German federal republic. The chapter therefore discusses only state-accredited private higher education. From a regulatory point of view accredited private higher education institutions are such higher education providers that have provided sufficient funding capacity and credentials to sustain a university and thus have been recognised by the German state in which they reside[2] as legitimate degree granting institutions. They can include aspiring universities as well as regional education providers, and provide both non-profit and for-profit edu-cation. Private higher education through governmental accreditation goes back to the 1980s and is a result of pressure by private founding initiatives in the late 1970s (Schily 2007). Compared to countries such as the US (Geiger 2014), private higher education is not something that arose in a period of loose state-control but rather a distinct entitlement arising out of a state with strong regulatory powers. They are therefore not private *per se* but private by public will.[3]

---

2 Within the federal political system of Germany, education has so far remained the sole re-sponsibility of the individual states.

3 Lorenz (1996) argues that this makes them public institutions, too.

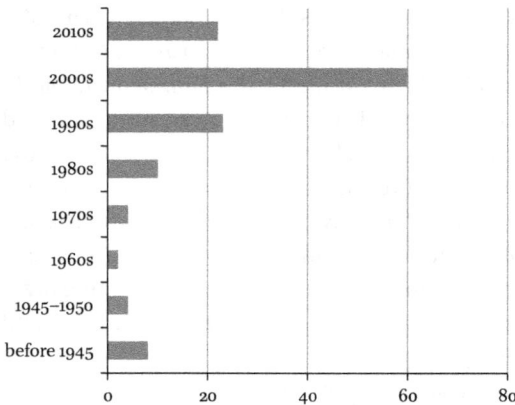

FIGURE 7.1 *Number of private universities founded, data from 2014*
SOURCE: *HOCHSCHULKOMPASS*, NOVEMBER 2014

While proponents of private higher education (Jansen 2007) have com-
plained that the accreditation procedures have become more complicated, the
number of newly accredited private providers suggests otherwise. In fact, the
expansion of student numbers is not met – as in the public sector – by a stable
number of existing universities but is paralleled by a rapidly expanding number of private higher education institutions. Brauns (2003) already counted 52
organisations in 2003 and remarked a considerable expansion since the 1990s,
the *Hochschulkompass* of the German rectors' conference now lists a total of
119 state accredited private universities to date (Figure 7.1).[4]

Private universities within the sector range from regional universities of applied sciences, large part-time and further education granting organisations, to
full-scale universities and aspiring top universities within a specific field that
have PhD and habilitation granting rights.[5]

Broadly speaking the purpose of private higher education in Germany within the overall higher education sector resonates with what Roger Geiger (1986)
called: "more, better or different". In his cross-country study of private higher
education, he concluded that private higher education occurred in

---

4 Several however belong to various groups of education providers (such as SRH higher education institutions or the medical schools in Hamburg and Berlin).

5 The German university system is traditionally divided between teaching-centered universities of applied sciences without PhD-granting rights and the research universities, *'Universität'*, with an equal focus on research and teaching. Most private universities belong to
   the first group. The Bologna Process has, however, equalised the degrees of the two types of
   institutions. I will only voice the distinction where necessary and speak of universities including both groups.

cases in which *more* higher education was demanded than was provided
by the state, *different* kinds of schools from those provided, and cases in
which qualitatively *better* education was sought.

GEIGER 1985, 387

As public higher education in Germany is free of charge,[6] and private universities need a considerable income in tuition fees to sustain themselves, private
higher education prospers where the public sector does not accommodate
demands by potential students. It traditionally covers demand from those having problems acquiring study places within the state system, those in search
of a degree to increase their career chances, and those who aim for a distinctive degree on the same level or above that of the public university sector. The
subjects indeed cover 'niche' degrees such as anthroposophy, social work and
religious studies, but also natural sciences at a few research universities, and
mainstream business related degrees (cf. WR 2012). Private universities have
also been innovative in offering degrees for job profiles that have hitherto been
dominated by apprenticeships (e.g. nursing) (cf. Schily 2007, 18; Brockhoff 2011).
Notwithstanding this spread of different disciplines, the majority of students
is inscribed in law, social sciences and business administration/economics
(*Wirtschaftswissenschaften*[7]) (68%). In fact half of all students study some
form of business administration/economics.[8] While some universities offer
research-intensive degrees (such as the Jacobs University in Bremen and the
University Witten-Herdecke) the majority of students is inscribed in professional social science programmes with a strong practical orientation (Sperlich
2008). This has also to do with the low organisational costs for social sciences
degrees. The costs for students are, however, comparatively high. In 2012 the
average tuition fee at a state accredited private university amounted to 578€
per month. The spectrum ranges from zero (state subsidised) in a very small
number of degrees to 4,166€ for MBAS and executive MBAS.[9]

---

6 There are small administration fees per semester that include services such as public
   transportation.

7 *Wirtschaftswissenschaften* is a classificatory degree combination that does not exist in this
   form in other countries. It combines economics, management and business administration.
   In the following I will refer to it as business administration/economics.

8 Most of the universities offer only a small number of degree programmes. More than half of
   them provide fewer than three disciplinarily distinct degrees. 64% of all degree programmes
   are cross-disciplinary and connected to business administration/economics.

9 If not explicitly stated, all figures arise from a 2012 in-depth analysis of the private higher education sector. We analysed mission statements, rankings, newspaper articles and organisational data of 105 state-accredited private higher education organisations. The data is based on

In order to survive private higher education institutions in Germany address all three rationales Geiger has described. They have to provide education that either differs considerably from public university degrees, responds to a growing demand for scarce public study places, or is better than what is offered in the public sector.

The strong tendency towards the field of business administration/economics as well as the rapid growth in the number of universities since 2000 indicates that the private sector has not reached a state of maturity. Compared to the public sector it is still rather unstable. Reisz and Stock (2009; same data: Lenhardt, Reisz and Stock 2012) show that between 1980 and 2006, 24 of 131 private universities closed down. In the same time period only 21 out of 292 state universities ceased to exist. While the authors do not refer to the aspirations of the closed down universities, they find no specific indicator to suggest why private higher education providers close.[10] Such closures have hit both regional private universities and those aspiring for the top. Of nine private universities that were described by Brauns as aiming to become top of their discipline in 2003 (one was not state accredited), two have already closed, one became insolvent in 2013, and two have considerable funding problems.

The reasons are mostly financial. Private higher education institutions in general have six financing options: tuition fees, foundation capital, private contributions, profit from further education, research and other offerings (e.g. event facilities), state subsidies, interest and profits from capital investment, and speculations (Brockhoff 2011, 19). Practice-oriented, non-aspiring private universities of applied sciences cover 55% of their budget through tuition fees. The minority of these are profit-oriented (WR 2012, 32). Their student-staff relations are in several cases worse than in the public sector. Non-profit universities in general benefit from tax exemptions and student support through the federal need-based funding scheme for students. In aspiring universities which emphasise research next to teaching and which are in all cases non-profit, tuition fees cover only around 30% of the budget (WR 2012, 52; Frank *et al.* 2010). These universities struggle to use the other financing sources to maintain and advance their offerings. The small group of leading private universities has either gained considerable support from non-profit foundations, has been

---

www.hochschulkompass.de and expanded through intensive research and actualisation via the websites of the respective private institutions (cf. Mitterle *et al.* Forthcoming; Mitterle & Stock 2015).

10   They test student numbers, founding date, size of the teaching body, PhD and habilitation granting rights, student-staff relations, completion rates.

successful in obtaining larger donations from various sources,[11] or has received state money and support.[12] While business schools are more successful in acquiring funds from various donors, aspiring universities in other fields are very often backed by a single large foundation. The 2000s in particular have seen the rise of the aspiring foundation-funded private university. The Hertie School of Governance in Berlin, the Bucerius Law School in Hamburg, the Zeppelin University in Friedrichshafen, are all dependent on regular contributions from their name-giving foundations. If such contributions dry out, problems arise (cf. Ibid. 48–49). This is the case for the Jacobs University in Bremen. All in all, decreases in donation willingness, changes in student flows or changes in decision making of the supporting foundations[13] can directly impact on the existence of private universities as none of them have to date built up and maintained considerable endowment funds.[14] Accreditation reports from the science council as well as data from Frank *et al.* (2010) suggest that most German private universities live from hand to mouth, struggling to expand their resources.

With a growing number of students in private higher education, this situation may improve. Non-aspiring universities of applied sciences can enrol more students, thereby increasing their funding range, and the competitive admission barriers at aspiring institutions may warrant tuition increases as well as donation money. Yet the expansion of the private sector also goes hand in hand with structural changes in the sector as a whole.

The Effects of Differentiation and Student Expansion on German Private Higher Education

The participation of an age cohort in higher education has been rising steadily since 2007 and has recently passed the 50% level. Whether this is an effect of

---

11   The implementation of the foundation law reform in 2002 (amended in 2007) positions donations to universities at the highest level of tax deduction among non-profit, common-good oriented corporations.

12   A survey by the Science Council (WR 2012, 46, 166) shows 24 out of 58 responding private universities receive some form of state subsidies (seed and project funding).

13   However, this is a long-term approach. The foundations have given funding warranties for the respective universities to obtain state accreditation.

14   As far as the data is accessible, the ESMT in Berlin seems to be backed by the largest endowment fund, covering more than 120 million euros, and is hence relatively stable, with a slight surplus since 2010 and annual expenses of around 33 million euros (cf. WR 2013, 72).

a long-term drift towards higher education (Frank & Meyer 2007; Baker 2014) and credentialism (Collins 1979) or whether this can be attributed to the Bologna Process is unclear. The Bologna Process, however, has introduced certain structural changes into higher education that have impacted on expansion and have given it a certain form that also has specific effects for private higher education. I will hence discuss how the distinction of "different, more or better" has been changing in recent years, and continues to do so.

'Different'?

The Bologna Process abandoned the old German degree structure of diploma and magister degrees, and replaced it with a two-tiered system of bachelor's and master's degrees. While the former ended after at least four to five years of studies with a master's equivalent degree, the new system introduced six or seven semester bachelor programmes usually followed by two to four semester master's. Not only did the Bologna Process introduce a hierarchy of degrees, each of which comes with a set of admission procedures, but it also changed the structure of the curricula. Until the reforms most degree programmes were highly regulated through so-called *"Rahmenprüfungsordnungen"* (Framework regulations for examination). These originated in a consensual decision process that codified the number of examinations and broad themes a discipline had to cover (Immer 2013). The themes were connected to respective sub-themes of a discipline and provided sufficient leeway for course offerings on the local level. It however maintained a common core within each discipline that suggested similar or equivalent education among the same degree programmes across Germany. Private education providers could hence offer education that cut across such disciplinary lines, that was more international, that was part-time or had a more practical approach than the discipline-driven degrees of the public sector. They could also be more innovative in offering bachelor's and master's degrees at a time when the public sector was still operating in the 'old' framework (Bloch 2009; WR 2012). With a re-drafting of the curricula in most degree programmes through the Bologna reforms, the framework regulations were abandoned in favour of a more or less voluntary quality assurance system that accredited both state and private universities within a discipline. Such an assessment was based less on disciplinary coherence but more on formal aspects of 'studyability' (*'Studierfähigkeit'*) and 'employability'. A "radical differentiation" (Schröder 2014) took place that led to a horizontal diversification of degree programmes on the public side. This means that the nationwide homogeneity of degree programmes was substituted by a variety of offers that were more interdisciplinary, more experimental or more specialised – or just had a new name.[15] The 'different' niche of private higher education now experiences competition from the public sector itself. It however also produces disorientation on the part of potential students as a larger variety of study options exists (Schneider & Franke 2014, 34). In these circumstances rankings and marketing aspects become more important, to which the private education providers have already developed consistent approaches.[16] Also the growing percentage of an age cohort going to university may create higher incentives for those without a degree programme to return – at least part-time – to a university in order to obtain a degree. As argued before, a large number of private universities have specialised in providing and adjusting to such educational demands. Apart from universities such as the "Fernuniversität Hagen" (Distance University of Hagen) the public higher education sector has so far only partially targeted these groups. According to the *Hochschulkompass* (accessed September 2014) around 60% of the degrees offered both, distance and part-time education are provided by private universities. Overall the age structure of students at private universities is more diverse than at public universities.[17]

'More'?

The expansion in overall student numbers has had mostly positive effects for the private higher education sector. The number of students applying to private higher education institutions is rising. Some reasons for this lie in the specific structure of the public higher education sector and a lack of proportionate funding increases for public higher education by the responsible ministries. In fact several state ministries have aimed at decreasing their spending following a prognosis of a soon-to-come decrease in student numbers (KMK 2012). Public higher education institutions are hence restrained in providing a sufficient number of study places for potential students. A potential lack of study places goes hand in hand with the specific form in which such places in Germany are distributed. While students are free to choose their own degree programme, the logic of German higher education policy has been strongly influenced by the demands of the labour market since the 1970s. This labour market was

---

15   Our own data shows a considerable variation, especially at the master's level, in the naming of political sciences and business administration/economics degrees (we used data from www.hochschulkompass.de in 2014 and then updated and expanded the given information via department websites).

16   While only the leading ones make much of rankings, most private universities have marketing personnel of some sort.

17   In 2012, 66% of students in the private higher education were under 30 years old, compared to 84% in the public sector (Stat. Bundesamt 2014a).

envisaged as providing a very stable job-structure that was populated by various streams of graduates. Within such a picture the rising student numbers, especially in the social sciences and humanities, led to cyclical discussions and fear of over-education. Governmental perspective was and is therefore more focused on introducing measures that respond to perceived deficiencies in specific disciplines (e.g. a regularly voiced lack of engineers) than responding to a growing student demand for a specific discipline (cf. Stock 2014).[18] While unemployment rates for graduates in specific disciplines influence potential students' choice of study, they do not seem to have much impact on students in social sciences and economics. Compared to teaching or engineering degrees, the degree choice of freshmen in social sciences and economics seem to not resonate with changes unemployment prospects (Reisz & Stock 2013, 149).

For a long time, higher education institutions were able to respond to variable demand-streams. Not because they were adequately equipped for asynchronous demand increases but because they were restrained from installing entrance barriers. According to a constitutional court decision in 1972, the German constitution entitles every citizen to pursue their chosen work-trajectory provided that they have obtained the necessary credential – in this case the highest secondary degree (*Abitur*). Consequentially higher education institutions are only allowed to implement admission procedures if they can prove that additional students would lead to an unintended prolongation of the study duration of the other students (cf. Mitterle *et al.* 2014; Winter 2013), i.e. that they do not have enough personnel to teach more students. With the considerable rise in freshmen numbers the capacity for taking in students without restrictions seems to have come more or less to an end in high-demand degree programmes. According to university self-reports, 45.5% of all degree programmes applied admission barriers in 2012 (Herdin & Hachmeister 2014). That the number is not higher is due to a lack of transparency in the German higher education sector and the main factor in university choice, which is still the distance to the potential student's home-town. Also there is a considerable preference for larger than for small cities (Herdin & Hachmeister 2014, 12). While potential students write a growing number of applications to universities in different cities there seems to be a considerable overlap of cities students want to go to. That other higher education institutions may have

---

18   The narrative of the taxi-driving philosopher is constantly voiced among students, and
      the press resonates with such a perception. However, as Reisz and Stock (2013) have
      shown, mismatches between graduates and job prospects are resolved to a large degree
      by a more flexible labour market.

places still available is beyond their reach.[19] In other words, in order to understand why private higher education is expanding despite its high tuition fees, a possible answer might lie in growing access problems to the public sector. This means potential students who want to take up a degree in a specific discipline that has high admission barriers in the public sector may opt to study at a private university; they are crowded out of the public sector.

It is however difficult to statistically ground such a hypothesis. So far there is no publicly available information on how many study places a university can provide and how many freshmen have chosen private universities, or for what reasons. It is, however, possible to look at data in the public and the private sector within a discipline to see whether developments in the public sector (e.g. student number growth) go parallel with developments in the private that would support such a hypothesis. There are two distinct transition points where crowding-out effects, i.e. access problems, into the private higher education sector are possible: First at the freshmen level and second with the transition from Bachelor to Master.

Given the dominance of business administration/economics in private higher education I will concentrate on this discipline to discuss crowding-out effects.[20] As argued above, at least business administration/economics intake numbers seem not to respond to employment prospects on the labour market.[21] They have been growing more steadily compared to other disciplines. As soon as the number of applications exceeds the number of places in the public sector, a growth in admission barriers should be visible. With more student applications than places in the given discipline, admission barriers are increasing. And indeed today around 78% of the public bachelor's programmes in business administration/economics have some form of admission barrier other than the *Abitur* installed. Parallel to the increasing admission barriers in the public sector the number of freshmen in private higher education increased. While in 2000 less than 1% of freshmen chose a private university, roughly 18% of all students in this discipline today study there (Stat. Bundesamt 2014a). Apart from health sciences (49% of all bachelor graduates in the field), which

---

19   A national internet platform for making open study places visible across Germany is still struggling for the necessary support from the higher education sector.

20   There are other important degree programmes in the private sector relative to the public sector, namely business engineering (9%), mining (10%), psychology (11%), design (11%), health sciences (42%) [relationship of enrolled students in private higher education to the overall student number (Stat. Bundesamt 2014a)].

21   www.hochschulkompass.de (September 2014) adjusted by data of all degree-providing faculty websites (including university-wide lists of restricted degree programmes).

can be explained by the rather recent academisation of programmes such as nursing or medical pedagogy ('different'), no other degree programme shows a similar expansion. Apparently a high number of access barriers in the public sector is paralleled by a rapid increase in private business administration/ economics enrolment numbers. As the data does not differ between students inscribed in bachelor's or master's programmes, the expansive effects are not directly traceable to a level of education. Neither is it so far clear whether similar crowding-out effects exist in the transition from bachelor's to master's level. The number of master's level students in private higher education can indicate whether the private sector profits from possible transition problems from bachelor's to master's level.[22] If it does not we can assume that the expansion in the private sector takes place mostly at undergraduate level. As there is no direct data on private master's freshmen per discipline available we have to draw on overall master-level completion rates (old system degrees + bachelor/ master), which to a certain extent lag behind rising enrolment numbers. The data clearly indicates that no overall expansion of the number of master's level students in the private sector has taken place. It remains rather stable at between 7,500 and 8,000 graduates a year. We can conclude that for this level a potential crowding-out effect into the private sector is not visible.

However, if we look at those universities that are classified as research oriented *Universität* the picture changes. Since 2008 the number of master's level graduates, while still rather small, has grown by 76% (Stat. Bundesamt 2014d; Stat. Bundesamt 2014b).

The data indicates that one can cautiously point to some kind of relationship between the high rise in the number of business administration/economics students in private higher education and the scarcity of equivalent places in public higher education at bachelor's level. While credential-seeking older professionals (see *"Different?"*) may also play a role, the majority of students are in their twenties and potentially compete for places in undergraduate degrees at public universities (Stat. Bundesamt 2014a). At master's level an expansion seems so far only to be taking place at universities that position themselves as equal or 'better' to the public sector. Here the subjects offered are more diverse and a crowding-out of good students from the public sector into master's degrees at aspiring private universities is at least questionable.

---

22   Overall my own calculations of the bachelor's graduates and master's freshmen do suggest transition problems within the classificatory field of law, social sciences and economics, if they are contrasted with surveys on transition willingness of undergraduate students.

'Better'?

If we now look at aspects of the 'better' of private higher education, the Bologna Process seems to have introduced ambivalent changes. On the one side the increasing horizontal differentiation in the public sector has made the borders between public and private more diffuse. In addition to the liberation of the curricula as argued above, the public sector has been experiencing liberation in governance regulation and an increase in competitive funding mechanisms (research and teaching). A growing horizontal differentiation with more formal quality assurance procedures initiated aspirations among some degree programmes in the public sector.[23] Also the publication of rankings (CHE, Shanghai ranking etc.) and the so called Excellence Initiative that granted the title 'elite university' to a small number of public universities led to a growing atmosphere of distinctiveness.

Especially aspiring private universities have argued and still are arguing that they provide a specific atmosphere – a 'spirit' as several call it, better study conditions, more internationality and career options than the public do. The product they provide is adequately remunerated through the high tuition fees they charge. Critics on the other hand argue that these fees primarily function as instruments for elite reproduction (cf. Friedrich 2009; Doelle 2014). Several such aspiring universities have however installed need-blind admission policies and they provide funding possibilities for those without the direct means to pay for their tuition fees. Also, social stratification research indicates that so far no elite universities have been established in Germany (Kaina 2004; Hartmann 2009).

In fact service offers that were traditionally stronger at aspiring private universities can now be found among most of the public universities (cf. Teichler and Mercator 2010). Nevertheless, aspiring private universities have on average far better professor-student relationships than public universities (WR 2012), which can be regarded as a strong indicator of study quality.

The growing number of students graduating at master's level at aspiring universities indicate that promising students are drawn to the private sector. This is also reflected in the proportionally high number of non-private, merit-based foundational scholarships awarded to students at these universities (WR2012). Yet from a sector analysis such stratificatory aspects are difficult to trace. Vertical differentiation is still a very new phenomenon in the rather egalitarian German higher education system (cf. Kreckel 2010). Thus to understand

---

23   This is the case for political science and business administration/economics, which our
     research group is studying in a follow-up project.

why aspiring universities may draw good students we have to look at stratification through qualitative research and on-site experience.

Next to various forms of vertical differentiation that can be both found in private and public universities (cf. Bloch *et al.* 2014), private universities as organisations that essentially produce a private good can be more clearly stratified on grounds of access and belonging. To a greater extent than public universities they can engage in a process that I call 'bordering' in order to improve their position. Bordering in this sense is a fine-grained process of relational formation that is somewhat restricted in public universities, as both their buildings and personnel are strongly rooted within the public space and domain.

Methodological Remarks: The Private Universities and Bordering Practices

Organisations do not function as monolithic blocs. They are moving targets that change their form depending on their perspective. They reach out, develop and depend on relations that reach beyond their walls (Czarniawska 2013; Latour 2013a). They cannot be understood without the outside but their relationship to the outside can vary. While it is common to describe organisational borders through forms of membership (Kühl 2011), it is less common to look at organising processes from a theoretical perspective that concentrates on bordering practices as a distinct socio-material movement. In the case of private education, this involves a perspective that follows the Latin origins of the word 'private' – *privatus, privare* – and looks for movements of dissection. The focus thereby is not on describing the excluded or included as a group *per se* but rather on describing the directed relations that form the border between a part of the organisation and something perceived as 'outside'. In other words, bordering is a collective engagement of human and non-human actors that defines some of these actors (a group, a person, an artefact etc.) as external to the organisation through the construction of some form of hurdle.[24] For example a wall only becomes a hurdle in such bordering practices if someone wants to reach something on the other side. What makes the private distinct in bordering practices is its difference to similar practices in public universities. While there is a stratificatory aspect to such bordering practices I will concentrate on explaining how such borders are built along three examples: admission

---

24   Organisational borders are blurry and mostly theoretical if they are not formed and visible through such specific processes (cf. Weick 1995).

policies, location and student ambassadors. I will also discuss why this can be attributed to aspiring private rather than public universities in Germany.

The examples draw on organisational case studies at three private universities (pseudonyms: Big Town Private University, Paxheim Private University, and International Private University). They were chosen from a leading cluster after a field analysis of all 105 state-accredited private universities in 2012 (Mitterle *et al.* Forthcoming). The universities at which the research takes place offer only a small number of degree programmes which lie within the broad disciplinary field of law, social sciences and business administration/economics, and finish with a master level degree.

Different to ethnographic approaches, the case studies do not involve participant observation within the universities over a longer time period. This is because access to private higher education institutions is rather difficult and raises cost issues.[25] Hence interviews with students, administration and academia undertaken between November 2012 and February 2015 are core to our case studies. These are contrasted by participant observation of specific events, namely enrolment and graduation ceremonies, career and networking events, extracurricular and public events, as well as single-time course participation. For the purpose of this chapter I narrow the analysis to interviews with students (N=50) and experience from participant observation. As explained above, the theoretical perspective aims at unravelling micro-situational relationships of bordering. It does not aim to provide a thick description of the organisational or disciplinary proceedings but rather detailed descriptions of relationships that help to explain cross-organisational similarities with regard to the private. Therefore, in order to maintain the anonymity of the studied organisations within the rather small field of private higher education, I will specify neither discipline nor location.

Bordering through Admission

As already shown, admission barriers are not uncommon in German higher education. In order to avoid negative court rulings, they are usually constructed along *Abitur* grades and involve the enrolment of students who apply, best grades first, until the degree programme reaches full capacity. The grade of

---

25   Courses are products the universities sell. They involve conditions of good student-staff relationships and a sense of familiarity. Intrusion over a longer time period by the researcher would raise several issues that would make universities and professors less likely to agree to cooperate. As our research on public degree programmes has not yet started, I lack comparative experience and hesitate to treat this experience as distinctive of private higher education.

the last enrolled student is the so-called *numerus clausus*-grade. While some programmes now include interviews and paper-based tests, they all refer to a maximum intake capacity which, as stated before, is a sign of programme overload. Public higher education institutions have thus only marginal control of their intake number (without risking law-suits) and can only introduce selective admission barriers if the degree is overcrowded. Therefore information on admission is scattered over their websites and, due to annual variations, in a majority of cases difficult to obtain (Mitterle *et al.* 2015; Bloch *et al.* 2015a).[26] For private higher education, however, constitutional restrictions do not apply. They can base admissions on reasons of quality, exclusivity, or to improve completion rates. They can also use admission to construct a visible border. Such borders are commonly seen as fissures that restrain people from entering, but by viewing them through the perspective of socio-material ordering they become the opposite. They are very densely tied networks that assemble various actors (cf. Latour 2013b) in order to create stratificatory visibility. At the outset, admission procedures at all the institutions demanded a large range of documents (language test, letters of reference, motivation letters, cv, GMAT etc.), followed by a multiple step procedure, including interviews and/or entry exams. While the careful choice of students may intentionally involve qualitative considerations, several aspects arise that are in no need of any legitimation. First, the multiple-step admission process makes it possible to visibly exclude students in order to position the university. State universities do not advertise the number of students that have applied or the numbers that have been accepted, but aspiring private universities state these publicly. The number of failed applicants is intentionally included in the border precisely in order to increase its visibility as a border. Second, the more steps admission procedures demand, the more challenging it seems to enter. While this may discourage some potential students from applying, it visibly expands the "sacrifices to get here", as one dean remarked (Field Notes EL II, Paxheim Private University).

> And one has to say, and I think that is a factor that is rather important, if you are accepted by [private university 1], ... you are flattered. Because this whole procedure, one goes through, I mean one meets with other people and it is constantly communicated: this is a really difficult entry exam and afterwards you have to go to the oral exam etc. And then it

---

26   This is the result of a review of admission procedures in business administration/economics and political sciences at all public higher education institutions which I undertook with Jörn Franke.

really is a procedure, which is different to if you just sent your Abitur to [a state university] and two weeks later you get a letter saying: "yes, that's ok".

> Transl. Student 1, Big Town Private U, l. 49–56

Crossing the border as a sharing experience that provides an initial reference point for the successful applicants also levers them in their self-perception.

> The big advantage is that they can choose whoever they want. [One of the professors] ... calls it the LEGO-theory. That means you can just choose the people here well and then have them play with LEGO the whole day. We would probably still go out and find our way. It is really difficult to measure what the impact of the university is.
>
> Transl. Student 2, International Private University, l. 1363–1368

Exactly because the entrants are contrasted to those that could not enter, and professors refer to this border crossing as being special, students perceive themselves as initially 'chosen', meant to 'find' their 'way'. It is these specific relationships and dimensions that form and evolve around borders. They visibly drop the unsuccessful, build seemingly uncrossable walls, elevate the successful, and, in a re-referral, increase the prestige of the organisation for being chosen by such students.

Locational Bordering

Another form of bordering that is visible in aspiring private universities is a spatial seclusion of the university's premises. While admissions create a relational border that surrounds the curriculum, two of the three universities we researched have installed very material borders. I will discuss these on the basis of quotes from field notes from two on-site visits. In the first case I was attending a course, in the second an evening event:

> I am standing ... in front of a glass door, 15 minutes too early. The door can only be opened with a chip [that is only distributed to members of the university]. I had specifically planned in some extra time as I knew I would not be able to get to the seminar room without the help of others. ... Nobody comes. [After a while] I see an international student approach the glass door from the other side. He opens the door .... He is very kind and allows me in. I walk down the corridor, make a turn at a side-corridor and am confronted with the next problem. The seminar room is further

down [the side-corridor] and likewise closed by as glass door. Students are sitting in the room and are working.

Transl. field notes, course II, International Private University

I say goodbye and leave the room. I don't get far. I stand in front of a glass door which leads into the entrance hall, which however I cannot open. I look for a button to pass the door but there isn't one. ... A student comes along and asks me whether I want to leave and how I got here in the first place. I tell him that I was at the event, while he uses his student id to open the door. I leave.

Transl. field notes, evening event I, Paxheim Private University

Both cases show how I was confronted with the material circumstances of a glass door within the university. As I do not have the respective key, I am locked out in the first case, locked in in the second. While for me the door creates an obstacle to moving through the university premises, students can easily pass through by swiping their ID card. At first glance the door seems to function as a gatekeeper (cf. Latour 1996) that dissects the non-members from the organisation. With the exception of medical premises, movement through public universities is not restricted. If doors are closed at public universities, they are usually also closed for enrolled students. This applies likewise to services such as the university archive or the library, which may include a small fee, but in general are open to the public. Libraries in private universities on the other hand may provide access under special circumstances but in all three cases are restricted to fee-paying students and enrolled PhD students. While moving through the narrow corridors of a private university may be in the interest of a researcher who studies this specific organisation, it is nothing the average person would want to do. In other words there is nothing worth mentioning with reference to the peculiarity of the private sector if all that counts is (not) moving through a glass door somewhere in an office building.

There is however another dimension to the glass door that is less about the excluded researcher and more about the student easily passing through. Installing visible borders that can be overcome with a swipe turns the organisational border into a relationship of inclusion. By being a student, the library, the study rooms, the corridors, the table football, all remain open for purpose-related usage by the student (24 hours at one, until midnight at the other). They can study, use their personal locker, meet for a coffee, grab a glass of wine after an evening presentation (which they have not necessarily attended) at all times, and thereby become a strong part of the organisational network. When I met a student for an interview in front of the premises of Paxheim

Private University he was himself unsure whether he could easily pass with his student ID as he had not been on the premises for a long time due to an internship. But by successfully opening the first door, he transformed into a host, asking me to follow him with a wide gesture of his arm. By entitling only a small group of students to move through the location, and inviting those they chose as worthy, the university provides trust to the students but also privilege that binds them to the institution. The following quote from a student at Big Town Private University, which has restricted access only to some rooms, including the library, but is situated in a location which is somewhat secluded from the rest of the town, illustrates this movement:

> Well, it [the campus] is very much for itself, very encapsulated. And notably in the first [study period], let's say one has to be here 40 hours a week, but if you want, you can also be here 80. Especially if you participate in all the student groups, if you work for the student representation, if you go to [champagne] receptions, if you take in all that is there, then you are basically always here. That means one becomes socialized ... here. And well, ... the leap [to build up a social life] outside [of Big Town Private University] take only a small number.
>
> Transl., Student 2, Big Town Private University, l. 501–519

By visibly setting borders that are easy to overcome for the chosen few, the premises become a place of one's own, a place of socialisation. Just as a door key confirms that the place you enter is your apartment, every time a student swipes his card at a seminar room or a library gate he reconfirms himself as being part of a private university network. It restates the privilege of being a student at this particular university.

Student Ambassadors as Borders

Being a privileged student at a particular university however also comes as a responsibility. The reference to purposeful behaviour above is contrasted by measures to control student behaviour, as the following quote shows.

> It's more that they, that the experience was that the ... people would come here on the weekends to ... for example watch a soccer game ... so they would come at two in the morning, ... and then there's like 20 people here drinking, maybe they leave their beer bottles around when they leave the school and then the cleaners in the morning find this and they don't agree with it. It's not your living room, you're not supposed to come here and entertain yourself in that sense if you don't have to be here to study.
>
> Student 3, Private International University, l. 972–978

While the measures the university undertakes to avoid the study rooms being used as a drinking venue address an internal problem, this construction of appropriate behaviour is also projected to the outside. I will discuss this in the context of the Private International University, but similar issues came up in interviews with students from the other private universities.[27] Students at Private International University talk about how the school asks them to reflect well on the institution by their behaviour in public:

> A code of conduct was presented ...; we protested, there is a passage in there that admonishes you to promote the image of [Private International University] in public, literally. Yes, this is about promotion, but not to damage the reputation. ... they said very clearly ... 'no, it's not meant that way', but for me that's a gagging order, that is somehow written into that thing. It won't have any consequences as such, but I think it is a joke. ... It is also in my study agreement, which is a bit like a contract. ... Among other things it says that you are an ambassador of the Uni and such ... if you are somewhere you leave a good impression, also for the institution.
>
> Student 4, International Private University, l. 472–531

> ... they talk about the school reputation a lot, and about how we're supposed to be, like the ambassadors of the school. And I know all school[s] ... do it. Um I mean I'm pretty sure [prestigious British university] does it (laughs). So, it- it- it belongs there, ah but I think this is one of the- or at least this is how I feel it. I feel it "Ok, I have to be really good", because I have to ... be good for myself, but then it's also like "I'm a [International Private University] student", and ... I don't I don't think... any of us would do something to damage the school reputation or something on purpose. But they- you- at least I'm made aware of it. Like I felt "Ok, this is something I have to watch out, because ... it says '[International Private University]' on my CV now", so I mean I'm gonna do it for myself anyway. Th- it's not that "I do it because it says '[International Private University]' on my CV", but because it says '[International Private University]' on my CV it's an extra- like people pay even more attention, or people who've heard about it anyway.
>
> Student 5, International Private University, l. 598–628

---

27 Private International University seems to be the most outspoken about such policies. This may however also have to do with the fact that the other two organisations set stronger focus on identifying the 'fitting' students during admission interviews (cf. Bloch *et al.* 2015b).

The first student discusses a self-declaration to promote the image of the university. He is opposed to it even though he does not see how it could be enforced by the school. While he talks about a "gagging order" (in German *"Maulkorb"*) the quote from the second student shows that such an ambassador status is much more nuanced. While she seems to be somewhat annoyed by the reputational aspect that is voiced by the school, on the other hand she agrees with the idea that with the way she acts, she acts in the name of the school: she uses the university to upgrade her CV and is treated as a relational part of the school by the outside: she is the border. With or without such a policy in place, in any potential discussion between students of these universities and outsiders, as other interviews indicate, their school may be a point of question, discussion or attack. By secluding the relational space, by charging tuition fees, by promoting the school widely through public relations staff, aspiring private universities perform a border along various relations that all invoke the organisation's name: especially towards students. They will be held to discuss their status, asked to narrate their experiences (such as they also did towards me) and make a choice on whether they promote their school.

In asking them to become ambassadors they create awareness of the individual role of the student with regard to the outside, and also ask them to engage actively in positive border building. Wherever the student goes s/he potentially transforms into the border of the university:

> ... at the event [he] constantly ‚wiggled around the students and invited them to take a photo with basically every politician that 'jumped' around that place.
>
> Conversation protocol 1, Student 6, International Private University

> I remember one panel discussion that we had that the [International Private School] was affiliated with, there was like the [international conference] ... was here .... And he [famous public figure] specifically came to us to basically say, you know can we have like you know a bunch of student ambassadors ... to basically you know assist us with the [conference] ....
>
> Student 7, International Private University, l. 651–660

By being in a photo that potentially shows up on the school's website or by becoming ambassadors of a school at a conference – just like the ambassador of a nation state – the students represent their organisation in a positive way. Rather than creating a fissure, they actually perform relationships with a constructed outside – that only becomes an outside through this specific movement – and that positively retranslates into alleviating the inside. This movement aims at slowly turning the name of a private university into an achievement. It aims at transforming the role of the educational organisation into a marker of excellence, a marker that makes being there more important than excelling there. While public universities do promote individual students as ambassadors for the university, they do not and they cannot transform the masses into ambassadors. Sometimes students may talk positively about a university but they also complain about overcrowded rooms and strange grading. Because public universities are larger in size students very often just remain anonymous, and they are not contested as stratificatory borders of their university.

Conclusion

Private higher education in Germany is experiencing an expansion that provokes questions on why and how it is expanding, as well as whether there is anything distinct about it. In addressing Roger Geiger's typification of private higher education as 'different', 'more' or 'better' than the public sector, and narrowing the focus down to state accredited private universities, I have shown that these forms do apply to the German sector. In the wake of the Bologna reforms, certain degrees in private higher education are indeed different, and there is an older age profile on degree programmes comparative to the public sector, but boundaries blur with stronger horizontal differentiation in the public sector. With regard to expansion ('more'), an increase in both student numbers and universities is visible. As private higher education still has considerable funding problems, the sector has not reached a state of maturity. The expansion in private higher education seems to be connected to the recent expansion of German higher education in general. With more and more public degree programmes reaching their maximum intake capacity and therefore introducing admission procedures, certain students seem to be crowded out into private undergraduate programmes, particularly in business administration/ economics. Thus, judged by an analysis of available numbers, the overall distinguishing feature of private higher education in Germany is its orientation towards students demand in less-cost intensive undergraduate programmes.[28]

In order to identify specific aspects of some of the private universities, namely those that aim at becoming 'better' than public universities, the perspective shifted from numbers to on-site experience at aspiring private universities. While public sector programmes have begun to engage in vertical differentiation, some private universities are still at the forefront of this development. In contrast to public higher education institutions, private universities can

---

28   For the university providing them.

forcefully engage in dissecting processes that aim at making borders visible and hence increase their status. Three such forms of 'bordering' were discussed as very distinct trajectories: admissions procedures produce a strict line between the inside and the outside, and attribute those as special who have crossed through this border. Glass doors then materialise a localisable border to visitors but also for those passing through on a daily basis. Localisable borders *include* in a specific way by constantly reinstating the privilege and the private space through which enrolled students pass. Student ambassadors finally are constructed as institutional borders themselves – either through performative acts from the public relations office, challenges from third persons or through school policy. By being challenged to defend or to perform the school students carry the school's border whereever they go. Such a process is not visible at public universities. While such bordering practices may indeed show up in specific degree programmes at public universities, there is something specifically private about them. These practices evolve around movements that dissect the inside from the outside – not by fissure but by specific forms of relations. The outside hereby is opposed to a public good that is potentially open to everybody. In all three cases belonging and transcending this belonging through materiality play an important role.

The private sector in higher education covers a wider range of universities. As state accredited private universities they receive more regulatory leeway but also have to finance themselves through tuition fees. Thus they follow and depend on student demand, not only for 'more' places but also for 'different' and 'better' programmes. And while demand orientation and bordering processes as discussed here seem to still be very much distinct to the sector, developments indicate that boundaries along specific purposes between the public and the private sector might become more diffuse in the future. Indeed public universities have started to offer further education programmes such as the MBA and also started charging tuition fees for non-undergraduate and non-consecutive graduate degrees.

Works Cited

Baker, David. 2014. *The Schooled Society: The Educational Transformation of Global Culture.* Stanford, CA: Stanford University Press.

Bloch, Roland. 2009. *Flexible Studierende? Studienreform und studentische Praxis.* Leipzig: Akademische Verlagsanstalt.

Bloch, Roland, Reinhard Kreckel, Alexander Mitterle, and Manfred Stock. 2014. "Stratifikationen im Bereich der Hochschulbildung in Deutschland". *Z Erziehungswiss* 17 (S3): 243–261.

Bloch, Roland, Marion Gut, Katja Klebig, and Alexander Mitterle. 2015a. "Die Auswahl der Besten? Auswahlverfahren an sich stratifizierenden Einrichtungen und Programmen im Hochschulbereich". In Werner Helsper and Heinz-Hermann Krüger (eds). *Auswahl der Bildungsklientel. Zur Herstellung von Selektivität in 'exklusiven' Bildungsinstitutionen.* Wiesbaden: VS Verlag für Sozialwissenschaften, 185–209.

Bloch, Roland, Lena Dreier, Katrin Kotzyba, Alexander Mitterle, and Mareke Niemann. 2015b. "Auswahlgespräche in ,exklusiven' Gymnasien, privaten Hochschulen und ,exzellenten' Graduiertenschulen: Die Überprüfung von Authentizität und Passung". *Zeitschrift für Pädagogik* 61 (1): 41–57.

Brauns, Hans-Jochen. 2014. "Private Hochschulen in Deutschland: Eine Bestandsaufnahme". WiSo Institut für Wirtschaft und Soziales GmbH. Unpublished manuscript, last modified 21January 2015, http://www.alpheios.de/fileadmin/dateien/Private _Hochschulen_in_Deutschland.pdf.

Brockhoff, Klaus. 2003. "Management privater Hochschulen in Deutschland". In Horst Albach and Peter Mertens (eds). *Hochschulmanagement,* 1–24. ZfB – Ergänzungshefte. Wiesbaden: Gabler Verlag.

Brockhoff, Klaus 2011. "Erfolgsfaktoren privater Hochschulen". *Z Betriebswirtsch* 81 (S4): 5–31.

Collins, Randall. 1979. *The Credential Society: An Historical Sociology of Education and Stratification.* New York: Academic Press.

Czarniawska, Barbara. 2013. "Organizations as obstacles to organizing". In Daniel Robichaud and François Cooren (eds). *Organization and organizing: materiality, agency and discourse.* Abingdon, New York: Routledge, 3–22.

Doelle, Joris. 2014. *Privathochschulen in Deutschland: Bildungsstätten der zukünftigen Wirtschaftselite.* Hamburg: Kovač.

Darraz Fernández, Enrique, Robert Reisz and Manfred Stock. 2009. *Private Hochschulen in Chile, Deutschland, Rumänien und den USA: Struktur und Entwicklung.* Arbeitsberichte / Institut für Hochschulforschung Wittenberg an der Martin-Luther-Universität Halle-Wittenberg 2009/3. Wittenberg: HoF.

Frank, Andrea *et al.* 2010. *Rolle und Zukunft privater Hochschulen in Deutschland: Eine Studie in Kooperation mit McKinsey & Company.* Positionen. Essen: Stifterverband für die Dt. Wiss.

Frank, David J. and John W. Meyer. 2007. "University expansion and the knowledge society". *Theory and Society* 36 (4): 287–311.

Friedrichs, Julia. 2008. *Gestatten: Elite: Auf den Spuren der Mächtigen von morgen.* 2. Aufl. Hamburg: Hoffmann und Campe.

Geiger, Roger L. 1985. "The private alternative in higher education". *European Journal of Education* 20 (4): 385–398.

Geiger, Roger L. 1986. *Private Sectors in Higher Education: Structure, Function, and Change in Eight Countries*. Ann Arbor, MI: University of Michigan Press.

Göschel, Hans. 2008. *Die Handelshochschule in Leipzig*. Leipzig: Handelshochschule.

Hartmann, Michael. 2009. "Wer wird Manager? Soziale Schließung durch Bildungsabschlüsse und Herkunft im internationalen Vergleich". In Rudolf Stichweh and Paul Windolf (eds). *Inklusion und Exklusion: Analysen zur Sozialstruktur und sozialen Ungleichheit*. Wiesbaden: VS Verlag für Sozialwissenschaften, 71–84.

Herdin, Gunvald and Cort-Denis Hachmeister. 2014. "Der CHE Numerus Clausus-Check 2013/14 Eine Analyse des Anteils von NC-Studiengängen in den einzelnen Bundesländern", https://www.che-consult.de/downloads/CHE_AP_178_Numerus _Clausus_Check_2013_14.pdf.

Immer, Daniel. 2013. *Rechtsprobleme der Akkreditierung von Studiengängen*. Göttingen: Univ.-Verl. Göttingen.

Jansen, Stephan A. 2007. "Forschungsorientierung privater Hochschulen in Deutschland – Ausgangssituation und Thesen". In Detlef Müller-Böling and Michael Zürn (eds). *Private Hochschulen in Deutschland – Reformmotor oder Randerscheinung? Symposium der Hertie School of Governance und des CHE, Centrum für Hochschulentwicklung, 7./8. November 2005*. Berlin: HSoG Publishing, 120–135.

Kaina, Viktoria. 2004. "Deutschlands Eliten zwischen Kontinuität und Wandel. Empirische Befunde zu Rekrutierungswegen, Karrierepfaden und Kommunikationsmustern". *Aus Politik und Zeitgeschichte* 10: 8–16.

Kämmerer, Jörn A. 2003. "Regulierung staatlicher und privater Hochschulen". In Jörn A. Kämmerer and Peter Rawert (eds). *Hochschulstandort Deutschland: Rechtlicher Rahmen – politische Herausforderungen*. Köln [u.a.]: Heymann, 119–141.

[KMK] Konferenz der Kultusminister der Länder in der Bundesrepublik Deutschland. 2012. "Vorausberechnung der Studienanfängerzahlen 2012–2025 – Fortschreibung – (Stand: 24.01.2012)". Unpublished manuscript, last modified 17 November 2014, http:// www.kmk.org/fileadmin/veroeffentlichungen_beschluesse/2005/2005_10_01-Studi enanfaenger-Absolventen-2020.pdf.

Konegen-Grenier, Christiane. 1996. "Private Hochschulen". In Winfried Schlaffke and Reinhold Weiß (eds). *Private Bildung – Herausforderung für das öffentliche Bildungsmonopol*. Köln: Dt. Inst.-Verl., 131–170.

Kreckel, Reinhard. 2010. "Zwischen Spitzenforschung und Breitenausbildung. Strukturelle Differenzierungen an deutschen Hochschulen im internationalen Vergleich". In Heinz-Hermann Krüger *et al.* (eds). *Bildungsungleichheit Revisited*. Wiesbaden: VS Verlag für Sozialwissenschaften, 237–258.

Kühl, Stefan. 2011. *Organisationen: Eine sehr kurze Einführung*. Wiesbaden: VS Verlag für Sozialwissenschaften.

Latour, Bruno. 1996. *Der Berliner Schlüssel*. Berlin: Akademie Verlag.

Latour, Bruno 2013a. "'What's the story?' Organizing as a mode of existence". In Daniel Robichaud and François Cooren (eds). *Organization and Organizing: Materiality, Agency and Discourse.* Abingdon, New York: Routledge, 37–51.

Latour, Bruno 2013b. *An Inquiry into Modes of Existence: an Anthropology of the Moderns.* Cambridge, MA: Harvard University Press.

Lenhard, Gero, Robert D. Reisz and Manfred Stock. 2012. "Überlebenschancen privater und öffentlicher Hochschulen im Ländervergleich". *Beiträge zur Hochschulforschung* 34 (2): 30–48.

Lorenz, Dieter. 1996. "Privathochschulen". In *Handbuch des Wissenschaftsrechts.* 2nd ed. Berlin [u.a.]: Springer, 1157–1184.

Merkator, Nadine and Ulrich Teichler. 2010. *Strukturwandel des tertiären Bildungssystems.* Düsseldorf: Hans-Böckler-Stiftung, www.boeckler.de/pdf/p_arbp_205.pdf.

Meyer, Heinz-Dieter. 1998. "The German Handelshochschulen 1898–1933: a new departure in management education and why it failed". In Lars Engwall and Vera Zamagni (eds). *Management Education in Historical Perspective.* Manchester: Manchester University Press, 19–33.

Mitterle, Alexander and Manfred Stock. 2015. "Exklusive Hochschulen". In Sandra Rademacher and Andreas Wernet (eds). *Bildungsqualen.* Wiesbaden: Springer Fachmedien Wiesbaden, 185–206.

Mitterle, Alexander, Robert D. Reisz and Manfred Stock. Forthcoming. *Rangdifferenzierung des privaten Hochschulsektors Eine explorative Studie zur Stratifizierung der Hochschulbildung in Deutschland: manuscript.* Halle (Saale). Under review.

Mitterle, Alexander, Carsten Würmann and Roland Bloch. 2015. "Teaching without faculty: policy interactions and their effects on the network of teaching in German higher education". *Discourse: Studies in the Cultural Politics of Education,* 36 (4): 560–577.

Pfeiff, Andreas. *Die Entstehung und Entwicklung der Handelshochschulen in Deutschland.* Frankfurt am Main, Mannheim: Lang.

Reisz, Robert D. and Manfred Stock. 2013. "Hochschulexpansion, Wandel der Fächerproportionen und Akademikerarbeitslosigkeit in Deutschland". *Z Erziehungswiss* 16 (1): 137–156.

Schily, Konrad. 2007. "Die Rolle privater Hochschulen in Deutschland". In Detlef Müller-Böling and Michael Zürn (eds). *Private Hochschulen in Deutschland – Reformmotor oder Randerscheinung?* Berlin: HSoG Publishing, 11–25.

Schneider, Heidrun and Barbara Franke. 2014. "Bildungsentscheidungen von Studienberechtigten: Studienberechtigte 2012 ein halbes Jahr vor und ein halbes Jahr nach Schulabschluss", http://www.dzhw.eu/pdf/pub_fh/fh-201406.pdf.

Schröder, Marco. 2013. "Radikale Differenzierung als nicht intendierte Nebenfolge des Bologna-Prozesses". Presentation at the 24. Kongress der Deutschen Gesellschaft für Erziehungswissenschaft, Berlin, 12 March.

Sperlich, Andrea. 2006. "Was heißt und zu welchem Ende gründet man eine private Hochschule? Gründungsmotive und Erfolgsdefinitionen privater Hochschulen in Deutschland". *die hochschule* 2: 138–156.

Sperlich, Andrea 2008. *Theorie und Praxis erfolgreichen Managements privater Hochschulen in Deutschland.* Berlin: BWV, Berliner Wissenschafts-Verlag.

Stannek, Antje and Frank Ziegele. 2005. "Private higher education in Europe: a national report on Germany". Gütersloh: Centrum für Hochschulentwicklung, http://www .che-ranking.de/downloads/Studie_Privathochschulen_AP71.pdf.

Statistisches Bundesamt. 2014. *Private Hochschulen. 2012. Fachserie 11 Reihe 4.2.* Wiesbaden.

Statistisches Bundesamt 2014a. *Prüfungen an Hochschulen. 2013. Fachserie 11 Reihe 4.2.* Wiesbaden.

Statistisches Bundesamt 2014b. *Studierende an Hochschulen. Wintersemester 2013/2014: Fachserie 11 Reihe 4.1.* Wiesbaden.

Statistisches Bundesamt 2014c. "Hochschulabsolventinnen und -absolventen nach Hochschularten, Hochschulen und Prüfungsgruppen: Zeitreihe: 2008–2012. Tab.2.5.47", http://www.datenportal.bmbf.de/portal/Tabelle-2.5.47.xls.

Steinkemper, Ursula. 2002. *Die verfassungsrechtliche Stellung der Privathochschule und ihre staatliche Förderung: Verantwortungsteilung im dualen Hochschulsystem.* Berlin: Duncker & Humblot.

Stock, Manfred. 2014. "'Überakademisierung'. Anmerkungen zu einer aktuellen Debatte". *die hochschule* 2: 22–37.

Technische Fachhochschule Georg Agricola zu Bochum [TFH Georg Agricola]. 2012. "Geschichte: TFH Georg Agricola zu Bochum", http://www.tfh-bochum.de/geschichte .html.

Trow, Martin. 1984. "The analysis of status". In Burton R. Clark (ed.). *Perspectives on Higher Education: Eight Disciplinary and Comparative Views.* Berkeley, CA, London: University of California Press, 132–164.

Weick, Karl E. 1995. *Der Prozess des Organisierens.* 1. Aufl. Frankfurt am Main: Suhrkamp.

Winter, Martin. 2013. "Studienplatzvergabe und Kapazitätsermittlung – Berechnungs- und Verteilungslogiken sowie föderale Unterschiede im Kontext der Studienstrukturreform". *Wissenschaftsrecht* 46 (3): 241–273.

[WR] Wissenschaftsrat. 2012. "Private und kirchliche Hochschulen aus Sicht der Institutionellen Akkreditierung". Drs. 2264-12, http://www.wissenschaftsrat.de/ download/archiv/2264-12.pdf.

[WR] Wissenschaftsrat 2013. "Stellungnahme zur Reakkreditierung (Promotionsrecht) der European School of Management and Technology (ESMT), Berlin". Frs. 3211-13, http://www.wissenschaftsrat.de/download/archiv/3211-13.pdf.

Afterword: Shifting Categories of Public and Private

Susan Wright

Academic literature is awash with texts bemoaning the commoditisation, marketisation and privatisation of higher education. These '-isation' words are often used to label processes as if they have uniform and predictable characteristics. This book admirably gets beneath the surface of these labels to explore, through ethnography and case studies in different parts of the world, how private universities were established, their social and political context and history, and their changing business models and operations.

Each of the chapters starts by setting out the extent of privatisation in a different context and variations in its meaning. It is clear that the place of private universities in each country's sector varies. Profanter's chapter shows how difficult it is to untangle differences between public and private universities in Saudi Arabia. Unlike most other countries, in the 1990s the late king devoted over 50% of the budget to human resource development, including higher education, and this was used both to maintain public universities and subsidise private ones. Now roughly half of the 52 universities are private. But the first private university eventually became public. Private universities often receive a lease on land from the royal family, and by law have to have multiple owners – in Profanter's case study a consortium of 52 Saudi business men worked with a group of 22 Texan universities. It is similarly complex in Sudan, where, as Ille describes, the private sector only caters for 19% of students, but the 1990s saw a sharp decrease in the funding of public universities, which shifted to charging student fees and seeking private investors. Wages are low, so academics employed in public universities also staff the private universities. In Egypt, according to Cantini, some public universities, faced with a collapse in their finances, have started charging fees for particular programmes in a form of internal privatisation. The categories public and private do not form a simple binary and they are not stable.

In some countries there is a clear hierarchy between public and private, whereas in others it is more complicated. For example, in the USA, as Cantini (Introduction) points out, 20% of the oldest and most distinguished universities are private-not-for-profit. One university, Cornell, is famously a part private not-for-profit Ivy League university, and part a federal land-grant public university. At the other end of the scale in the USA, a plethora of for-profit colleges includes Apollo's Phoenix University, which has come under censure from a U.S. federal jury in 2008 for 'knowingly and recklessly' misleading investors (Hotson 2011), and been severely criticised by a U.S. Senate Report for 'prioritis[ing] financial success over student success' (U.S. Senate Report 2012: 292; Shore and Wright forthcoming). In Peru, as described in Irigoyen's chapter, the public universities were proselytised by the Shining Path movement, which the state forces attacked, so that they became viewed as unsafe. Instead, new private and very expensive for-profit universities attracted the social and cultural elite and symbolised efficiency and quality. But more recently a new group of low-fee private universities has been established, costing half the price charged by the prestigious private universities. These low-fee universities focus on increasing social mobility and employment through professional and technical training. Thus private universities can have different locations in local university hierarchies; and in some places they have even more of a social purpose than the public universities, while in others they are primarily concerned with profit extraction.

Cantini's introduction points out that one of the benefits of an ethnographic approach is that it can highlight different 'bordering' processes and practices between these interwoven public and private spheres. The cases from Sudan and Saudi Arabia refer to state forces or the religious police patrolling private universities. The state is ever-present, and in Sudan all universities have to promote the regime's idea of creating an Islamic community and morality. One bordering practice mentioned in many chapters is the different admission requirements of private and public universities. In Peru, even though the public universities had lost prestige, their entry requirements were still higher than private universities, while in Sudan, students who can pay have lower entry requirements. In Germany, private higher education is expanding despite high fees because students are crowded out of some disciplines in the public sector by high admission barriers. Yet the private universities adopt a 'multiple step' admission procedure, which makes those who are chosen feel they have achieved something special and have crossed a visible border to join a prestigious institution. Mitterle's chapter on Germany uses his participant-observation research to provide the most vivid examples of bordering practices. The private university's use of entry cards to open glass doors both on the exterior of the building and internally in the corridors, and both on the way in, and in order to get out, create a feeling of being 'insiders'. Outsiders can look in through the glass; only accepted students can move into and through the space. This sense of privilege is conveyed in talk of the students being the university's ambassadors: they are to behave in public in certain ways to protect the university's reputation and thereby enhance their own.

This ethnography generates a very sophisticated understanding of what is often referred to as 'the student as consumer'. Several chapters refer to the loss of higher education as a public right and the move to paying for education as a positional good and an entry qualification for the labour market. This claim often seems not to be realised, as many chapters refer to fears about graduate unemployment, and only in the Peruvian example has widened access to professional education resulted in expanded employment opportunities and increased wages. The Peruvian focus on professional and technical education is however at the expense of no longer foregrounding active citizenship and critical thought. In Sudan, where universities have a duty to promote a particular version of community and duty to the country, Ille's study is of a very interesting case of a university set up with the purpose of discriminating in favour of women so as to influence the gender balance in Sudan. Whilst being avowedly 'non-political' in the sense of averting external political pressures, the purpose of the university is to prepare women 'to become change agents in their families and communities and to assume leadership positions in society'. This is a private university espousing a strong notion of citizenship rather than consumership.

The chapters also reveal the different roles that private universities play in relation to economic development. In Saudi Arabia, state investment in public and private education is part of a policy to move away from an oil economy and establish a knowledge economy – in which universities are crucial. The royal family and members of the elite have invested heavily in foundations to fund new universities, and the case study is of a university that had the patronage of the regional governor. Some of these universities have risen quickly up the rankings (e.g. the THE's 'new university ranking') but the chapter questions how well this economic strategy will succeed when freedom of thinking and limitations on women are so heavily patrolled by the religious police on campus. In Egypt, the new universities are part of an economic strategy to move the middle class out of Cairo and into new suburbs in the desert, provided with all necessary facilities, including new universities. The working class does the long commute daily from Cairo just to do menial work at the university, not to study. Private universities are clearly playing a role in class differentiation in Egypt. In contrast, in Turkey the philanthropists specifically established a new university in a poor neighbourhood in order for it to have transformative effects, both by improving opportunities for study and by providing employment. However, the philanthropists sought to expand their operations and entered into an arrangement with the US-based company, Laureate. The study shows in graphic detail how Laureate used its funding of former U.S. President Bill Clinton's charity to call on him to create good relations with the Turkish authorities. Although Turkish law stated that for-profit higher education was not allowed, Laureate used a service agreement to extract profit – a method used widely by private higher education providers elsewhere in the world.

Within three years the Laureate cuckoo had taken over the whole university. The chapters show the different ways that private universities are entangled with political elites and national politics.

The ethnographies in this book are clearly able to highlight complexities in the development and operations of private universities. I have identified some of the important themes that cut across the chapters but it behoves a postscript to also point forward, to themes that could be taken up for future work.

Future Research

First, referring to the Turkish example, further work is needed on the strategies of for-profit 'education providers' to erode the purpose and operations of not-for-profit or public universities from within. In England, companies are experimenting with ways to turn public or not-for-profit universities into a carapace and to privatise internal operations. Privatisation of catering, security and cleaning happened long ago. Now some universities are setting up a service company to run all their administration, apart from the vice-chancellor's powers (Wright 2015). When they have their company running, they will then tender to take over all the operations of another university, or neighbouring colleges and schools. As in the case with Laureate, profit is extracted by way of a 'management fee'. Pearson, the major publishing company, has recently sold some of its leading titles to reposition itself in global education provision. Its CEO was the lead author in a recent think-tank report, *The Avalanche is Coming*, which set out the future extent of this erosion from within: it envisaged 'unbundling' the university into separate operations – not only HR, accounts, and other administration, but curriculum development, delivery of teaching and exam marking would all be outsourced in short term contracts to private companies or self-employed academics. In this way, the university would diminish its fixed costs of buildings and permanent staff. This follows a model devised by manufacturing industry for unbundling and outsourcing its operations around the world in the 1990s (Harvey 1990) but some firms have now realised the shortcomings and are bringing operations back in house.

A second theme is the way profit-making in higher education is rarely achieved without public funding. In England, the coalition government ceased funding higher education (except in STEM subjects) and offered students a loan to pay for fees, which were tripled to £9000 per year, and to cover living costs. Students at for-profit colleges became eligible for these loans. New colleges sprang up, offering sub-degree higher education and charging a fee of £6000 per year. For example, St Patrick's International College was too small to register for public-backed loans for students in 2011–12 but grew within a year to 4,000 students, and received £11 million in public-backed funding in 2012–13, but its students had a very low completion rate. Its owner is a Dutch company whose majority shareholder is the Russian Etingen family – beyond the reach of UK jurisdiction (Wright 2015). In the USA, Apollo has come under severe criticism for aggressive selling to under-qualified applicants, who take out a government loan which haunts them for life. After they have paid their fees, they find out they cannot do the course and drop out. The college seems not to employ its staff until after the drop-out period, so as to minimise their costs and maximise the government-funded profits. President Obama has declared it an aim to restore free public education at two-year community colleges, and several states have already implemented this. As the business models of Apollo and similar companies are affected in the USA, it can be expected that they will intensify their search for risk-free, state-funded profit in England and other parts of the world.

A third issue for future research is to explore not just the meaning of 'private' but also of 'public'. The constitution of the 'public' varies in former state social-ist countries as against former colonial regimes, in Islamic regimes such as Su-dan (Ille's chapter), and between liberal and social democracies. In Germany (Mitterle's chapter) and England the oldest universities were always private in the sense that they are independent corporations, but founded with a public purpose. Marquand (2004) sheds light on this English meaning of 'public' by making a distinction between 'public domain' and 'public institutions' or 'pub-lic sector'. He shows how the idea of a public domain emerged in nineteenth century England out of resistance to both an elite governing through purchas-ing positions and family and political patronage – called 'Old Corruption' – and *laissez faire* commodification of land, labour and money traded through supposedly self-regulating markets. In a piecemeal fashion, the public domain developed as a 'space' that was governed not by family interests or market im-peratives, but by norms of disinterested service to a public good. Universities were central to developing this idea amongst the social actors involved in de-veloping and defending the public domain. The ancient universities educated the next generation of the ruling elite in the humanities and inculcated them with an ethos of service to a disinterested public good. Gradually they reduced corruption in parliament and, following the 1854 Northcote-Trevelyan report, created a non-partisan bureaucracy recruited and promoted on merit and serving ministers by offering independent advice (Marquand 2004: 47). The universities also educated newly organised professions of lawyers, architects and surveyors who established a social compact based on the trust that they would sell services to clients without abusing their monopoly position. By 1893, 500,000 women had also espoused this ethos of working for the public good by 'serving' the poor (Ibid.: 51). For this new middle class, the public domain did not just mean the public sector: it encompassed civil servants paid by the state, professionals who worked for profit, and the voluntary sector.

The public domain was conceived of as a realm of debate and argument, a strenuous, testing, collective moral enterprise where active citizens would strive to reflect on their own ideas and persuade each other in order to reach disinterested judgement about how to serve the public good (Ibid.: 72). However, this was not democracy. As Williams (1960: 349) makes clear, 'service' was an elite concept, a virtuous desire to improve the lives of the poor and feckless, that nestled within a 'larger selfishness': a 'command to conformity' with the existing, inviolate framework for the distribution of property, education and respect. At the same time the lower-middle and working classes were organising their own, marginalised, public domain in the form of cooperative societies, educational institutes and savings and burial associations (Yeo and Yeo 1981). Williams espouses the more inclusive, working class idea of mutual responsibility in opposition to the elitist notion of public service when setting out his aspiration to establish a 'fully democratic' process of continually contesting and redefining a 'common culture' (Williams 1960: 352).

After the Second World War, the role of government increased, and the notion of a state-funded, public sector grew. At this point, universities could be considered 'public' in multiple senses. They came to be considered part of the public sector, as they were increasingly dependent on state funding, albeit via an arms-length arrangement (Shattock 1994). They were also 'public' in that they took students from a much wider sweep of the population than the previous elite, and they contributed to the public domain by educating them to be critical thinkers and cultivated citizens who would build up the institutions of the post-war welfare state and bring prosperity to the country. Sixteen 'green field' campus universities were built in the 1960s for a massive expansion of student numbers (from 100,000 full time students in 1958–1959, to 235,000 in 1970–1971 and 370,000 in 1990–1991) (Willetts 2013: 9, 24). New polytechnics also focussed on the professional and vocational training needed for the urban economy (advanced engineering and applied science, law, architecture, management, business, accounting, journalism, town planning, IT). A national system of grants was set up in 1962 to cover all tuition and maintenance grants for poorer and middle class students, and a means test to decide the parental contribution to be paid by richer families. The very influential Robbins Report in 1963 established the principle that:

> Courses of higher education should be available for all those who are qualified by ability and attainment to pursue them and who wish to do so.
> ROBBINS 1963: 8

By the mid-1960s, a national system of free and publicly funded higher education had been established. Ideally universities would help form a public domain in which all could be involved in debating and contesting a 'common culture' and the definition of 'public good', and universities would equip students from all classes with the critical skills that enable them to engage in this debate and the ethos of active citizenship that inspires them to do so. This model of state funded but autonomous universities, with fee-free access to all students based on merit and supported by state grants, and with an aspiration to turn the public domain into a participatory democracy was only in place in England for about 30 years, yet it became a model of 'public' universities that was associated with modernisation and democracy and was exported to Britain's colonies and around the world.

International Policy

Signs of this model of 'public' universities are seen in Ille's chapter on Sudan, and another area of future research would be to locate ethnographies about public and private universities in the wider policies and international political economy. In Africa, in the last years of colonial rule, Britain established university colleges such as Makerere in 1948 and Ibadan and Legon in 1949, with 'umbilical ties' to London University (Lebeau and Mills 2008: 61). With the coming of independence, in 1963 a UNESCO *Conference on the Development of Higher Education in Africa* explored how universities could loosen their proximity to ruling elites, become more publicly accountable, and spearhead national development efforts, creating the professionals needed to run the public administration and to develop agriculture, industry, health, education and other services. American foundations, notably the Rockefeller and Ford foundations and the Fulbright programme, invested heavily in Sub-Saharan African universities and US-African academic staff exchange.

Just as this model of not-for-profit universities serving a public domain began to be undermined by the Thatcher government in Britain, several chapters refer briefly to the ways public universities in developing countries were affected by the Washington Consensus. By the 1980s, when African economic growth had faltered and graduate unemployment and student unrest had grown, World Bank reports claimed that state-controlled development in Africa had been a failure and Structural Adjustment Policies were imposed with drastic cuts in public expenditure. Whereas overall World Bank lending for higher education, science and technology development grew from $2.5 billion in the 14 years 1970 to 1984, to a further $2.5 billion in the next six years, 1985–1991, Africa's share of the World Bank's education spending fell from 17% in 1985–9 to 7% in 1996–9 (Lebeau and Mills 2008: 67, 84). The World Bank's analyses claimed there were greater 'rates of return' from investing in basic, not higher, education. By 1994, the World Bank's *Higher Education: the Lessons of Experience*, identified the resulting drop in student enrolment and in academic research, but used this to legitimise market-driven reform, further reductions in state funding and students and their families 'sharing' the cost of higher education (Lebeau and Mills 2008: 68). Several of the chapters refer to cuts in public funding and new laws to introduce private universities in the 1990s.

During the same period, in 1995, the World Trade Organisation (WTO) set in train negotiations for a General Agreement on Trade in Services (GATS), which was to come into force in 2005. GATS encouraged countries to include their higher education sectors in this free trade agreement, not only in the form of cross-border mobility of students and teachers, but foreign investment in educational institutions, and this market was expected to increase especially in developing countries (Mazzella, this volume). But the WTO set no standards or quality controls to regulate this trade. A UNESCO expert meeting in 2001 identified the need for global quality initiatives:

> There were fears that unmonitored free trade would be an invitation for fraudulent operators, especially in parts of the world where there was little or no consumer protection and potential students did not have reliable information on which to judge where and how to invest their education and their future.
>
> MATHIESEN 2007: 270

The meeting ended with the establishment of a Global Forum for a dialogue between academic and market values on quality assurance, accreditation and the recognition of qualifications. Simultaneously the OECD held forums in different parts of the world, initially in favour of trade in higher education but eventually concluding that guidelines were needed. But, unlike UNESCO, the OECD did not have powers to make international agreements (Ibid.: 275). The OECD approached UNESCO to establish 'Guidelines for Quality Provision in Cross-Border Higher Education' (UNESCO/OECD 2005). However, UNESCO's General Conference felt these guidelines made too many concessions to education service providers and demoted it to a document of the UNESCO Secretariat, which was neither standard-setting nor enforceable (Hartmann: 2015: 104).

Enforceable international standards for the quality of cross-border higher education providers are especially needed in countries which do not have the capacity to do this themselves. For example, in a study of Senegal's moves to become a higher education 'hub' for students in West Africa, public officials were candid that they did not have the resources to set up an effective quality control system. They did not have a list of all private higher education providers and there was no national system of accreditation (Michelsen 2007: 287). Mazzella's account (this volume) of Tunisia as a higher education hub offers a similarly complex picture. How is the quality of private and commercial universities assured when they have up to 80 shareholders and offer 80 high-fee courses for students predominantly from Gabon, Cameroon and other sub-Saharan countries? Is it through fear of embarrassing their high level contacts, when the Tunisian ambassador hosts the directors of Tunisian private universities on their visits to recruit students, or when ministers attend their functions? These Tunisian private universities are also setting up foreign campuses or franchising local institutes to provide the first two years of study for students 'at home', before they move to Tunisia to complete their qualification. Many English public universities are establishing similar operations in other parts of the world, and as these commercial and international operations are so complex, how can students be sure of high quality education? This remains an unanswered question.

A new role for universities in leading development arose with the OECD's (1996) argument that the future lay in a global knowledge-based economy. In 1998, UNESCO, which had opposed the World Bank's policy, now promulgated a new attitude towards the role of higher education in development at its first World Conference on Higher Education. The World Bank did a u-turn in 2000 and told African governments that it was economically beneficial to invest in higher education after all. The World Bank's Task Force on Higher Education and Society (2000) and subsequent report (2002) argued that 'developing and transition' countries could leapfrog stages of development if their universities improved their production of the raw materials for the new economy: knowledge and graduates.

At the 2015 African Higher Education Summit, the World Bank was castigated for the fact that its policies had degraded African higher education:

> Many of those in the audience had, publicly and repeatedly over the years, said that one of the World Bank's most shameful policies was to insist for decades during the second half of the 20th century that Africa did not need to focus on higher education but on the school sector – the implication being that Africa was never going to fully develop.
>
> Conditions attached to [World Bank] loans obliged African countries to spend on primary and not higher education, and the result over many years was the degradation of universities that had been growing in the

post-colonial period. This was exacerbated by marginalisation of universities by many despotic African governments that saw them as hotbeds of opposition.

MACGREGOR 2015

Claudia Costin, a senior director at the World Bank, told the 2015 African Higher Education Summit that public investment is now considered central to building 'quality and capacity in universities and to create skills that remain on the continent' (quoted in MacGregor 2015). The World Bank has invested more than US$1 billion in African higher education since 2000, and current commitments to higher education represent about 20% of its investment in Africa (MacGregor 2015). Yet by 2000, the cost of restoring higher education was beyond the capacity of the public purse. The World Bank's solution is further to promote private investment, on a philanthropic or for-profit basis, by local elite families or foundations, or by for-profit western companies, seeing this as a new market.

The World Bank has engaged in a drastic *volte face*. In the 2000s it also started providing loans to other world regions to develop private higher education, as mentioned in the chapter on Egypt. Even in countries such as Vietnam, whose state socialism was opposed to the establishment of new private universities, the World Bank offered funding for the government to develop its universities by choosing from a smorgasbord of policy options, all of which ended up in introducing ideologies of competition, 'cost-sharing' and the market into public universities (Dang 2009). In South America, military coups and the neoliberal 'shock doctrines' of the Chicago Boys in the 1980s had privatised public services, including higher education. Chile has ended up with the highest university fees in the world, and after students sustained a protest for over a year, the World Bank recently sent a mission to try to help the government find ways to reform and 're-publicise' the entire education system (Shore and Wright forthcoming).

Conclusion

The future of public and private higher education are both in flux. Will international operations such as Laureate and Pearson expand their for-profit operations world-wide? Will local and governing elites, supported by World Bank funding, use universities to try to consolidate their power? Will countries such as Chile find a way to 're-publicise' their universities? If so, which meanings of 'public', 'public sector', 'public good', public domain' or local meanings of 'community' or 'social purpose' will become dominant? Or will aspects of private and public interweave? The strengths of the book are its ethnographic detail, which shows the complexity and fast changing forms of private higher education, and its reluctance to jump to simplified labelling of public and private, which would camouflage these differences. The book acts as a model for further ethnographic studies of the detail of local developments in higher education, set within national contexts – and even more widely, within the international policy context and political economy of the sector.

Works Cited

Dang, Que Anh. 2009. "Recent Higher Education Reforms in Vietnam: the Role of the World Bank". Working Papers on University Reform no. 13. Copenhagen: Danish School of Education, Aarhus University, http://edu.au.dk/fileadmin/www.dpu.dk/forskning/forskningsprogrammer/epoke/workingpapers/WP_13.pdf.

Hartmann, Eva. 2015. "The educational dimension of global hegemony". *Millenium: Journal of International Studies* 44: 89–108.

Harvey, David. 1990. *The Condition of Postmodernity: An Enquiry into the Origins of Cultural Change*. Oxford: Blackwell.

Hotson, H. 2011. "Short Cuts". *London Review of Books*, 33 (11), http://www.lrb.co.uk/v33/n11/howard-hotson/short-cuts.

Lebeau, Yann and David Mills. 2008. "From 'crisis' to 'transformation'? Shifting orthodoxies of African higher education policy and research". *Learning and Teaching: The International Journal of Higher Education in the Social Sciences* 1 (1): 58–88.

MacGregor, Karen. 2015. "Higher education is key to development – World Bank". *University World News* 362, http://www.universityworldnews.com/article.php?story=20150409152258799.

Marquand, David. 2004. *Decline of the Public*. Cambridge: Polity.

Mathisen, Gigliola. 2007. "Shaping the global market of higher education through quality promotion". In D. Epstein, Rebecca Boden, Rosemary Deem, Fazal Rizvi and Susan Wright (eds). *Geographies of Knowledge, Geometries of Power: Framing the Future of Higher Education, World Yearbook of Education 2008*. New York: Routledge: 266–279.

Michelsen, Gunnar Guddal. 2007. "The rise of private education in Senegal". In D. Epstein, Rebecca Boden, Rosemary Deem, Fazal Rizvi and Susan Wright (eds). *Geographies of Knowledge, Geometries of Power: Framing the Future of Higher Education, World Yearbook of Education 2008*. New York: Routledge: 280–298.

OECD. 1996. *The Knowledge-based Economy*. Paris: OECD.

Robbins, Lionel. 1963. *Higher Education: Report of the Committee Appointed by the Prime Minister under the Chairmanship of Lord Robbins, 1961–63.* Cmnd 2154. London: HMSO.

Shattock, Michael. 1994. *The UGC and the Management of the British Universities.* Buckingham: Society for Research into Higher Education.

Shore, Cris and Susan Wright. Forthcoming. "Privatising the Public University: Key Trends, Counter-trends and Alternatives". In Cris Shore and Susan Wright (eds). *Death of the Public University? Uncertain Futures for Higher Education in the Knowledge Economy.* Oxford: Berghahn.

UNESCO/OECD. 2005. *Guidelines on Quality Provision in Cross-border Higher Education: Quality, Accreditation and Qualifications.* Paris: UNESCO.

United States Senate Committee on Health, Education, Labor and Pensions. 2012. "For Profit Higher Education: The Failure To Safeguard The Federal Investment and Ensure Student Success". Washington, DC: US Government Printing Office, https://www.gpo.gov/fdsys/pkg/CPRT-112SPRT74931/pdf/CPRT-112SPRT74931.pdf.

Willetts, David. 2013. *Robbins Revisited: Bigger and Better Higher Education.* London: Social Market Foundation, http://www.smf.co.uk/wp-content/uploads/2013/10/Publication-Robbins-Revisited-Bigger-and-Better-Higher-Education-David-Willetts.pdf.

Williams, Raymond. 1960. *Culture and Society 1780–1950.* New York: Doubleday.

World Bank. 1994. *Higher Education: the Lessons of Experience.* Washington, DC: World Bank.

World Bank. 2000. *Higher Education in Developing Countries. Peril and Promise.* Washington, DC: World Bank, International Bank for Reconstruction and Development, Task Force on Higher Education and Society.

World Bank. 2002. *Constructing Knowledge Societies: New Challenges for Tertiary Education.* Washington, DC: World Bank.

Wright, Susan. 2015. "Anthropology and the 'imaginators' of future European universities". *Focaal* 71 (Spring): 6–17.

Yeo, Eileen and Yeo Stephen (eds). 1981. *Popular Culture and Class Conflict 1590–1914: Explorations in the History of Labour and Leisure.* Sussex: Harvester Press.

Index

www.ingramcontent.com/pod-product-compliance
Lightning Source LLC
Chambersburg PA
CBHW070920030426
42336CB00014BA/2466